Understanding Macroeconomic Theory

GW00762698

At each point in time, individuals in an economy are making choices with respect to the acquisition, sale, and/or use of a variety of different goods. Such activity can be summarized by aggregate variables such as an economy's total production of various goods and services, the aggregate level of unemployment, the general level of interest rates, and the overall level of prices. Macroeconomics is the study of movements in such economy-wide variables as output, employment, and prices.

The focus of this book is on developing simple theoretical models that provide insight into the reasons for fluctuations in such aggregate variables. These models explore how shocks or "impulses" to the economy impact individuals' behavior in specific markets and the resulting implications in terms of changes in aggregate variables.

Understanding Macroeconomic Theory will provide the reader with an in-depth understanding of standard theoretical models: Walrasian, Keynesian and neoclassical. It is written in a concise, accessible style and will be an indispensable tool for all students who wish to gain firm grounding in the complexities of macroeconomic theories.

John M. Barron is the Loeb Professor of Economics in the Krannert School of Management at Purdue University.

Bradley T. Ewing is the Jerry S. Rawls Endowed Professor in Operations Management in the Rawls College of Business at Texas Tech University.

Gerald J. Lynch is Professor of Economics in the Krannert School of Management at Purdue University.

Routledge Advanced Texts in Economics and Finance

Financial Econometrics
Peijie Wang

Macroeconomics for Developing Countries 2nd edition
Raghbendra Jha

Advanced Mathematical Economics
Rakesh V. Vohra

Advanced Econometric Theory
John S. Chipman

Understanding Macroeconomic Theory
John M. Barron, Bradley T. Ewing and Gerald J. Lynch

Understanding Macroeconomic Theory

John M. Barron, Bradley T. Ewing
and Gerald J. Lynch

Routledge
Taylor & Francis Group

NEW YORK AND LONDON

First published 2006
by Routledge
711 Third Avenue, New York, NY 10017

Simultaneously published in the UK
by Routledge
2 Park Square, Milton Park, Abingdon, Oxon OX14 4RN

Routledge is an imprint of the Taylor & Francis Group, an informa business

© 2006 John M. Barron, Bradley T. Ewing and Gerald J. Lynch

Typeset in Times New Roman by
Newgen Imaging Systems (P) Ltd, Chennai, India

Library of Congress Cataloging in Publication Data
Barron, John M.
    Understanding macroeconomic theory / John M. Barron,
  Bradley T. Ewing and Gerald J. Lynch.
      p. cm.
    Includes bibliographical references and index.
     1. Macroeconomics. I. Ewing, Bradley T. II. Lynch, Gerald J. III. Title.
   HB172.5.B3753 2006
   339–dc22   2005026372

British Library Cataloguing in Publication Data
A catalogue record for this book is available from the British Library

ISBN13: 978–0–415–70195–2 (hbk)
ISBN13: 978–0–415–70196–9 (pbk)
ISBN13: 978–0–203–08822–7 (ebk)

Contents

1 Introduction

The topics of macroeconomics

At each point in time, individuals in an economy are making choices with respect to the acquisition, sale, and/or use of a variety of different goods. Such activity can be summarized by aggregate variables such as an economy's total production of various goods and services, the aggregate level of employment and unemployment, the general level of interest rates, and the overall level of prices.[1] Macroeconomics is the study of movements in such economy-wide variables as output, employment, and prices.

The focus of this book will be on developing simple theoretical models that provide insight into the reasons for fluctuations in such aggregate variables. These models explore how shocks or "impulses" to the economy (e.g., changes to technology, the money supply, or government policy) impact individuals' behavior in specific markets and the resulting implications in terms of changes in aggregate variables.

An overview of some facets of theoretical macroeconomic analysis

Given the breadth of economic activity in an economy, the study of macroeconomics must involve an examination of a variety of different markets. For instance, it is common for macroeconomic analysis to consider exchanges of labor services in the labor markets, of consumption and capital goods in the output markets, and of financial assets in the financial markets. The fact that macroeconomics simultaneously analyses exchanges of different goods in different markets means that macroeconomic theory is a *general equilibrium theory*. That is, macroeconomic theory must by necessity incorporate the links across markets that are fundamental to general equilibrium analysis. As we will see throughout this book, a key reflection of the links across markets is Walras' law, named in honor of the nineteenth-century French economist, Leon Walras.[2] Simply put, Walras' law notes that the budget constraints faced by individual agents in the economy suggest that if $n - 1$ of the n markets in the economy are in equilibrium, then the nth market must be in equilibrium. We will repeatedly rely on Walras' law or variants of it to simplify macroeconomic analysis.

While macroeconomic theories have in common (a) an attempt to explain fluctuations in aggregate variables and (b) a general equilibrium character, there remain wide differences among macroeconomic models. Below we break down these differences across macroeconomic models in several ways in order to make some sense of what passes for simple theoretical macroeconomic analysis.

Static, dynamic, and stationary analysis

One way of breaking down macroeconomic analyses is into static models, dynamic models, and stationary analysis of dynamic models. Static macroeconomic models analyze the economy at a point in time. They consider the determination of production, exchange, and prices of various goods only for the markets that currently exist. John Hicks (1939) sketched out an analysis of "spot" or "temporary" equilibrium. The advantage to such an approach is that it provides for rather simple "comparative static" analysis of the effects of changes in a variety of exogenous variables on the endogenous variables.[3] Such static analysis is useful in providing insight into a variety of questions of interest.

Static macroeconomic analysis can be viewed as a modification of a Walrasian general equilibrium analysis, or what is commonly referred to as "Arrow–Debreu theory" (Arrow and Hahn 1971; Debreu 1959). In Arrow–Debreu theory, each commodity is described by its physical characteristics, its location, and its date of availability. It is assumed there are a complete set of spot and forward markets. Prices adjust to clear all markets. However, if one restricts attention to just spot markets, then one moves from traditional Walrasian general equilibrium to an analysis of "temporary equilibrium," a phrase coined by Hicks (1939). This restriction to spot markets is one element of static macroeconomic analysis.[4]

A second element of static models is that if there is a future, then static macroeconomic analysis simply assumes given expectations of future prices and environment. How expectations of future events are formed is left unspecified, so that expectations of future prices become simply an element in the set of exogenous variables.[5]

While static analysis provides insights, there are several disadvantages of static analysis severe enough that it alone does not provide an adequate grounding in macroeconomic analysis. The key disadvantage of static analysis is that it breaks ties between current events and future events. To show the limitations of static analysis, let us suppose that underlying a simple static macroeconomic analysis of current markets is a microeconomic analysis of individuals' decisions that identifies the anticipated future level of prices as one of the exogenous variables affecting current behavior. As we have seen, static analysis takes expectations of such variables as future prices as exogenous variables. Doing so, however, results in (a) an incomplete enumeration of exogenous variables that can impact current economic activity and (b) a potentially incomplete accounting of the effects of the impact on current economic activity of a change in those exogenous variables that are identified by the analysis.

To illustrate the first point of an incomplete listing of exogenous variables, let us suppose that the static model identifies changes in the current money supply as one factor that influences current prices. This suggests that if we replicate the static analysis in future periods, changes in the money supply in the future would be shown to affect prices at that time. It seems natural to then presume that individuals' anticipation of future prices would incorporate this link between changes in the future money supply and future prices in forming their expectations of future price levels, so that the anticipated future money supply becomes a determinant of current activity.[6] Yet static analysis, since it does not analyze markets beyond the current period, will not identify the potential impact of future changes in the money supply on current activity.[7]

To illustrate the second point of an incomplete accounting of the effects of a change in an exogenous variable, let us suppose that underlying the static macro-economic analysis of current markets is a microeconomic analysis of firms' current investment behavior that identifies the anticipated future tax levels as well as future prices as two exogenous variables affecting investment decisions. Thus, static analysis would suggest that a change in future tax levels will impact current activity through the direct effect on current investment. It is not hard to see, however, that (a) the current change in investment means a different future capital stock and (b) the change in future tax levels could affect future as well as current investment. Either or both of these changes would likely impact future prices and, if such an impact were anticipated, be a second way that future tax changes impact current activity.[8]

An obvious way to avoid the above problems is to introduce forward markets, so that the macroeconomic analysis determines the prices of goods to be traded in the future along with the prices of goods traded at the current time.[9] In doing so, we have moved from static to dynamic analysis. That is, the macroeconomic models now determine the paths of variables (such as prices) over time rather than prices (and other variables) at only one point in time.

In a deterministic setting, this expansion of dynamic analysis incorporates the notion of "perfect foresight," in which individuals correctly anticipate all future prices. If there were uncertainty, the analysis indexes goods by both the date of trade and the "state of nature," with trades contingent on the realized state of nature.[10] The result is that at each date there is a distribution of potential prices at which trade for a good could occur and, given common knowledge of likelihood of the states of nature, expectations of future prices would be defined by the analysis ("rational expectations").

Once dynamic analysis is introduced, we can consider a special limiting form of dynamic analysis, termed stationary analysis. The aim of stationary analysis is to identify in the context of a dynamic model the limiting tendencies of endogenous variables such as the capital stock or the rate of growth in prices given that the exogenous variables remain constant or stationary over time.[11]

While stationary analysis is distinct from static analysis, in some cases one can think of static analysis as a form of stationary analysis. That is, static analysis in some cases can be viewed as the outcome that would emerge each period given that the exogenous variables remain constant (or in some cases grow at a steady rate over time) *and* given that one picks the correct fixed level of certain key exogenous variables (e.g., the capital stock and the rate of change in the money supply). Note, however, that this implies that for static analysis to perfectly mimic stationary analysis, one must to all intents and purposes have first executed the underlying dynamic analysis.

Period (discrete) versus continuous-time analysis

Macroeconomic analysis can be broken down into period or discrete-time macro-economic models and continuous-time macroeconomic models. Substantive differences in terms of theoretical predictions do not exist between these two types of analyses if one is careful to assure identical underlying assumptions. Yet the two analyses do differ in the analytical techniques used. For instance, while discrete macroeconomics relies on the techniques of dynamic programming and difference equations to characterize elements of the model, in similar circumstances con-tinuous macroeconomic analysis turns to the techniques of optimal control and differential equations.

Although substantive issues are not raised by the discrete- versus continuous-time dichotomy, it is sometimes argued that one is preferred to the other. For instance, an attractive feature of the continuous-time analysis is that it highlights quite clearly the distinctions between stocks and flows, something that is not so clearly discernable in discrete analysis. On the other hand, an attractive feature of discrete analysis is that it makes more transparent the link between the theoretical analysis and empirical testing, since such analysis coincides with the obvious fact that empirical data on macroeconomic variables is discrete.

New classical economics versus non-market-clearing

Classical analysis refers to the widely adopted view of how the macroeconomy should be modeled that existed prior to the experience of the Great Depression and John Maynard Keynes' *General Theory of Employment, Interest, and Money* (1936). In classical theory, the real side of the economy was separate from the money side. Classical analysis of the "real" side of the economy is aimed at determining such variables as total production, relative prices, the real rate of interest, and the distribution of output. Classical analysis of the money side of the economy meant analysis is aimed at determining money prices and nominal interest rates.

The separation of the monetary side from the real side in classical or neoclassical analysis led to the prediction that monetary changes do not have any effect on real variables such as total output.[12] A similar prediction is often obtained by more recent macroeconomic analysis, and this is one reason why this more recent analysis is referred to as the new classical economics.[13] Alternative labels of these new classical models include: rational expectations models with market clearing, neoclassical models of business fluctuations, and equilibrium business cycle models.

A common feature of the analyses of new classical economics, besides the fact that it suggests a divorcement of monetary changes from the real side of the economy, is that prices are determined in the analysis so as to clear markets. This view that prices serve to equate demands and supplies, a view common to microeconomics, is taken as an important strength of the analysis for it means that the models have consistent "microeconomic foundations." One implication of the market-clearing assumption is the same as in microeconomics – the analysis suggests that all gains to exchange have been extracted.

Contrasting the new classical economics with what preceded it helps one put this rebirth of classical analysis into perspective. Following the Great Depression, macroeconomic analysis took as its main premise the idea that markets did not clear – in particular, that prices did not adjust. In this context, the business cycle was defined by "market failure," and the role of government to stabilize the economy was clear. There are a number of different types of non-market-clearing, or Keynesian, models. One version of such Keynesian models, that popularized by Patinkin (1965, chapters 13–14), Clower (1965), and Barro and Grossman (1971), takes as given output prices, such that the output market fails to clear. A second model, popularized by Fischer (1977), Phelps and Taylor (1977), and Sargent (1987a) as an alternative formalization of the Keynesian model, takes as given the price of labor, such that the labor market fails to clear.

The common theme of these non-market-clearing analyses is that for various reasons prices do not clear markets and concepts such as excess demand and supply play a role in the analysis. Yet no concise reason is given as to why there is market failure other than suggesting such items as "coordination problems" and "transaction costs."[14] The result is that such analysis is challenged by the new classical economics as lacking the microeconomic foundations for price determination. As Howitt (1986: 108) suggests, such a view "forces the proponent of active stabilization policy to explain the precise nature of the impediments of transacting and communicating that prevent private arrangements from exhausting all gains from trade."[15] This is not an easy task according to Howitt, since "impediments to communication in a model simple enough for an economist to understand will typically also be simple enough that the economist can think of institutional changes that would overcome them" (1989: 108).

Microeconomic foundations and aggregation issues

An important feature of macroeconomic analysis is that it reflects the aggregation of individual decisions. A common approach to such aggregation is to assume "representative" agents, characterize their optimal behavior, then use such behavioral specifications in building the macroeconomic model. Thus, much of macroeconomic analysis entails looking at individuals' decisions, such as households' decisions to work, consume, and save or firms' decisions to produce, borrow, and invest in capital.

These characterizations of optimizing individual behavior make up part of the building blocks, or "microeconomic foundations," of macroeconomic analysis. Yet microeconomic foundations of macroeconomics are not restricted to such analysis. For instance, such foundations also include a characterization of how prices in individual markets are determined, as we saw in our discussion of new classical economics.

In developing the microeconomic foundations of macroeconomic models, we will often be struck by the extent to which the analysis restricts any role for heterogeneity or diversity among the individual agents in the economy. Yet such diversity can in certain instances be critical to the analysis. One attempt to introduce diverse or heterogeneous agents into macroeconomic analysis is represented by the overlapping generations models. These models also have the advantage of being genuinely dynamic in nature, and as such represent one area of macroeconomics that has recently received significant attention.

Deterministic versus stochastic

In recent years, an important element to macroeconomic models has been to introduce stochastic elements. The rationale is clear: the presence of uncertainty as to future events is real. As noted by Lucas (1981: 286),

> the idea that speculative elements play a key role in business cycles, that these events seem to involve agents reacting to imperfect signals in a way which, after the fact, appears inappropriate, has been commonplace in the verbal tradition of business cycle theory at least since Mitchell . . . It is now entirely practical to view price and quantity paths that follow complicated stochastic processes as equilibrium "points" in an appropriately specified space.

As the quote suggests, in dynamic models, especially for new classical economics where market clearing is presumed, stochastic elements are incorporated into the analysis, so that the role played by shocks to an economy in a dynamic setting can be well defined.

2 Walrasian economy

Introduction

This chapter develops a competitive model of the economy. The key assumptions needed for this model are spelled out in detail. One important aspect of this model is the "numeraire" or the commodity price that is used as a reference in the model. A distinction is made between accounting prices and relative prices and it is seen that traditional general equilibrium analysis does not determine the level of accounting prices, but rather simply relative prices. A number of modifications to the model are mentioned and add a sense of "realism" to the framework. These modifications include the introduction of futures markets, quantity constraints, and the costs associated with carrying out a transaction.

The chapter continues by considering individual decision-making and the theory of the consumer and how this relates to the determination of market demand. The general equilibrium conditions are stated in terms of relative prices and allocations. A theme carried throughout this book is emphasized, and that is the use of the aggregate budget constraint. Finally, it is shown that explicitly excluding money as a "market" allows one to understand how Say's conclusion that "supply creates its own demand" is arrived at in an economy composed of a single, aggregate commodity.

A simple Walrasian model

As discussed previously, the idea that prices adjust to clear markets is common to much of new classical macroeconomics. Thus we begin our examination of macroeconomic analysis by considering an economy consisting of perfectly competitive markets. This means that individuals take prices at which exchanges can be made as parametric, and prices adjust to eliminate excess demands so that individuals' plans at given prices are feasible. As the title to this section suggests, such a characterization is sometimes referred to as being indicative of a "Walrasian" economy. Walras described the process by which prices adjust to excess demand or supply as a groping or *tatonnement* process (see Walras 1954).[1] A fictitious auctioneer calls out different prices for the various markets and no exchange occurs until equilibrium prices are reached.[2]

Our analysis also begins at a very simple level. The term "simple" reflects at least the following three characteristics of the economy that we consider:

1   It is a barter economy. That is, any commodity can be freely traded for any other commodity. There is no role for a medium of exchange (money) in reducing the costs of arranging exchanges.
2   It is an exchange economy. That is, there is no production. Instead, individuals have initial fixed endowments of various commodities.
3   It is a timeless economy. Goods are indexed by physical characteristics and location but not dated according to availability. This rules out futures markets or the formation of expectations of future events and planning. Such an economy was suggested by Hicks (1939). Patinkin (1965: Chapter 1) and Hansen (1970: Chapter 4) provide a more detailed view of such an economy. An actual example of a pure barter exchange economy is offered by Radford (1945). The simple model of the economy developed below is useful in highlighting such concepts as: relative prices, the numeraire, individual versus market experiments, aggregation issues, conditions for general equilibrium, and Walras' and Say's laws.

The first model developed below also takes an approach to modeling the economy that is in vogue in current theoretical macroeconomics. As Sargent (1987b) states, the "attraction of (such) general equilibrium models is their internal consistency: one is assured the agents' choices are derived from a common set of assumptions."

Yet this advantage of general equilibrium analysis is not fully exploited until the elements of time, money, and production are introduced, and so we will expand the discussion in subsequent sections by introducing such features. Below we introduce in more detail some of the key assumptions underlying the simple Walrasian model we start with.

Key assumptions underlying a simple Walrasian model

As noted by Debreu (1959: 74), "an economy is defined by m consumers (characterized by their consumption sets and their preferences), n producers (characterized by their production sets), and the total resources (the available quantities of the various commodities which are *a priori* given)." As discussed above, we consider a special case of Debreu's "concept of an economy," one in which production is absent. As the following set of assumptions makes clear, we also restrict our analysis to private ownership economies with a price system. In particular, assume (partial listing):

Assumption 2.1   There are m individuals (agents) in the economy, indexed by $a = 1, \ldots, m$. There are T commodities, indexed by $i = 1, \ldots, T$.[3] Agent a's initial endowment of commodity i is denoted by $\bar{c}_{ai}$, $\bar{c}_{ai} \geq 0$, $i = 1, \ldots, T$. Naturally,

$$\sum_{a=1}^{m} \bar{c}_{ai} = \bar{c}_i > 0.$$

Note that this assumption reflects an exchange economy in which private property rights exist. "Private property rights" means that for each unit of each good, the exclusive right to determine use has been assigned to a particular individual.

Assumption 2.2   All exchanges occur at a single point in time.

Assumption 2.3   Each individual confronts the same known set of prices at which exchange can occur.[4] A *relative* (purchase) price of commodity i indicates the units of commodity j required to purchase one unit of commodity i. A *relative* (sale) price of commodity i indicates units of commodity j received when one unit of commodity i is sold.

Assumption 2.4   Purchase and sale prices are identical for each commodity. This means that there are no "price spreads" which would suggest either a gain to an individual buying and selling the same commodity or the presence of costs to making an exchange.[5] Thus, for the T commodities there are T^2 exchange rates, or relative prices, taking two commodities at a time.

The numeraire

While there are T^2 exchange rates, the complete set of exchange rates can be deduced directly or indirectly by the set of $T - 1$ relative prices:

$$(\pi_{1j}, \ldots, \pi_{j-1,j}, \pi_{j+1,j}, \ldots, \pi_{Tj}),$$

where the π_{ij} denotes the price of commodity i in terms of commodity j.[6] In the listing of relative prices, $(\pi_{1j}, \ldots, \pi_{j-1,j}, \pi_{j+1,j}, \ldots, \pi_{Tj})$, commodity j is referred to as the "numeraire."

To see how the set of relative prices reduces to $T - 1$, we rely on the fact that $\pi_{hh} = \pi_{hj}/\pi_{hj}$ for all h, j, and k. Let us see what this means for a simple example of three commodities, h, j, and k. There are then T^2 or nine different relative prices, which are: $\pi_{hh}, \pi_{jj}, \pi_{kk}, \pi_{hj}, \pi_{jh}, \pi_{hk}, \pi_{kh}, \pi_{jk}$, and π_{kj}. But, we can use the relationship $\pi_{hh} = \pi_{hj}/\pi_{hj}$ to reduce this to $T - 1 = 2$ relative prices with informational content. In particular, we know that:

1   $\pi_{hh}, \pi_{hk}/\pi_{hj}$, and similarly for π_{jj}, and π_{kk}, when $h = j = k$. In other words, the exchange rate of a commodity with itself is unity. This reduces from nine to six the number of relative prices for which information is required.

2   $\pi_{jh} = 1/\pi_{hj}$ when $k = j$ (such that $\pi_{kj} = \pi_{kk} = 1$). Similarly $\pi_{hk} = 1/\pi_{kh}$ and $\pi_{jk} = 1/\pi_{kj}$. For example, if the jth commodity is pears and the hth

commodity is oranges, then if $\pi_{jh} = 3$ (3 oranges = 1 pear), $\pi_{hj} = 1/3$ (1/3 pear = 1 orange). This reduces from six to three the number of relative prices for which information is required to reconstruct the complete set of relative prices.

3   Finally, $\pi_{kh} = \pi_{kj}/\pi_{hj}$ (for $k \neq j \neq h$). For example, if the jth commodity is pears, the kth commodity is apples, and the hth commodity is oranges, then if $\pi_{kj} = 3$ (3 pears = 1 apple) and $\pi_{hj} = 1/3$ (1/3 pears = 1 orange), then $\pi_{kh} = 9$ (9 oranges = 1 apple). That is, with 9 oranges, you can get 3 pears, which in turn will purchase 1 apple. This drops us from three to two relative prices required to reconstruct the complete set of relative prices. Since the number of commodities $T = 3$, we have shown how the T^2 relative prices can be constructed from $T - 1$ relative prices.

In subsequent discussions, we will arbitrarily let commodity T be the numeraire, such that the set of relative prices can be summarized by

$$(\pi_{1T}, \ldots, \pi_{T-1,T}).$$

For simplicity, let us change notation such that $\pi_{iT} = \pi_i, i = 1, \ldots, T$. Thus the set of relative prices can be rewritten as

$$(\pi_1, \ldots, \pi_{T-1}).$$

Note that $\pi_T = 1$ since we are assuming the Tth good is the numeraire.

In traditional general equilibrium theory there is a concept of "accounting prices" as well as the concept of relative prices. Accounting prices can be represented by a set of real numbers (say, $p_i, i = 1, \ldots, T$) attached to the T commodities.[7] The relationship between these accounting prices and the set of relative prices that do impinge on behavior is that $\pi_i = p_i/p_T, i = 1, \ldots, T$ (for $P_i \neq 0$). As we will see, traditional general equilibrium analysis does not determine the level of accounting prices, but rather simply relative prices.[8]

Anticipating future modifications

Before continuing, it might be useful to anticipate some of the subsequent changes we will make in the characterization of the economy. Besides the introduction of production, we will:

- introduce time, implying either forward (futures) markets or an important role for expectations of future spot prices;
- introduce quantity constraints that can arise if prices are fixed at non-market-clearing levels (i.e. depart from a Walrasian framework); and
- introduce the cost of carrying out an exchange.

With respect to point (c), such costs have been characterized by Coase (1960) as "transaction costs" arising from the costs "necessary to discover who it is that one wishes to deal with and to inform people that one wishes to deal," the costs of "conduct[ing] negotiations leading up to a bargain and to draw up a contract," and the costs "to undertake the inspection needed to make sure that the terms of the contract are being observed."[9] Such costs will alter the nature of contracts (exchange agreements) formed and may provide the reason for "price rigidities." Such costs also suggest a role for money.

Transaction costs are assumed to be zero in the simple Walrasian system outlined above. Sometimes this is referred to as a situation where there is "perfect information" or where markets are complete and "perfectly competitive."

Individual experiments

General equilibrium analysis can be divided into what Patinkin (1965) refers to as "individual experiments" and "market experiments." In the context of the simple Walrasian barter exchange economy, individual experiments consider the behavior of individual agents given an initial endowment and preferences when confronted with a set of prices. Market experiments consider the resulting determination of prices.

In the simple Walrasian model under consideration, individual experiments replicate standard microeconomic analysis of consumer behavior. In particular, assume:

Assumption 2.5   Individual a's preferences are described by his utility function $u^a(c_{a1}, \ldots, c_{aT})$ where $c_{a1}, \ldots, c_{aT}$ denote agent a's consumption bundle, $c_{ai} \geq 0$, $i = 1, \ldots, T$. u^a maps the set of all T-tuples of non-negative numbers into the set of all real numbers ($u^a : R_+^T \to R$). We make the appropriate assumptions with respect to individuals' preferences such that a utility function exists and is well behaved.[10]

Assumption 2.6   Individual a will choose the most preferred consumption bundle from the set of feasible alternatives (rationality). Given the possibility of costless exchange at the set of relative prices represented by $(\pi_1, \ldots, \pi_{T-1})$, feasible consumption bundles or sets $(c_{a1}, \ldots, c_{aT})$ are defined by:

$$\sum_{i=1}^{T} \pi_i \bar{c}_{ai} - \sum_{i=1}^{T} \pi_i c_{ai} \geq 0,$$

where $\sum_{i=1}^{T} \pi_i \bar{c}_{ai}$ denotes the initial endowment of individual a in terms of commodity T. The above expression defines the budget set.

The consumer problem

From Assumptions 2.5 and 2.6, individual a's optimum consumption bundle is the solution to the problem

$$\max_{c_{a1},\ldots,c_{aT}} u^a(c_{a1},\ldots,c_{aT})$$

subject to

$$\sum_{i=1}^{T} \pi_i \bar{c}_{ai} - \sum_{i=1}^{T} \pi_i c_{ai} \geq 0, c_{ai} \geq 0, \quad i = 1,\ldots,T.$$

The constrained maximization problem can be translated into the unconstrained Lagrangian expression:

$$\max_{c_{a1},\ldots,c_{aT},\lambda} L(c_{a1},\ldots,c_{aT},\lambda) = u^a(c_{a1},\ldots,c_{aT}) + \lambda\left(\sum_{i=1}^{T} \pi_i \bar{c}_{ai} - \sum_{i=1}^{T} \pi_i c_{ai}\right),$$

with first-order (necessary) conditions being[11]

$$\frac{\partial L}{\partial c_{ai}} \leq 0, \quad i = 1,\ldots,T,$$

$$\frac{\partial L}{\partial c_{ai}} c_{ai} = 0, \quad i = 1,\ldots,T,$$

$$c_{ai} \geq 0, \quad i = 1,\ldots,T,$$

$$\frac{\partial L}{\partial \lambda} \geq 0,$$

$$\lambda \frac{\partial L}{\partial \lambda} = 0,$$

$$\lambda \geq 0.$$

The constrained maximization problem can be translated into the unconstrained Lagrangian expression:

$$\max_{c_{a1},\ldots,c_{aT},\lambda,\mu_1,\ldots,\mu_T} \bar{L}(c_{a1},\ldots,c_{aT},\lambda,\mu_1,\ldots,\mu_T) = u^a(c_{a1},\ldots,c_{aT})$$

$$+ \lambda\left(\sum_{i=1}^{T} \pi_i \bar{c}_{ai} - \sum_{i=1}^{T} \pi_i c_{ai}\right),$$

with the necessary conditions being

$$\frac{\partial \overline{L}}{\partial c_{ai}} = 0, \quad i = 1, \ldots, T,$$

$$\frac{\partial \overline{L}}{\partial \lambda} \geq 0,$$

$$\lambda \frac{\partial \overline{L}}{\partial \lambda} = 0,$$

$$\frac{\partial \overline{L}}{\partial \mu_i} \geq 0, \quad i = 1, \ldots, T,$$

$$\mu_i \frac{\partial \overline{L}}{\partial \mu_i} = 0, \quad i = 1, \ldots, T,$$

$$\lambda \geq 0,$$

$$\mu_i \geq 0, \quad i = 1, \ldots, T.$$

Individual demands and excess demands

The optimal consumption bundle for agent a is defined by the above first-order conditions and will be denoted by the (demand) set

$$(c_{a1}, \ldots, c_{aT}), c_{ai} \geq 0, \quad i = 1, \ldots, T.$$

Individual a's demand functions will be of the form

$$c_{ai}^d \left(\pi_1, \ldots, \pi_{T-1}, \sum_{i=1}^{T} \pi_i \bar{c}_{ai} \right), \quad i = 1, \ldots, T.$$

That is, individual a's demand (consumption) of commodity i depends on the $T-1$ relative prices of commodities and the initial endowment. Note that the form of the utility function implies the utility-maximizing consumption bundle meets the budget constraint with equality. Thus at the optimal bundle we have

$$\frac{\partial L}{\partial \lambda} = \sum_{i=1}^{T} \pi_i \bar{c}_{ai} - \sum_{i=1}^{T} \pi_i c_{ai}^d = 0.$$

An important point to note about demand functions is that they are homogeneous of degree zero in what might be called accounting prices.[12] Accounting prices are defined such that $p_i = \pi_i \cdot p_T, i = 1, \ldots, T$, so it is clear that if all prices increase by the multiple θ, relative prices and the initial endowment are unchanged.

Individual a's excess demand function for commodity i is defined by $z_{ai} = c_{ai}^d - \bar{c}_{ai}$. If z_{ai} is positive, agent a is a net buyer of commodity i, while if z_{ai} is negative, the agent is a net seller of commodity i. The market value (in terms of the numeraire) of the quantity of the ith commodity that individual a seeks to exchange (buy or sell) is then given by $\pi_i z_{ai}$. From the budget constraint, we know that $\sum_{i=1}^{T} \pi_i(c_{ai}^d - \bar{c}_{ai}) = 0$ or $\sum_{i=1}^{T} \pi_i z_{ai} = 0$. In other words, for each individual the market value (in terms of commodity T) of individual excess demands must sum to zero. This rather obvious finding generates what is referred to as Walras' law, as we will see.

Market experiments

In the previous section, we reviewed the nature of individual demand functions and individual excess demand functions. Now consider the collection of m individuals. Aggregating or summing individual demand functions, we obtain an aggregate or "market" demand function for commodity i of the form

$$
c_i^d \left(\pi_1, \ldots, \pi_{T-1}, \sum_{i=1}^{T} \pi_i \bar{c}_{i1}, \ldots, \sum_{i=1}^{T} \pi_i \right) \equiv \sum_{a=1}^{m} c_{ai}^d(\cdot).
$$

Similarly, summing agents' excess demand functions for commodity i gives us the aggregate or "market" excess demand function for commodity i of the form

$$
z_i \equiv \sum_{a=1}^{m} (z_{ai}) \equiv \sum_{a=1}^{m} (c_{ai}^d - \bar{c}_{ai}).
$$

Note that a zero *aggregate* excess demand for commodity i does not imply that no exchange of commodity i occurs among the m agents. However, as we have seen, a zero *individual* excess demand for commodity i does imply no exchange of commodity i by that particular individual.

Aggregation issues

So far, our aggregations have remained true to the underlying microeconomic analysis. Yet this is rarely the case in macroeconomic analysis, which typically abstracts from what might be termed "distributional" effects. An example of this in the above context, as we will see later, is to ignore the effects of the distribution of initial endowments across individuals on market demands, such that the market demand function for commodity i is assumed to be of the form

$$
c_i^d \left(\pi_1, \ldots, \pi_{T-1}, \sum_{i=1}^{T} \pi_i \bar{c}_i \right),
$$

where

$$
\sum_{i=1}^{T} \pi_i c_{ai} \equiv \sum_{a=1}^{m} \left(\sum_{i=1}^{T} \pi_i \bar{c}_{ai} \right).
$$

As you can see, with heterogeneity (either in initial endowments or preferences), such a posited aggregate market demand function is unlikely to follow exactly from the underlying microeconomic analysis. One should keep in mind such approximations when interpreting macroeconomic analysis.

Equilibrium: an isolated market

With respect to a single market, equilibrium is characterized by an accounting price p_i and implied relative price $\pi_i = p_i/p_T$ such that $c_i^d = \bar{c}_i$ (demand equals fixed endowment) or equivalently $z_i = 0$ (excess demand equals zero). The tatonnement process is the description of how prices change to clear the market. In the Walrasian model, movement toward equilibrium, the tatonnement process, involves two facets:

1 *The Walrasian excess demand hypothesis*, which indicates that the accounting price of commodity i rises if there is excess demand and falls if there is excess supply. That is,

$$dp_i = f_i(z_i), \quad i = 1, \ldots, T, \qquad f_i(0) = 0, \qquad \frac{df_i}{dz_i} > 0.$$

In terms of relative prices,

$$d\pi_i = \frac{dp_i}{p_T} = \frac{f(z_i)}{p_T}, \quad i = 1, \ldots, T - 1.$$

Note that the change in price is *not* across time, since each market is assumed to clear instantaneously at the same point in time.

2 *The recontracting assumption*, which states that offers to buy or sell at various relative prices are not binding unless market(s) clear. Only when the equilibrium price (or price vector) is obtained are contracts then made final.

General equilibrium (conditions)

A general equilibrium will be characterized by a set of $T - 1$ relative prices $(\pi_1^*, \ldots, \pi_{t-1}^*)$ and allocations $(c_{a1}^*, \ldots, c_{aT}^*)$ for individual a, $a = 1, \ldots, m$, such that:

$$c_{ai}^* = c_{ai}^d \left(\pi_1^*, \ldots, \pi_{t-1}^*, \sum_{i=1}^{T} \pi_i \bar{c}_{ai} \right), \quad i = 1, \ldots, T; a = 1, \ldots, m \qquad (2.1)$$

$$\Rightarrow c_i^* \equiv \sum_{a=1}^{m} c_{ai}^* = \sum_{a=1}^{m} c_{ai}^d \equiv c_i^d;$$

$$c_i^* = \bar{c}_i, \quad i = 1, \ldots, T. \qquad (2.2)$$

Equation (2.1) indicates that the equilibrium allocation must be *optimal* in that it must satisfy all demands for commodities at the specified set of prices. Equation (2.2) indicates that such an allocation must be *feasible*, that is, sum to total resource endowment. Together these two conditions imply a set of relative prices such that excess demands are zero, or

$$c_i^d = \bar{c}_i, \quad i = 1, \ldots, T.$$

For questions concerning the existence, uniqueness, and stability of general equilibrium, consult Varian (1992), Debreu (1959) and Arrow and Hahn (1971).

Walras' law and Say's law

Note that the above statement of general equilibrium involves setting T excess demand equations equal to zero, but there are only $T - 1$ unknowns (relative prices). Walras solved this problem by showing that one of the equations, arbitrarily chosen, can be deduced from the other $T - 1$ equations. In other words, there are only $T - 1$ independent equations. To show the dependency, remember that the budget constraint for each individual is given by

$$\sum_{i=1}^{T} \pi_i c_{ai}^d - \sum_{i=1}^{T} \pi_i \bar{c}_{ai} = 0.$$

Summing across all individuals, it must then be the case that

$$\sum_{a=1}^{m} \left(\sum_{i=1}^{T} \pi_i \bar{c}_{ai} - \sum_{i=1}^{T} \pi_i c_{ai}^d \right) = 0.$$

Rearranging and substituting in c_i^d for $\sum_{a-1}^{m} c_{ai}^d$ and $\bar{c}_i$ for $\sum_{a-1}^{m} \bar{c}_{ai}$, we obtain:

$$\sum_{i=1}^{T} \pi_i (c_{ai}^d - \bar{c}_{ai}) = 0 \quad \text{or} \quad \sum_{i=1}^{T} \pi_i z_i = 0.$$

The above is an explicit statement of Walras' law. Walras' law states that the sum of the excess demands across all markets must be zero. Note that in summing, the excess demand of each commodity is weighted by its relative price, so that we are summing common units (i.e. all excess demands are in units of the numeraire). The above aggregate budget constraint is sometimes referred to as Say's law or Say's identity. If there is a distinction between the two, it is that Say's law explicitly excluded money as a "market." In this setting, one can understand how Say's conclusion that "supply creates its own demand" is arrived at in an economy composed of a single, aggregate commodity.

Conclusion

This chapter has developed a general equilibrium framework that sets the stage for a thorough understanding of how the macroeconomy works. Particular attention has been paid to the development of relative prices, and the development of aggregate demand through a process of many individual consumers operating in an environment in which they set out to maximize their own utility. This framework, and the tool of constrained optimization, is used throughout this book.

3 Firms as market participants

Introduction

In this chapter the simple Walrasian model is discussed in the context of money, financial assets, and production. The chapter clearly illustrates the firm's objective, that is, to maximize profits. However, the firm is constrained in that it must finance purchases of capital and equipment as well as pay its workers. Moreover, attention is paid to all the costs faced by the firm, not just the obvious ones. The investment and financing decisions of firms are discussed and issues related to Tobin's Q and debt-to-equity are explored. This chapter provides a detailed examination of the role that firms play in the macroeconomy.

A simple Walrasian model with money, financial assets, and production

In the exchange economy we just considered, endowments of the commodity good were magically bestowed on individuals each period. We now introduce production as the source of commodities. At the start of each period, there now exists a "labor" market in which labor services are exchanged. New agents, denoted "firms," hire the labor services provided by households. During the period, firms combine the labor services with an existing capital stock to produce output (commodities), which is sold in the output market net of output retained to replace capital used up during production. Revenues from the sale of output are distributed to "households" in the form of wages during the period. At the end of the period, interest payments and dividends are made to households out of revenues. Each period firms also enter the output market to augment their capital stock, with such purchases financed by the issue of bonds and a new financial asset denoted "equity shares." In particular, we assume:

Assumption 3.1 There are new agents in the economy, denoted as "firms." These agents are initially endowed at time t with a capital stock $\overline{K}$ and a technology for transforming capital services from a capital stock and labor services into a single, "composite" commodity. The technology is summarized by the production function

$$y_t = f(N_t, \overline{K}),$$

where $\overline{K}$ denotes the capital stock the firm inherits at time t, N_t denotes the employment of labor services arranged at time t for period t (from time t to time $t + 1$) and y_t denotes the constant rate of production of the commodity for period t (from time t to time $t + 1$).[1] Similarly, for period i ($i = t + 1, t + 2, \ldots$), which runs from time i to time $i + 1$, output produced is given by[2]

$$y_i = f(N_i, K_i).$$

Assumption 3.2 During each period, firms sell the output produced in the output market. For output produced during period t (from time t to time $t+1$), let p_t denote its price when it is sold during the period up to and including time $t + 1$. Let p_{t+1} denote the price of output produced during period $t + 1$ that is sold beyond time $t + 1$ up to and including time $t + 2$, and so on. At time t, the price level associated with the prior period is denoted by $\bar{p}$.

Assumption 3.3 At the start of each period, households rent their labor services to firms for the period. At the start of period t, agreements to exchange the N_t labor services during period t (from time t to $t + 1$) are entered into at the money wage rate denoted by w_t. Similarly, at the start of period $t + 1$, N_{t+1} labor services are exchanged at the money wage rate w_{t+1}, and so on.[3]

Assumption 3.4 At the end of each period, two types of financial assets are exchanged, bonds (in the form of perpetuities) and equity shares. Bonds promise to pay a fixed money (coupon) payment z each future period in perpetuity. Let $\bar{p}_b$, p_{bt}, and $p_{b,t+1}$ denote the money price of such bonds in markets at the end of periods $t-1, t$, and $t+1$, respectively; the gross (nominal) interest rates over period t (from time t to time $t + 1$) and over period $t + 1$ (from time $t + 1$ to time $t + 2$) are then given by:[4]

$$1 + \bar{r} = (z + p_{bt})/\bar{p}_b,$$
$$1 + r_t = (z + p_{b,t+1})/p_{bt}.$$

Note that if $r_i = r_t$, $i = t + 1, \ldots$, then successive substitution for the price of bonds in future periods will result in the following expression for the price of bonds at time t:

$$\bar{p}_b = \frac{1}{1+\bar{r}}(z + p_{bt}) = \frac{1}{1+\bar{r}}\left[z + \sum_{i=1}^{\infty} \frac{z}{(1+r_t)^i}\right]$$
$$= \frac{1}{1+\bar{r}}\left(z + \frac{z}{r_t}\right),$$

where $p_{bt} = z/r_t$. The number of previously issued bonds outstanding at time t is denoted by $\overline{B}$.[5]

Assumption 3.5   Equity shares are the second type of financial asset exchanged at the end of each period. Equity shares ("stocks") are contracts that obligate the issuer (firms) to pay to bearers at the end of each future period the income from the sale of output produced during the period net of other contractual obligations of the firms (e.g., wage payments to suppliers of labor services and interest payments to holders of bonds issued by firms). Let $\overline{S}$ denote the number of previously issued equity shares outstanding at time t. Holders of these equity shares are the "owners of the firms." Let $\bar{p}_e$, p_{et}, and $p_{e,t+1}$ denote the money price of equity shares exchanged in markets at the end of periods $t-1$, t, and $t+1$, respectively. The gross (nominal) rate of return on equity shares over period t (from time t to time $t+1$) and period $t+1$ (from time $t+1$ to time $t+2$) is then given by:[6]

$$1 + \bar{r}_e = [(p_t d_t/\overline{S}) + p_{et})]/\bar{p}_e,$$
$$1 + \bar{r}_{et} = [(p_{t+1} d_{t+1}/S_t) + p_{e,t+1})]/\bar{p}_{et},$$

where $p_t d_t$ and $p_{t+1} d_{t+1}$ denote total nominal dividend payments made at the end of periods t and $t+1$ (at time $t+1$ and time $t+2$), respectively. S_t denotes the anticipated number of equity shares outstanding after the equity market at the end of period t.[7] Note that the price of an equity share indicates the fact that the purchase of an equity share entitles the holder to a portion of future (not current) dividends.

Assumption 3.6   Households view bonds and equity shares as perfect substitutes. "Perfect substitutes" means that if equality in yields did not hold, households would refuse to purchase the asset with the lower yield, forcing an adjustment in its price that would result in equivalent yields.[8] With bonds and equity shares as perfect substitutes, we can speak of a single "financial asset market" that incorporates both bonds and equity shares and determines a single "interest rate."

Assumption 3.7   There are incomplete markets. Let p_i^e, $i = t+1, t+2, \ldots$, denote the expectation formed in period t concerning the price of the consumption good over period i.[9] Similarly, in period t we have p_{ei}^e, $i = t+1, \ldots$, and w_i^e, $i = t+1, \ldots$. Such expectations are assumed to be held with subjective certainty, allowing us to abstract from risk considerations for the moment.

Assumption 3.8   There are positive transaction costs to arranging exchanges of the consumption commodity during each period t. Money holdings serve to reduce the transaction costs of arranging exchanges during a period.[10]

Assumption 3.9   It is prohibitively costly for individuals to directly store the "composite" commodity for consumption in future periods. However, output not consumed during the period can be transformed (by "firms") into output in the subsequent periods through the augmentation of the capital stock, which permits higher rates of production of output in future periods.

Individual experiments: firms

As always, we start our analysis at the individual level. The behavior of two types of agents must now be considered – firms and households. We start with firms. In doing so, we consider a "representative" agent, a unit whose behavior, except for scale, is identical to the behavior of the aggregate of such units. Thus, the same notation will be used to represent both the individual unit and the aggregate of all units. In addition, we consider an infinite time horizon.

You should now recognize that an analysis of a representative unit neglects certain potentially important "distributional" aspects of the problem. For instance, for households the "real indebtedness effects" of a price change on demand may not be offsetting in the aggregate, but that potential impact is ignored.[11] For firms, the distribution of the initial capital stock can, given adjustment costs, affect total employment and output, but that too is ignored.[12]

To consider the behavior of a firm (or, more specifically, the manager who directs production for the representative firm), we assume:

Assumption 3.10   Technology is represented by the concave production function

$$y_t = f(N_t, \overline{K}),$$

where y_t denotes the firm's planned (at time t) constant rate of output for the time period from time t to $t+1$ to be sold during the period and at time $t+1$, N_t denotes the firm's planned (at time t) rate of employment of labor during period $(t, t+1)$, with labor services purchased in the labor market at time t, and $\overline{K}$ denotes the firm's planned capital stock for period t. Recall that to simplify matters, we take the capital stock for the current period, $\overline{K}$, as fixed at the individual firm level. This would be the case given appropriate capital adjustment costs.[13]

Assumption 3.11   The representative firm will choose the most preferred input combination, and implied output, given technology and prices (both current and anticipated future prices). At time t, the objective of the firm is to maximize the expected real market value of the $\overline{S}$ equity shares:

$$V_t = \frac{\bar{p}_e \overline{S}}{\bar{p}}$$

where $\bar{p}_e$ is the price of equity shares at the end of period $t-1$ (at time t).[14]

A restatement of the firm's objective

We have indicated that the objective of the firm at time t is to maximize the real market value of the $\overline{S}$ equity shares as given by

$$V_t = \frac{\bar{p}_e \overline{S}}{\bar{p}}.$$

To understand what underlies this market value of the firm, we have to define the elements underlying the price of equity shares and dividends. We start by examining what lies behind the price of equity shares.

The assumption that equity shares and bonds are perfect substitutes means that the price of an equity share can be expressed as

$$\bar{p}_e = [p_t d_t / \overline{S} + p_{et}]/(1 + \bar{r}),$$

where d_t denotes real dividends at the end of period t, so that $p_t d_t$ denotes nominal dividends, $\overline{S}$ denotes the number of equity shares outstanding at time t, p_{et} is the price of equity shares at the end of period t, and $\bar{r}$ denotes the interest rate over period t (i.e., from time t to $t + 1$).

By successively substituting in a similar expression for the price of equity shares in the next period, we obtain for an infinite horizon that:[15]

$$\bar{p}_e = [1/(1 + \bar{r})] \left[p_t d_t / \overline{S} + \sum_{k=1}^{\infty} [(p_{t+k} d_{t+k})/S_{t+k-1}] / \prod_{j=1}^{k} (1 + r_{t+j-1}) \right].$$

That is, the price of an equity share at the end of period $t - 1$ (at time t), $\bar{p}_e$, reflects the anticipated discounted future stream of nominal dividends per share.[16]

Since the real value of the firm is given by $V_t = \bar{p}_e \overline{S}/\bar{p}$, we can now express the value of the firm as:

$$V_t = [\overline{S}/\bar{p}(1 + \bar{r})] \left[p_t d_t / \overline{S} + \sum_{k=1}^{\infty} [(p_{t+k} d_{t+k})/S_{t+k-1}] / \prod_{j=1}^{k} (1 + r_{t+j-1}) \right],$$

which means that the objective of the firm can be stated in terms of maximizing the discounted stream of current and future dividends. Before examining what determines dividends each period, let us simplify the above expression for V_t by putting it in terms of real dividends each period. To do so, note that, by definition,

$$p_t \equiv \bar{p}(1 + \bar{\pi}),$$

$$p_{t+k} \equiv \bar{p}(1 + \bar{\pi}) \left(\prod_{j=1}^{k} (1 + r_{t+j-1}) \right), \quad k = 1, 2, 3, \ldots,$$

where π_{t+j} denotes the rate of change in the price level between period $t + j$ and $t + j + 1$. Thus, we have:

$$V_t = (\overline{S}/R) \left[d_t / \overline{S} + \sum_{k=1}^{\infty} [d_{t+k}/S_{t+k-1}] / \prod_{j=1}^{k} R_{t+j-1} \right],$$

where $\bar{R} = (1+\bar{r})/(1+\bar{\pi})$ and $R_i = (1+r_i)/(1+\pi_i)$ denotes the real gross rate of interest for period i (from time $i+1$ to time $i+2$, $i = t, t+1, \ldots$). Our next step in outlining the firm's problem is to obtain an expression for real dividends in each period.

Dividends and the firm distribution constraint

In general, we may denote real dividends at the end of any period as the difference between a firm's total real revenues during the period and the total costs incurred during the period. Total revenues derive from the sale of output produced during the period. In addition, one could add revenues from a change in the number of equity shares outstanding or a change in the number of bonds outstanding at the end of the period.[17] Total costs to the firm in any period include the agreed upon wage payments to the labor hired during the period, payments to replace depreciated capital, plus coupon payments at the end of the period to holders of previously issued bonds. Payments at the end of the period for the purchase of capital and associated adjustment costs could be counted as well.[18] That is, firms are constrained to have

dividends = revenue from sale of output

− wages

− interest payments

+ funds from change in outstanding bonds and stocks

− costs to replace depreciated capital, add new capital,

and capital adjustment costs.

The above constraint is typically divided into two separate constraints. One constraint earmarks funds raised from the change in outstanding bonds and equity shares at the end of the period to pay for or "finance" the installation of new capital stock during the period plus any capital adjustment costs. This is the "firm financing constraint." The remaining revenues minus expenditures then determine the level of dividends. This part is called the "firm distribution constraint."

The firm distribution constraint simply states that the revenues from the sale of output that exceed expenditures to meet wage payments, purchases of capital to replace that used up in the production process, and interest payments to bond holders at the end of the period, are distributed at the end of the period to households as dividends. Thus, real dividends at the end of period t are given by:

$$d_t = y_t - (w_t/p_t)N_t - z\bar{B}/p_t - \delta\bar{K}.$$

According to this expression, real dividends at the end of period t equal real revenues derived from the sale of output, y_t, produced during period t minus costs to the firm during period t that reflect the real wage, w_t/p_t, times the quantity of labor hired, N_t, less real coupon payments at the end of the period on previously issued bonds, $z\overline{B}/p_t$, plus purchases of capital during the prior period to replace that used up in the production process, $\delta\overline{K}$.[19]

In similar manner, real dividends for periods $t+1$ and $t+2$ (paid at the end of each period) are given by:

$$d_{t+1} = y_{t+1} - (w_{t+1}/p_{t+1})N_{t+1} - zB_t/p_{t+1} - \delta K_{t+1},$$
$$d_{t+2} = y_{t+2} - (w_{t+2}/p_{t+2})N_{t+2} - zB_{t+1}/p_{t+2} - \delta K_{t+2}.$$

We can rewrite the above definition of dividends to see more clearly why it is also termed the "firm distribution constraint." This constraint simply says that revenue from the sale of output net of that retained to replace capital used up in the production process (i.e., "net product") is distributed to households either as wage payments, interest payments, or dividends. That is,

$$d_t + (w_t/p_t)N_t + z\overline{B}/p_t = y_t - \delta\overline{K},$$
$$d_{t+1} + (w_{t+1}/p_{t+1})N_{t+1} + zB_t/p_{t+1} = y_{t+1} - \delta K_{t+1},$$
$$\ldots.$$

The firm financing constraint

The second part of the general constraint that firms' total expenditures equal revenues is that changes in the firm's holdings of capital, as well as any associated adjustment costs, are financed by a change in outstanding equity shares and/or bonds. This linking of funding for capital purchases to the issuing of equity shares and bonds is denoted the "firm financing constraint." For instance, at the end of periods $t+1, t+2, \ldots$, we have the following firm financing constraints:

$$K_{t+1} - \overline{K} + \psi(I_{nt}) = [p_{et} \cdot (S_t - \overline{S}) + p_{bt} \cdot (B_t - \overline{B})]/p_t,$$
$$K_{t+2} - K_{t+1} + \psi(I_{n,t+1}) = [p_{e,t+1} \cdot (S_{t+1} - S_t) + p_{b,t+1} \cdot (B_{t+1} - B_t)]/p_{t+1},$$

where $\psi(I_i)$ denotes the costs of installing new capital at rate I_i during period i (between time i and time $i+1$), a cost that depends directly on the rate of net investment ($I_{ni} = K_{i+1} - K_i$) planned at time t to occur between time i and $i+1$.[20] Recall that we assume that firms' plans with respect to the number of stocks and bonds that will be outstanding following the financial market at the end of period i (time $i+1$) mirror households' expectations concerning the number of bonds and stocks that will be outstanding, so we do not distinguish between firms' plans and households' expectations with respect to these variables.

Since bonds and equity shares are perfect substitutes, we can rewrite the above firm financing constraints in the simpler form

$$I_{nt} + \psi(I_{nt}) = A_t - \overline{A}_t = \text{net } A_t,$$

$$I_{n,t+1} + \psi(I_{n,t+1}) = A_{t+1} - \overline{A}_{t+1} = \text{net } A_{t+1},$$

where I_{ni} denotes net real investment (i.e., $K_{i+1} - K_i$), A_i denotes the *real* planned (at time t) value of total equity shares and bonds to be outstanding after the financial market at the end of period i, and $\overline{A}_i$ denotes the initial real value of equity shares and bonds for period i reflecting financing and capital decisions in prior periods but period i prices. For instance:

$$A_t = [p_{et}S_t + p_{bt}B_t]/p_t \quad \text{and} \quad \overline{A}_t = [p_{et}\overline{S} + p_{bt}\overline{B}]/p_t,$$

$$A_{t+1} = [p_{e,t+1}S_{t+1} + p_{b,t+1}B_{t+1}]/p_{t+1} \quad \text{and}$$

$$\overline{A}_{t+1} = [p_{e,t+1}S_t + p_{b,t+1}B_t]/p_{t+1}.$$

There are several aspects of interest with respect to the firm financing constraints. First, note that net capital purchases planned for period i to be installed between time i and time $i + 1$ are paid for at the end of period i when completely installed from the sale of financial assets at that time.

Second, note that firms purchase the output of the composite good to augment the capital stock. That is, we have a "one-sector" model in which the same good serves both households (for consumption) and firms (for investment). There is only a single commodity price. A typical extension is a two-sector model in which two goods are produced, a consumption good and a capital good. In such cases, a new variable, the relative price of the capital good in terms of the consumption good, is introduced.

Third, note that the firm financing constraint holds whether the firm finances capital with new bonds, new equity shares, or "retained earnings." Suppose, for instance, that a firm plans to add 100 units to its capital stock by buying a new piece of machinery. If the firm issues a bond with real value of 100 to pay for the machinery, then there is a direct 100 unit increase (the new bond) in the value of the financial assets issued by the firm. Note that the value of the current shareholders' stock is unchanged in this case of bond financed investment. While it is true that the tangible assets of the firm have increased by the 100 addition to capital, this benefit to shareholders is exactly offset by the fact that the firm's debt has also increased by 100.[21]

If the firm finances the 100 net investment by issuing new shares of stock equal to 100, again there is a 100 unit increase (the new equity shares) in the real value of the financial assets issued by the firm. As with bond financing, however, the real value of the initial shareholders' stock is unchanged when the firm finances its capital purchases by issuing new equity shares. The new shares do not dilute the value of the shares of the initial shareholders since the capital purchase increases the firm's tangible assets by 100, which is exactly the real value of the new equity shares issued.

Finally, if the firm finances the 100 net investment through retained earnings, there is, in essence, a 100 unit increase in the value of the financial assets issued by the firm for the following reason. When a firm retains earnings in order to finance a capital purchase, the current stockholders own the right to the income generated from the additional capital. As a consequence, the value of their equity shares rises to reflect the value of the new capital owned by the firm. We could equivalently view this as the firm paying out 100 units in dividends to its initial shareholders who then use the dividends to buy additional "constant value" equity shares equal to the value of the capital purchased by the firm. In other words, when the firm uses retained earnings to finance its investment spending, it is implicitly issuing new financial assets – equity shares.

The nature of capital adjustment costs

An important aspect of the above financing constraint is that it incorporates potential adjustment costs to purchases of capital as captured by the terms $\psi(\cdot)$, which depend on $I_{nt}, I_{n,t+1}, \ldots$, where I_{ni} denotes the planned (at time t) net rate of investment for period i.[22] The total cost of capital purchases is thus the sum of (a) the real payments (or receipts if negative) involved in the purchase (or sale if negative) of capital in the output market and (b) potential real payments, denoted "installation" or adjustment costs, associated with new capital acquisitions. For period t, adjustment costs are given by $\psi(I_{nt})$, where I_{nt} denotes net investment between time t and $t+1$. Gross investment for period t is given by $I_{nt} + \delta \overline{K}$. Note that we can thus decompose gross investment over the period into the change in the capital stock, $K_{t+1} - \overline{K}$, which is termed "planned net investment," and the replacement of capital used up in the production process, $\delta \overline{K}$, which is termed "depreciation."[23]

To understand the conversion of the above analysis to continuous time, we note that, in general, adjustment costs over period t of length h are given by $h\psi(I_{nt}/h)$, where the limit of the term I_{nt}/h defines the *rate* of net investment. That is, in continuous time the planned *rate* of investment would be defined by the rate of gross investment,

$$i_t = \lim_{h \to 0} \frac{I_t}{h} = \lim_{h \to 0} \frac{K_{t+h} - \overline{K} + h\delta \overline{K}}{h} = \dot{K}_t + \delta K_t,$$

and the adjustment cost function in continuous time would be $\psi(i_{nt})$.

For the aggregate rate of gross investment (a flow) to be defined by the above expression, K must equal $\overline{K}$. To achieve this, one of two approaches is typically taken. One approach assumes zero adjustment costs, in that $\psi \equiv 0$. This situation, sometimes referred to as the case of "perfect malleability," means that the rate of investment may not be defined at the level of the individual firm. That is, if the existing capital stock were higher or lower than the planned level, investment would be infinitely positive or negative. However, it can be shown that with zero adjustment costs, the output market in a continuous-time model at a point in time is simply a "capital market" and the expression $K_t = \overline{K}$ emerges as an equilibrium condition with respect to the capital market at time t.[24] Thus, we can apply L'Hospital's rule to define the aggregate rate of (net) investment in the continuous-time model with zero adjustment costs as:[25]

$$i_t = \lim_{h \to 0} \frac{K_{t+h} - \overline{K}}{h} = \frac{\lim_{h \to 0} d(K_{t+h} - \overline{K})/dh}{\lim_{h \to 0} dh/dh} = \dot{K},$$

where i_t is rate of investment.

In contrast to the case of zero adjustment cost, one can assume adjustment costs that take the following form:

$$\psi(0) = 0,$$

$$\psi(\beta) > 0, \text{ if } \beta > 0, \psi'' > 0, \text{ and } \lim_{\beta \to \infty} \psi(\beta) = \infty$$

$$\psi(\beta) < 0, \text{ if } \beta < 0$$

The above set of assumptions reflects the presumption that adjustment costs increase at an increasing rate with the rate of change in capital, and that it is infinitely costly to change the capital stock arbitrarily fast. The result of such adjustment costs in both discrete-time analysis and continuous-time analysis is that at time t the firm chooses $K_t = \overline{K}$. That is, at time t the firm views the inherited capital stock as optimal since it is prohibitively costly to change the capital stock at a point in time given such adjustment costs.[26]

As we will see, with "costs of installing a unit of new capital," there will be a difference between the market value of capital goods in place and their replacement cost. In particular, the ratio of these two values, known as "Tobin's Q," will exceed one. In addition, adjustment costs will mean that the firm's decision with respect to investment will not be myopic (i.e., plans will not be based on forecasts that extend only one period into the future). Rather, the firm will consider all future periods in making current investment decisions.

The firm problem: a general statement

One way to state the optimization problem faced by the firm is to say that at time t the firm makes plans with respect to current and future employment of labor $(N_t, N_{t+1}, \ldots)$, the future employment of capital $(K_{t+1}, K_{t+2}, \ldots)$, the stock of outstanding bonds $(B_t, B_{t+1}, \ldots)$, and the stock of outstanding equity shares $(S_t, S_{t+1}, \ldots)$ in order to maximize the real value of the previously issued equity shares outstanding at time t, with that real value given in general form by

$$V_t = (\overline{S}/\overline{R}) \left[d_t/\overline{S} + \sum_{k=1}^{\infty} [d_{t+k}/S_{t+k-1}] / \prod_{j=1}^{k} R_{t+j-1} \right].$$

Such plans are subject to the combined distribution and financing constraints listed above as well as to the production function. That is, in general the firm's problem can be stated as:[27]

$$\max(\overline{S}/\overline{R}) \left[d_t/\overline{S} + \sum_{k=1}^{\infty} [d_{t+k}/S_{t+k-1}]/ \prod_{j=1}^{k} R_{t+j-1} \right],$$

subject to the financing constraints

$$- [K_{t+1} - \overline{K} + \psi(K_{t+1} - \overline{K})] + (p_{et}/p_t) \cdot [B_t - \overline{B}]$$
$$+ (p_{bt}/p_t) \cdot (S_t - \overline{S})] = 0,$$
$$- [K_{t+2} - K_{t+1} + \psi(K_{t+2} - K_{t+1})] + (p_{e,t+1}/p_{t+1}) \cdot [B_{t+1} - B_t]$$
$$+ (p_{b,t+1}/p_{t+1}) \cdot (S_{t+1} - S_t)] = 0,$$

$$\ldots,$$

and the distribution constraints

$$d_t = y_t - (w_t/p_t)N_t - z\overline{B}/p_t - \delta\overline{K}$$
$$d_{t+1} = y_{t+1} - (w_{t+1}/p_{t+1})N_{t+1} - zB_t/p_{t+1} - \delta K_{t+1}$$
$$d_{t+2} = y_{t+2} - (w_{t+2}/p_{t+2})N_{t+2} - zB_{t+1}/p_{t+2} - \delta K_{t+2}$$

$$\ldots,$$

and given the production functions

$$y_t = f(N_t, \overline{K}),$$
$$y_{t+1} = f(N_{t+1}, K_{t+1}),$$

$$\ldots,$$

for $i = t, t+1, \ldots$.

The above problem has a recursive nature to it. At the start of any given period, the firm inherits a stock of capital, an outstanding stock of bonds, and an outstanding stock of equity shares.[28] These variables are state variables. Each period the firm chooses a set of the "control" variables – employment, investment. These choices, in conjunction with the production function, result in outcomes in terms of (a) a one-period return (dividends) at the end of the period and (b) a new set of "state" variables – capital stock and stock of financial assets (equity shares and bonds) – inherited in the subsequent period. Further, note that the objective of the firm is additive in these one-period returns (dividends). Thus, the problem is one to which we can apply Bellman's dynamic programming technique.

To reformulate the problem facing the firm as a dynamic programming problem, we use the conventional notation of dynamic programming problems.[29]

Specifically, the above problem can be viewed as involving:

(a) A set of "control" variables each period,

$$z_t = \{N_t, I_{nt}\}, z_{t+1} = N_{t+1}, I_{n,t+1}, \text{ etc.}$$

(b) A set of "state" variables each period,

$$x_t = \{\overline{K}, \overline{B}, \overline{S}\}, x_{t+1} = \{K_{t+1}, B_t, S_t\}, \text{ etc.}$$

(c) "Transition functions" that link the choices, specifically the choice of net investment during the period, to the capital stock available at the start of the next period as well as the stock of financial assets outstanding in the subsequent period. For instance, the choice of the net investment rate, I_{nt}, during period t dictates K_{t+1} given $\overline{K}$, since

$$K_{t+1} = I_{nt} + \overline{K}.$$

From the firm financing constraint, we know that the choice of the investment rate also determines the real stock of financial assets:

$$(p_{et}/p_t)[B_t - \overline{B}] + (p_{bt}/p_t)[S_t - \overline{S}] = I_{nt} + \psi(I_{nt}).$$

(d) A set of one-period return functions (evaluated at the end of period t):[30]

$$r_t(\overline{K}, \overline{B}, \overline{S}) = d_t, r_{t+1}(K_{t+1}, B_t, S_t) = \overline{S}d_{t+1}/S_t R_t, \text{ etc.}$$

Since bonds and equity shares are perfect substitutes, the above problem cannot be solved for a unique optimal number of bonds or equity shares to have outstanding each period. Thus, without any loss of generality, we may restrict our focus to either bond or equity share financing. That is, we can hold constant either bonds (i.e., $B_i = \overline{B}$, $i = t, t + 1, \ldots$) or equity shares (i.e., $S_i = \overline{S}$, $i = t, t + 1, \ldots$). Alternatively, we can combine the distribution and financing constraints into a single expression for dividends and hold constant both equity shares and bonds. In this case, we have "retained earnings" financing of changes in the capital stock. It is this case that we consider below.[31]

Simplifying the firm problem: "retained earnings financing"

If we assume that capital expenditures are financed from "retained earnings," there is a single state variable, the stock of capital. The problem facing the firm then can be simply stated as follows. The Bellman equation for period t given inherited capital stock $\overline{K}$ is

$$W(\overline{K}) = \max_{N_t, I_{nt}, K_{t+1}} \{d_t + W(K_{t+1})\},$$

subject to the transition function

$$K_{t+1} = I_{nt} + \overline{K},$$

and given the following definitions for real dividends and output for period t:

$$d_t = y_t - (w_t/p_t)N_t - \delta\overline{K} - z\overline{B}/p_t - I_{nt} - \psi(I_{nt}),$$

$$y_t = f(N_t, \overline{K}).$$

Substituting the above definitions for real dividends and output into the Bellman equation and substituting in the transition function, the first-order conditions are:

$$\frac{\partial f_t}{\partial N_t} - \frac{w_t}{p_t} = 0, \tag{3.1}$$

$$-(1 + \psi_t') + \frac{dW(K_{t+1})}{dK_{t+1}} = 0, \qquad \text{where } \psi_t' = \frac{d\psi(I_{nt})}{dI_{nt}}. \tag{3.2}$$

Equation (3.1) is the standard condition that labor is employed up to the point where the real marginal gain for an additional unit of labor in terms of the increase in output attained in the current period (i.e., the marginal product of labor, $\partial f_t/\partial N_t$), equals the real marginal cost as reflected by the real wage, w_t/p_t. Equation (3.2), indicating the optimal choice of investment, is discussed in the next section.

Optimal investment (and the future capital stock): zero adjustment costs

To express the optimal condition for investment and thus the future capital stock in a more transparent form, we need to expand upon the effect of an increase in the capital stock on the value function for period $t+1$. In other words, we need to clarify the nature of the term $dW(K_{t+1})/dK_{t+1}$ in Equation (3.2). To do so, let us consider the Bellman equation for period $t+1$. To simplify matters, we initially focus on the case of zero adjustment costs (i.e., that $\psi \equiv 0$, implying that $\psi_i' = 0$, $i = t, t+1, \ldots$). Given the inherited capital stock K_{t+1} for period $t+1$ and a fixed stock of equity shares, the Bellman equation for period $t+1$ is

$$W(K_{t+1}) = \max_{N_{t+1}, I_{n,t+1}, K_{t+2}} \{d_{t+1}(R_t)^{-1} + W(K_{t+2})\}$$

subject to the transition function

$$K_{t+2} = I_{n,t+1} + K_{t+1}$$

and (assuming retained earnings financing of capital changes and zero adjustment costs) the following definitions for real dividends and output for period $t+1$:

$$d_{t+1} = y_{t+1} - (w_{t+1}/p_{t+1})N_{t+1} - \delta K_{t+1} - zB_t/p_{t+1} - I_{n,t+1},$$

$$y_{t+1} = f(N_{t+1}, K_{t+1}),$$

Thus, we have:[32]

$$\frac{dW(K_{t+1})}{dK_{t+1}} = \frac{1}{R_t}\left(\frac{\partial f_{t+1}}{\partial K_{t+1}} - \delta\right) + \frac{dW(K_{t+2})}{dK_{t+2}}. \tag{3.3}$$

We can use first-order conditions for the Bellman equation for period $t+1$ to clarify the nature of $dW(K_{t+2})/dK_{t+2}$ in Equation (3.3). In particular, we have that the optimal choice of investment in period $t+1$ satisfies

$$-\frac{1}{R_t} + \frac{dW(K_{t+2})}{dK_{t+2}} = 0. \tag{3.4}$$

Substituting (3.4) into (3.3), we obtain the following expression for the effect of a change in the inherited capital stock on the value function for period $t+1$:

$$\frac{dW(K_{t+1})}{dK_{t+1}} = \frac{1}{R_t}\left(\frac{\partial f_{t+1}}{\partial K_{t+1}} - \delta\right) + \frac{1}{R_t}. \tag{3.5}$$

Substituting (3.5) into equation (3.2) and recalling our assumption that $\psi' = 0$, we thus have that the optimal choice of investment in period t satisfies

$$-1 + \frac{1}{R_t}\left(\frac{\partial f_{t+1}}{\partial K_{t+1}} - \delta\right) + \frac{1}{R_t} = 0. \tag{3.6}$$

The above expression can be rearranged to obtain:

$$\frac{\partial f_{t+1}}{\partial K_{t+1}} = m_t - \delta, \tag{3.7}$$

where m_t, Fisher's expected real rate of interest, equals $R_t - 1$ or $(r_t - \pi_t)/(1+\pi_t)$. The interpretation of (3.7) is fairly straightforward. Each period the firm chooses labor and capital such that the marginal gain in the subsequent period in terms of increased output equals the real marginal cost. For capital, the marginal cost is the rate of depreciation plus the expected real rate of interest. An explanation of this real "user" or "rental" cost of capital follows.

Over period t, the firm pays for one unit of capital at price p_t. Since the firm could have instead used these funds to reduce the outstanding stock of bonds by p_t, the cost of this capital (reduced dividends) in nominal terms is $p_t(1 + r_t)$. In real terms, the cost one period later is anticipated to be $p_t(1 + r_t)/p_{t+1}$. After one period, $1 - \delta$ of the capital remains, so that the sale of the remaining capital after one period of use (or the reduced purchases of new capital) reaps a nominal return of $(1 - \delta)p_{t+1}$ and real return $(1 - \delta)$. The real rental cost of the unit of capital is thus:[33]

$$p_t(1 + r_t)/p_{t+1} - (1 - \delta) = (1 + r_t)/(1 + \pi_{t+1}) - 1 + \delta$$
$$= (r_t - \pi_t)/(1 + \pi_t) + \delta$$
$$= m_t + \delta.$$

Summarizing our discussion, in the case of zero adjustment costs the optimal behavior of firms in periods t and $t+1$ is given by the following demand functions for period t and $t+1$:

$$N_t^d = N^d(w_t/p_t, \overline{K}),$$

$$I_{nt}^d = I_n^d(m_t + \delta, w_{t+1}/p_{t+1}, \overline{K}),$$

where $I_{nt}^d = K_{t+1}^d - \overline{K}$ and $K_{t+1}^d = K_t^d(m_t + \delta, w_{t+1}/p_{t+1})$. Note that the anticipated real wage next period affects I_{nt}^d since changes in the real wage affect the employment of labor and thus, assuming $\partial^2 f/\partial N \partial K$ does not equal zero, the marginal product of capital. A similar statement explains why $\overline{K}$ enters as an argument in the labor demand function.

An important feature of the above is that planned investment demand when there are zero adjustment costs simply depends on adjacent expected real user costs of capital and real wages. This reflects the fact that, with zero adjustment cost, capital demand is a function of the expected real user cost of capital and the real wage over the next period alone.

Financing choices and different debt-to-equity ratios: a digression

We have characterized the above choice of the capital stock under the presumption that the firm finances capital purchases through retained earnings. Yet we can show that the planned (at time t) choice of the optimal capital stock at time $t+1, t+2, \ldots$ is independent of the method of financing given that (a) bonds and equity shares are assumed to be perfect substitutes and (b) there is no cost to arranging the exchange of financial assets (otherwise, the retained earnings financing method is preferred). This result is sometimes referred to as the "Modigliani–Miller theorem" which states that the total value of the firm is independent of its financial structure. That is, the present value of the stream of dividends to the initial owners is independent of how liabilities are divided between bonds and equity shares. The result is that the capital structure is indeterminant.

The view that the method of financing capital purchases is largely irrelevant is a very useful simplification for macroeconomic analysis. However, you should be aware of some complicating factors that we are ignoring, factors that can cause firms to care about the method by which they finance their capital purchases.

When a firm issues bonds, the value of its outstanding debt rises. When it issues stocks, the value of its outstanding equity shares increases. Thus, the method of financing capital purchases affects what is known as the firm's debt-to-equity ratio.[34] Financing capital purchases with bonds will increase the firm's debt-to-equity ratio, while financing capital purchases with equity shares (either explicitly or implicitly by using retained earnings) will reduce the firm's debt-to-equity ratio. Two factors that can influence a firm's desired "capital structure" are tax considerations and bankruptcy costs.[35]

The corporate taxes that firms pay are calculated as a percentage of earnings. For tax purposes, corporate earnings are equal to total revenue net of costs, where costs are calculated as including not only wages and payments for raw materials and intermediate goods but also interest payments to bondholders. If a firm finances its purchases of capital using bonds, the interest it pays in the future will reduce its taxable earnings and thus the taxes that it has to pay. This means that a firm can lower its future tax liability by raising its debt-to-equity ratio – that is, by financing new capital purchases with new bonds rather than equity shares.

Raising the debt-to-equity ratio, however, is generally not without costs, which are typically referred to as "bankruptcy costs." Unlike equity shares which promise shareholders dividend payments if profits are sufficiently high, bonds promise *fixed* payments to their holders. Greater debt thus increases the fixed obligations that firms must meet in the future. This means that a fall in future revenues is more likely to force the firm into bankruptcy.

Bankruptcy occurs when a firm's revenues do not cover its costs and it is forced to default on its obligations to bondholders. Associated with bankruptcy are bankruptcy costs, the most obvious being the hefty legal costs associated with either reorganizing or undergoing a court-supervised liquidation. The existence of bankruptcy costs serves to limit the amount of borrowing a firm will undertake. It will hesitate to increase its debt-to-equity ratio beyond some level since the gain in tax savings will be offset by the costs associated with an increased likelihood of incurring bankruptcy costs.

To summarize, a firm can be viewed as having an optimal debt-to-equity ratio that reflects a tradeoff of tax and bankruptcy cost considerations. Table 3.1 lists the general level of debt-to-equity for a sample of industries in US manufacturing. Note that the debt-to-equity ratios vary widely among the industries in the sample, ranging from significantly over one to significantly less than one. The ratio is highest in the steel industry, where the value of debt is close to 1.7 times the

Table 3.1 Debt-to-equity ratios across select industries

	Book value of equity	Market value of equity
Steel	1.973	1.665
Petroleum refining	1.548	1.117
Textiles	1.405	1.296
Motor vehicles	0.922	0.594
Plastics	0.843	0.792
Machine tools	0.472	0.425
Pharmaceuticals	0.194	0.079

Source: Kester (1986). The book value of equity is computed from accounting sources, while the market value of equity is obtained by multiplying the number of outstanding shares by the current market price of the outstanding shares.

market value of outstanding market shares. In contrast, for pharmaceuticals the debt-to-equity ratio is only 0.079, indicating that the industry uses bond financing very little, instead financing its investment activities almost exclusively through the issuance of equity.

Adjustment costs for capital and Tobin's Q

Let us now consider the choice of capital when there exist adjustment costs. To keep the maximization problem simple, we shall continue to assume "retained earnings" financing of changes in the capital stock; we would, however, obtain identical results with bond or equity share financing. As we have seen, in the case of retained earnings financing the problem facing the firm is:

$$W(\overline{K}) = \max_{N_t, I_{nt}, K_{t+1}} \{d_t + W(K_{t+1})\}$$

subject to the transition function

$$K_{t+1} = I_{nt} + \overline{K},$$

and given the following definitions for real dividends and output for period t:[36]

$$d_t = y_t - (w_t/p_t)N_t - \delta\overline{K} - z\overline{B}/p_t - I_{nt} - \psi(I_{nt}),$$

$$y_t = f(N_t, \overline{K}).$$

As before, substituting the above definitions for real dividends and output into the Bellman equation and substituting in the transition function, the first-order conditions are:

$$\frac{\partial f_t}{\partial N_t} - \frac{w_t}{p_t} = 0 \tag{3.1}$$

$$-(1 + \psi_t') + \frac{dW(K_{t+1})}{dK_{t+1}} = 0, \quad \text{where } \psi_t' = \frac{d\psi(I_{nt})}{dI_{nt}}. \tag{3.2}$$

The problem facing the firm in period $t+1$, assuming retained earnings financing of capital changes, is:

$$W(K_{t+1}) = \max_{N_{t+1}, I_{n,t+1}, K_{t+2}} \{d_{t+1}/R_t + W(K_{t+2})\}$$

subject to the transition function

$$K_{t+2} = I_{n,t+1} + K_{t+1},$$

and given the following definitions for real dividends and output for period t:[37]

$$d_{t+1} = y_{t+1} - (w_{t+1}/p_{t+1})N_{t+1} - \delta K_{t+1} - z\overline{B}/p_{t+1} - I_{n,t+1} - \psi(I_{n,t+1}),$$

$$y_{t+1} = f(N_{t+1}, K_{t+1}).$$

Again, we can substitute the above definitions for real dividends and output into the Bellman equation for period $t+1$ and, substituting in the transition function (in particular, note the fact that $dK_{t+2}/dI_{n,t+1} = 1$), obtain the following first-order conditions:

$$\frac{\partial f_{t+1}}{\partial N_{t+1}} - \frac{w_{t+1}}{p_{t+1}} = 0, \tag{3.8}$$

$$-(1 + \psi'_{t+1}) + \frac{dW(K_{t+2})}{dK_{t+2}} = 0, \qquad \text{where } \psi'_{t+1} = \frac{d\psi(I_{n,t+1})}{dI_{n,t+1}}. \tag{3.9}$$

Finally, from our expression for the value function at time $t+1$, $W(K_{t+1})$, we have that

$$\frac{dW(K_{t+1})}{dK_{t+1}} = \frac{1}{R_t}\left(\frac{\partial f_{t+1}}{\partial K_{t+1}} - \delta\right) + \frac{dW(K_{t+2})}{dK_{t+2}}. \tag{3.10}$$

Substituting (3.9) into (3.10), and then substituting the resulting expression for $dW(K_{t+1})/dK_{t+1}$ into the first-order condition for I_{nt} (equation (3.2)), we obtain:

$$-(1 + \psi'_t) + \frac{1}{R_t}\left(\frac{\partial f_{t+1}}{\partial K_{t+1}} - \delta d\right) + \frac{1 + \psi'_{t+1}}{R_t} = 0. \tag{3.11}$$

Rearranging and simplifying, we have that

$$\frac{\partial f_{t+1}}{\partial K_{t+1}} = m_t + \delta + (m_t + 1)\psi'_t - \psi'_{t+1},$$

where $\psi'_t = \psi'(I_{nt}^d)$ and $\psi'_{t+1} = \psi'(I_{n,t+1}^d)$. An important feature of adjustment costs that is highlighted by the above equation is that the choice of investment in period t is now linked to the optimal choice of investment next period. Since this holds for each period in the future, the choice of investment today is linked to investment decisions over *all* subsequent periods.

We can simplify and rearrange the above first-order condition for investment in period t to obtain what is known as "Tobin's Q." To do so, let us first assume an identical real rate of return over time: in particular, we then have $R_i = R_t = 1+m$, $i = t+1, t+2, \ldots$, where $(1+m) \equiv (1+r)/(1+\pi)$. Let us also assume the firm has attained its optimal capital stock so that $K_{t+1}^d = \overline{K}$ and $I_{nt}^d = 0$. If the production function is separable into capital and labor, then the assumption of an invariant real interest rate implies that I_{ni}^d, $i = t+1, t+2, \ldots$, equal zero as well.[38] In this case, ψ'_t and ψ'_{t+1} can be replaced by a common $\psi'(0) > 0$. Then we may write the first-order condition as:

$$\partial f_{t+1}/\partial K_{t+1} - m - \delta = \psi'_m.$$

Dividing by m and adding one to both sides, we have:

Tobin's "marginal" $Q \equiv 1 + [\partial f_{t+1}/\partial K_{t+1} - m - \delta]/m = 1 + \psi' > 1.$

$$\tag{3.12}$$

The above provides the definition for Tobin's Q.[39] More precisely, we have Tobin's "marginal" Q, for it represents the ratio of the market value of an *additional* unit of capital to its replacement cost.

Given adjustment costs, the market value of an additional unit of capital exceeds its replacement cost, so Tobin's marginal Q is greater than one. Since investment demand planned over the coming period determines marginal adjustment costs $\psi'(I_{nt}^d)$, we see that investment can be written in terms of Tobin's Q.[40] The optimal rate of investment is that rate for which $Q - 1$ is equal to the marginal cost of installation. Thus, net investment demand is sometimes expressed as:

$$I_{nt}^d = I_{nt}^d(Q - 1), \quad \frac{dI_{nt}^d}{d(Q - 1)} > 0$$

The Q theory of investment is not operational as long as Q is not observable. While marginal Q is not typically apparent, with some additional assumptions we can show that the expression known as Tobin's "average" Q is identical to "marginal" Q. Tobin's "average" Q is defined as the ratio of the total value of the firm's existing capital (the market value of its equity shares) to its total replacement cost, and these variables are more easily measured.[41] In particular, for a one-sector model in which the cost of capital and output are identical:[42]

$$\text{Tobin's "average" } Q \equiv \frac{V}{K}.$$

Hayashi (1982) has shown that if the firm is a price-taker, if the production function is linear homogeneous in K and N, and if expectations of future real interest rates and real wages are static, then the marginal and average Q are identical.[43] To see why this is the case, note that if the real interest rate and real wage are invariant and the firm is at the optimal level of capital so that the capital stock is invariant over time, then, omitting time identifiers, we have

$$V = \sum_{k=1}^{\infty} d/R^k,$$

where (since $\psi(I_{nt}^d) = \psi(0) = 0$)

$$d = y - (w/p)N - \delta K.$$

Thus,

$$V = [y - (w/p)N - \delta K]/m,$$

where $m \equiv R - 1$. By Euler's theorem for a linear homogeneous production function (i.e., $K(\partial f/\partial K) = y - N(\partial f/\partial N)$) and the marginal productivity condition for labor (i.e., $w/p = \partial f/\partial N$) which reflects the price-taker assumption, the first two terms in the expression become $K(\partial f/\partial K)$.[44] Dividing by K, we thus obtain

Tobin's "average" $Q \equiv V/K = [\partial f/\partial K - m - \delta]/m + 1,$

which, as we can see, is the same expression as that for Tobin's marginal Q. Alternatively we can write the above as

$$V = [\partial f/\partial K - m - \delta]/m + 1 = (Q - 1)\,([\partial f/\partial K - m - \delta]/m)\,.$$

Adjustment costs for labor: labor as a "quasi-fixed factor"

Our prior characterization of the optimal choice of labor reflects an underlying production process that incorporates a very simple view of labor. For instance, labor markets are restricted to be only spot markets. That is, we rule out multiperiod labor contracts. Yet there is an extensive body of literature that investigates various rationales for and the implications of such multiperiod (implicit) labor contracts. One reason why long-term contracts might emerge is an attempt by firms who are less risk-averse than workers to smooth out income over time.[45]

A second reason why multiperiod labor contracts might emerge is if there are "adjustment costs" to changes in the size of the labor force. Adjustment costs could reflect the fact that in order to hire new workers, firms must incur hiring and training costs. Adjustment costs mean that a firm would view potential new hires and previously employed workers as imperfect substitutes, and this would provide an impetus for multiperiod labor contracts. The absence of adjustment costs simplifies the analysis by eliminating a rationale for multiperiod labor contracts and a choice of labor given adjustment costs. It also simplifies the analysis in two other ways.

First, the absence of adjustment costs suggests that we can measure labor services as the product of the fraction of the period each labor supplier works and the number of individuals hired. That is, given no adjustment costs, differences in "hours worked" and "number employed" that leave total work hours unchanged are viewed by the firm as equivalent in terms of production. In contrast, with positive adjustment costs, firms would have a preference for meeting temporary changes in output by changing hours rather than by changing the number employed.

A second implication of the absence of adjustment costs is that the employer views as equivalent two workers working at "half-speed" (and receiving "half-wages") and one worker working at "full-speed" for "full-wages." In contrast, given adjustment costs, firms would have a preference for meeting temporary output changes by altering not only hours per worker but also the intensity that each employee was asked to work. In fact, output per work hour, or "labor productivity," does typically increase more rapidly during a recovery, suggesting a more intensive use of labor.

In contrast, labor productivity growth is typically less rapid when the growth in total output slackens. This phenomenon is due in part to employers' hoarding labor in slack times so as not to lose trained employees whom they will want when there is an upturn in demand. (That is, to reduce subsequent adjustment costs given a future upturn in production.) Hoarding labor means that employers keep on more workers than necessary to produce the current output, so that each worker has less work to do than normal. The labor hoarding phenomenon, also referred to as the labor reserve hypothesis, is the formal term for changes in the "intensity" at which labor is used, and explains lower output per work hour during periods of slack demand.[46]

Conclusion

The nature of the firm was discussed with the emphasis on profit maximization. Decisions of firm owners facing a variety of constraints and costs were analyzed, with particular attention paid to how financing constraints and adjustment costs affected firm profits and the ability to adjust production levels. A link was made between households and firms that will lead us into the next chapter. Firms hire workers who, of course, constitute households in the economy. Workers are paid wages, as costs to the firm, but are an integral part of the production process. Moreover, firms may face costs of adjustment and other costly phenomena associated with decisions to alter the use of workers in the production process. Taken together, then, we see a link between firms and households as firm decisions have the propensity to affect consumer income.

4 Households as market participants

Introduction

This chapter brings the household into our model of the macroeconomy. Specifically, the household's ability to obtain utility through consumption and the labor supply decision is modeled within a choice framework. The solution is then used to formulate predictions about labor supply. The concept of time is critical to a thorough understanding of household behavior in the marketplace and a good deal of this chapter is spent analyzing intertemporal choices.

The life-cycle and permanent income hypotheses are introduced and a theory of portfolio choice is developed. Finally, the chapter ties many of these issues together and addresses the macroeconomic questions of absence of money illusion, the real balance effect, and the real indebtedness effect.

Individual experiments: households

Two agents inhabit our expanded macroeconomic model with production, firms and households. Having just discussed the nature of decisions confronting firms, we turn now to those confronting households. These decisions can be broken down into three types: consumption/saving, portfolio, and labor supply. Consider now the first two decisions, which should be familiar:

The "consumption/saving" decision. The representative household must determine at time t the consumption purchases over each period at the implied rate $c_t, c_{t+1}, \ldots$. We term this problem the "Fisherian" problem.

The "portfolio" decision. The individual must determine at time t the collection of assets to hold at the end of each period. In our expanded economy, there are ostensibly three types of assets:

1 nominal money balances planned at time t to be held at the end of period i, M_i, $i = t, t+1, \ldots$;

2 the nominal value of bonds planned at time t to be held at the end of period i, $p_{bi}B_i$, $i = t, t+1, \ldots$, where B_i denotes the planned number of bonds held and p_{bi} denotes the money price of bonds at the end of period i; and

3   the nominal value of equity shares planned at time t to be held at the end of period i, $p_{ei}S_i$, $i = t, t+1, \ldots$, where p_{ei} denotes the money price of an equity share at the end of period i and S_i denotes the number of equity shares planned at time t to be held at the end of period i.

Since bonds and equity shares are perfect substitutes, we can consider them as a single entity with respect to households' portfolio decisions. We will let A_i denote the *real* holdings of financial assets planned at time t to be held at the end of period i, $i = t, t+1, \ldots$. That is, for period t,

$$A_t = [p_{et}S_t + p_{bt}B_t]/p_t,$$

and so on. Excluding current dividend and interest payments, the real value of inherited financial assets at the end of period i reflecting portfolio decisions in the prior period will be denoted by $\overline{A}_i$, $i = t, t+1, \ldots$. For instance,

$$\overline{A}_t = [p_{et}\overline{S} + p_{bt}\overline{B}]/p_t,$$
$$\overline{A}_{t+1} = [p_{e,t+1}S_t + p_{b,t+1}B_t]/p_{t+1}.$$

The household problem

We start our analysis of the representative household, as usual, by discussing the household's preferences, constraints, and objectives. In particular, we make the following assumptions:

Assumption 4.1   The representative household's preferences are described by the utility function

$$u(c_t, c_{t+1}, \ldots, M_t/p_t, M_{t+1}/p_{t+1}, \ldots, 1-N_t, 1-N_{t+1}, \ldots),$$

where c_i denotes the household's planned (at time t) rate of consumption during period i (from time i to time $i+1$), M_i denotes the representative household's planned (at time t) nominal holdings of money at the end of period i, and N_i denotes the household's planned (at time t) rate of supply of labor services during period i (from time i to time $i+1$), such that $1-N_i$ denotes the planned rate of leisure during period i. It is assumed that $\partial u/\partial c_i > 0$, $\partial u/\partial(M_i/p_i) > 0$, and $\partial u/\partial(1-N_i) > 0$, $i = t, t+1, \ldots$. Macroeconomics often assumes a time-separable utility function, a form of the utility function that ensures "time consistency."[1] In particular, following the tradition of macroeconomics, we will assume that the total utility for the representative household at time t with an infinite planning horizon is given by

$$\sum_{i=t}^{\infty} \beta^{i-t} u(c_i, M_i/p_i, 1-N_i),$$

where β denotes the fixed personal or "utility" discount factor, with $0 < \beta < 1$.[2] In the above, note that the one-period utility function for period t (time t to $t + 1$) is $u(c_t, M_t/p_t, 1 - N_t)$, for period $t + 1$ (time $t + 1$ to $t + 2$) it is $u(c_{t+1}, M_{t+1}/p_{t+1}, 1 - N_{t+1})$, and so on. Further, note the infinite time horizon.

Assumption 4.2   Individuals will choose the most preferred sequence of consumption, money holdings, and labor supply from the set of feasible alternatives (rationality). The feasible set of consumption, money holdings, and leisure,

$$(c_t, c_{t+1}, \ldots, M_t/p_t, M_{t+1}/p_{t+1}, \ldots, 1 - N_t, 1 - N_{t+1}, \ldots),$$

is defined by the set of equalities:

$$(w_t/p_t)N_t + z\overline{B}/p_t + \overline{A}_t + \overline{M}/p_t - [c_t + M_t/p_t + A_t] = 0,$$

$$(w_{t+1}/p_{t+1})N_{t+1} + zB_t/p_{t+1} + \overline{A}_{t+1} + M_t/p_{t+1}$$
$$- [c_{t+1} + M_{t+1}/p_{t+1} + A_{t+1}] = 0,$$

$$\cdots$$

Note that we assume the budget constraints are met with equality. Further, note that the sum of dividends, wage payments, and interest payments equals total output minus depreciation. For instance, for period t,

$$(w_t/p_t)N_t + d_t + z \cdot \overline{B}/p_t = y_t - \delta\overline{K},$$

and so on. This is simply the firm distribution constraint for period t.

Several aspects of the above problem deserve further elaboration. First, a word on notation for future variables. It is common in macroeconomics to derive the microeconomic theoretical restrictions for the aggregate model under the condition of certainty even though the analysis is then applied to situations that involve potential stochastic elements. One obvious way to eliminate considerations of uncertainty from the analysis is to assume perfect foresight. A second way is to assume that individual expectations of future events are point estimates held with subjective certainty. Note that either approach simplifies the analysis, and in many cases this simplification gives us results that are not overturned if risk were to be systematically incorporated into the analysis.

In the analysis of individual behavior below, we will often, for notational simplicity, not distinguish between future prices and the expectations of future prices. Assuming expectations are held with subjective certainty, this lack of distinction will not be serious in discussing the result of the optimization problems. That is, the findings for perfect foresight can be made identical to those without the assumption of perfect foresight by switching actual future prices for expected prices. Sometimes, for clarity, we will explicitly denote expected future prices (point estimates held with subjective certainty) by the superscript "e."

A second aspect of the above analysis that may initially appear odd concerning the above one-period utility function for period i (from time i to time $i+1$) is that it seems that we are mixing money balances that occur at one time with consumption and leisure that occur at an earlier time. The reason for this is that money balances are a stock variable, and we are recording their value at the end of each period i, that is, at time $i+1$.[3] The following scenario for the discrete-time analysis may help clarify what is going on.

At time t the labor market takes place and agreements are made to exchange labor services at rate N_t over the period $(t, t+1)$ for the money wage w_t. During the period, an output market operates in which firms sell output produced at rate y_t. During the period, households receive money wages w_t. At the end of the period (time $t+1$), households anticipate real interest payments $z\overline{B}/p_t$ from their prior purchases of bonds $(\overline{B})$ and real dividends d_t from their prior purchase of equity shares stock $(\overline{S})$.[4] Given the above income sources as well as inherited nominal holdings of money $(\overline{M})$ and the anticipated value of inherited financial asset $\overline{A}_t$ at the end of the period, households plan an average rate of consumption c_t during the period.

At the end of period t, after all income is received and final planned purchases of consumption goods are made, the remainder reflects households' planned (at time t) end-of-the-period change in real money balances $((M_t - \overline{M})/p_t)$ and planned changes in real financial assets holdings $(A_t - \overline{A}_t)$. For financial assets, the real price for bonds at the end of period t is p_{bt}/p_t and the real price for equity shares is p_{et}/p_t.

According to the above scenario, the sale of labor services at rate N_t and rate of consumption c_t over the period from time t to $t+1$ tend to coincide, while real money balances M_t/p_t and real financial asset holdings A_t can be viewed as the planned (at time t) real stocks of such assets to be held at the end of period t. In continuous-time analysis, as the length of the period, h, goes to zero, the rate at which leisure is lost from supplying labor services during the period (N_t), the rate of consumption (c_t), and the stocks of real money and real financial asset holdings would coincide.

A third aspect of the above analysis is that we have interpreted $1 - N_i$ as the portion of the period of length 1 that the individual spends at leisure given the supply of labor at rate N_i. This is a simplification, however, for at the same time we have suggested that the "utility yield" of money is derived from its ability to reduce the transaction costs in arranging exchanges, with such transaction costs reflecting, at least in part, a loss of leisure. To explicitly incorporate such a view of money, leisure during a period i of length h given the sale of labor services N_i and the real money balances M_i/p_i held at the end of the period would be given by $h(1 - N_i - \Gamma(M_i/p_i))$, where the function $\Gamma(M_i/p_i)$ reflects transactions costs in terms of the loss of leisure. The fact that $\Gamma' < 0$ indicates that increased money holdings raise utility by reducing leisure lost in arranging transactions. In this case, the one-period utility function would formally be given by $u(c_i, 1 - N_i - \Gamma(M_i/p_i))$, with $\partial u/\partial c_i > 0$ and $\partial u/\partial(1 - N_i - \Gamma(M_i/p_i)) > 0$.

The general solution to the household problem

We can express the household problem in terms of a set of Bellman equations. Assuming perfect foresight (or, equivalently, interpreting future prices, dividend, etc. as expectations of such variables held with subjective certainty), we thus have for period t (time t to $t + 1$):

$$W(\bar{x}_t) = \max_{\substack{c_t, N_t \\ M_t/p_t, x_{t+1}}} [u(c_t, M_t/p_t, 1 - N_t) + W(x_{t+1})]$$

subject to the transition function

$$x_{t+1} = R_t[\bar{x}_t + (w_t/p_t)N_t - c_t] - [R_t - R_{mt}]M_t/p_t$$

and given $\bar{x}_t$. R_{mt} is the real gross rate of interest on money, that is, the gross real rate of return on money, and equals one divided by one plus the rate of inflation $(1/(1 + \pi_t))$. The term $\bar{x}_t$ is the total value in period t derived from the "inherited" holdings of money, bonds, and stocks. This total value is the sum of current dividends and interest (received at the end of period t) on stock and bond holdings acquired previously, the real value of these financial assets at the end of period t exclusive of these current interest and dividend payments, and the real value of previously acquired money holdings:

$$\bar{x}_t \equiv d_t + z\overline{B}/p_t + \overline{A}_t + \overline{M}/p_t,$$

where

$$\overline{A}_t \equiv [p_{et}\overline{S} + p_{bt}\overline{B}]/p_t.$$

The difference between the total real value derived in period t from inherited bonds, stocks, and money balances plus real wage income, $\bar{x}_t + (w_t/p_t)N_t$, and consumption in period t, c_t, reflects the acquisition of bonds, equity shares, and money holdings at the end of period t by the representative household. Letting A_t denote the planned holdings of financial assets at the end of period t, we thus have from the household budget constraint that

$$A_t + M_t/p_t = \bar{x}_t + (w_t/p_t)N_t - c_t,$$

where

$$A_t \equiv [p_{et}S_t + p_{bt}B_t]/p_t.$$

Recall that R_t, the gross real rate of return on financial assets, equals one plus the nominal interest rate divided by one plus the rate of inflation $((1 + r_t)/(1 + \pi_t))$. Thus in period $t + 1$, and given our definition of R_{mt}, the inherited real value of bonds, stocks, and money balances, including dividends and interest payments, is given by

$$x_{t+1} = R_t A_t + R_{mt} M_t / p_t.$$

Substituting in the expression for A_t derived from the household budget constraint (i.e., $A_t = x_t + (w_t/p_t)N_t - c_t - M_t/p_t$) and rearranging, we obtain the transition function:

$$x_{t+1} = R_t[x_t + (w_t/p_t)N_t - c_t] - [R_t - R_{mt}]M_t/p_t.$$

Substituting the transition function into Bellman's equation for period t, we have the following first-order conditions for c_t, N_t, and M_t/p_t assuming interior solutions (i.e., $c_t > 0$, $1 > N_t > 0$, and $M_t/p_t > 0$):

$$\partial u_t/\partial c_t - (\partial W(x_{t+1})/\partial x_{t+1})R_t = 0, \tag{4.1}$$

$$\partial u_t/\partial(1 - N_t) + (\partial W(x_{t+1})/\partial x_{t+1})R_t(w_t/p_t) = 0, \tag{4.2}$$

$$\partial u_t/\partial(M_t/p_t) - (\partial W(x_{t+1})/\partial x_{t+1})(R_t - R_{mt}) = 0. \tag{4.3}$$

The above conditions indicate that for period t (time t to time $t + 1$) we have from equations (4.1) and (4.2) that:

$$\frac{\partial u_t/\partial(1 - N_t)}{\partial u_t/\partial c_t} = \frac{w_t}{p_t}. \tag{4.4}$$

In words, the optimal choice of leisure is such that the marginal value of leisure in terms of consumption, that is, the marginal rate of substitution between leisure and consumption as given by

$$\frac{\partial u_t/\partial(1 - N_t)}{\partial u_t/\partial c_t}$$

equals the marginal cost of leisure in terms of consumption forgone in the current period as given by the real wage w_t/p_t.

From equations (4.1) and (4.3) we have for period t that:

$$\frac{\partial u_t/\partial(M_t/p_t)}{\partial u_t/\partial c_t} = (R_t)^{-1}(R_t - R_{mt}).$$

In words, the optimal choice of real money balances is such that the marginal rate of substitution between real money balances and consumption as given by

$$\frac{\partial u_t/\partial(M_t/p_t)}{\partial u_t/\partial c_t}$$

equals the marginal cost in terms of the present value of the loss in interest income in the subsequent period due to the holding of money balances instead of financial assets as given by the expression $(R_t)^{-1}(R_t - R_{mt})$. Recall that $R_t - R_{mt}$ equals $(1 + r_t)/(1 + \pi_t) - (1/(1 + \pi_t))$, which is simply $r_t/(1 + \pi_t)$, or essentially the anticipated nominal rate of interest. Given that $R_t = (1 + r_t)/(1 + \pi_t)$, we thus have that $(R_t)^{-1}(R_t - R_{mt}) = r_t/(1 + r_t)$.

We can expand upon the above discussion of the first-order conditions for period t by first noting that $W(x_{t+1})$ is defined by

$$W(x_{t+1}) = \max_{\substack{c_{t+1}, N_{t+1} \\ M_{t+1}/p_{t+1}, x_{t+2}}} [\beta u(c_{t+1}, M_{t+1}/p_{t+1}, 1 - N_{t+1}) + W(x_{t+2})],$$

where

$$x_{t+2} = R_{t+1}[x_{t+1} + (w_{t+1}/p_{t+1})N_{t+1} - c_{t+1}] - [R_{t+1} - R_{m,t+1}]M_{t+1}/p_{t+1},$$

given

$$\bar{x}_{t+1} \equiv d_{t+1} + zB_t/p_{t+1} + \overline{A}_{t+1} + M_t/p_{t+1},$$

$$\overline{A}_{t+1} \equiv [p_{e,t+1}S_t + p_{b,t+1}B_t]/p_{t+1}.$$

Again, substituting the transition function into the Bellman equation for period $t + 1$, we have the following first-order conditions for period $t + 1$:

$$\beta \partial u_{t+1}/\partial c_{t+1} - (\partial W(x_{t+2})/\partial x_{t+2})R_{t+1} = 0, \tag{4.1'}$$

$$- \beta \partial u_{t+1}/\partial(1 - N_{t+1}) + (\partial W(x_{t+2})/\partial x_{t+2})R_{t+1}w_{t+1}/p_{t+1} = 0, \tag{4.2'}$$

$$\beta \partial u_{t+1}/\partial(M_{t+1}/p_{t+1}) - (\partial W(x_{t+2})/\partial x_{t+2})(R_{t+1} - R_{m,t+1}) = 0. \tag{4.3'}$$

Now, consider the impact of the change in x_{t+1} on the value function $W(x_{t+1})$. The above first-order conditions imply that the indirect effects of the change in x_{t+1} on $W(x_{t+1})$ through the effect of such a change on the choice of the optimal values of consumption, labor supply, and real money balances for period $t + 1$ are zero.[5] This is simply an application of the envelope theorem, which states that the change in the objective function adjusting the choice variables optimally is equal to the change in the objective function when one does not adjust the choice variables. This fact, along with the transition function for x_{t+2}, gives us

$$\partial W(x_{t+1})/\partial x_{t+1} = (\partial W(c_{t+2})/\partial x_{t+2})R_{t+1}. \tag{4.5}$$

Substituting equation (4.1') into (4.5), we obtain

$$\partial W(x_{t+1})/\partial x_{t+1} = \beta \partial u_{t+1}/\partial c_{t+1}. \tag{4.6}$$

Alternatively, by substituting in (4.2'), we can obtain:[6]

$$\partial W(x_{t+1})/\partial x_{t+1} = \beta[\partial u_{t+1}/\partial(1 - N_{t+1})]p_{t+1}/w_{t+1}. \tag{4.7}$$

Combining equations (4.1) and (4.6) gives us the standard Fisherian solution for the optimal allocation of consumption between period t (time t to $t + 1$) and period $t + 1$ (time $t + 1$ to $t + 2$):

$$\frac{\partial u_t/\partial c_t}{\beta \partial u_{t+1}/\partial c_{t+1}} = R_t.$$

Combining equations (4.3) and (4.6), we obtain the standard expression for the optimal portfolio choice of money:

$$\frac{\partial u_t/\partial(M_t/p_t)}{\beta \partial u_{t+1}/\partial c_{t+1}} = R_t - R_{mt}.$$

Combining equations (4.2) and (4.7) gives us an expression for the optimal allocation of labor supply over time:

$$\frac{\partial u_t/\partial(1 - N_t)}{\beta \partial u_{t+1}/\partial(1 - N_{t+1})} = \frac{p_{t+1}}{w_{t+1}} R_t \frac{w_t}{p_t}. \tag{4.8}$$

Having discussed the "Fisherian problem" and the "portfolio problem" confronting the household, we turn our attention in the next section to the "labor supply problem" as captured by equations (4.4) and (4.8). Before doing so, however, a general comment should be made with respect to the discussions to follow, as well as the preceding discussions of the Fisherian problem and the portfolio decision.

In focusing on first-order conditions with respect to the particular variables at issue (i.e., first-order conditions for consumption now and next period for the Fisherian problem, first-order conditions for real money holdings and future consumption for the portfolio problem, and first-order conditions for labor supply now and next period for the labor supply decision), one has a tendency to forget that the optimizing problem involves the simultaneous choice of consumption, portfolio, and leisure. In general, this means that the analysis is often not as straightforward as it may first appear. For instance, a change in the current real wage or an expected real interest rate can affect the first-order condition concerning the choice of labor supply through its impact on the choice of consumption if $\partial^2 u/\partial c \partial N \neq 0$, for then the change in consumption alters the "marginal utility" of leisure. One simple way to abstract from these "indirect" effects is to assume that the utility function is separable not only across time but also with respect to consumption, leisure, and real money balances each period, such that $\partial^2 u/\partial c \partial N = \partial^2 u/\partial c \partial(M/p) = \partial^2 u/\partial N \partial(M/p) = 0$.

The choice of hours within a period

Equation (4.4) indicates that at the optimal labor supply the household cannot be made better off by trading consumption for leisure within periods at the expected real wage for the period. Equation (4.8) indicates that at the optimum the household cannot be made better off by trading leisure across periods given the relevant real wages and the real interest rate.[7] Figure 4.1 captures the first situation, that is, the optimal choice of consumption and leisure within a period.

For the moment, let us hold anticipated real interest rates constant. Further, let us assume unit elastic expectations with respect to wages as well as prices, so that a change in the current wage or price level that alters the current real wage changes future expected real wages as well, so that there is no change in the current real wage *relative to* future expected real wages. In addition, let us hold constant for the moment the effect on current real money balances of a change in the current real wage. These assumptions help us to mimic the traditional "static" or single-period analysis (e.g., Patinkin) of the effect of a change in the current period's anticipated real wage on individuals' labor supply during period t. Under such circumstances, an increase in the real wage for period t can have ambiguous effects. As Patinkin (1965) states: "for simplicity, it is ... assumed that [labor] supply is an increasing function of the real wage, though there are well known reservations on this score."

To understand what Patinkin is referring to, consider an increase in the real wage due to a rise in the money wage w_t. Consider one possible result on the household's labor supply decision. The increase in the net real wage means a steeper budget line, as the household's optimal leisure–consumption combination changes from $1 - N_t^s$ and c_t^d (call this choice A) to $(1 - N_t^s)'$ and $(c_t^d)'$ (choice C).

An increase in the real wage has two conceptually distinct effects on the household's labor supply decision: an income effect and a substitution effect. The income effect refers to the fact that an increase in the real wage makes the household better off because it leads to an increase in the household's feasible consumption set in

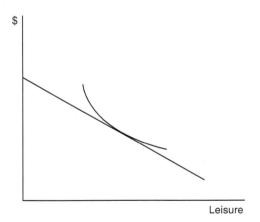

Figure 4.1 Consumption and leisure.

the current period. The higher real wage means that the household, if it so desires, can increase both its leisure and consumption. Thus, the household is able to reach a higher indifference curve, which has associated with it a higher utility level. The substitution effect refers to the fact that the increase in the real wage makes an hour of leisure relatively more expensive in terms of consumption that must be forgone.

To isolate the substitution and income effects of the change in the net real wage, suppose that after the real wage increases we temporarily take away just enough of the household's nonlabor income so that it is just able to attain its original indifference curve. The household's choice of leisure and income would then be $(1 - N_t^s)''$ and $(c_t^d)''$ (call this choice B). Thus, if we hold the household's utility level constant, the increase in the real wage leads unambiguously to a lower level of leisure: since an hour of leisure is relatively more expensive, the household substitutes away from leisure, choosing to work more hours. The movement from choice A to choice B constitutes the pure "substitution effect" of the higher net real wage.[8]

Now suppose that we give the household back the nonlabor income that we temporarily took away. This causes an outward shift in the budget line, and the household's new choice of leisure and consumption would be $(1 - N_t^s)'$ and $(c_t^d)'$ (choice C). The movement from B to C constitutes the "income effect" of the change in the net real wage. In the present case, the income effect on the choice of leisure is positive, reflecting the assumption that leisure is a normal good.

Note that the substitution and income effects on leisure work in opposite directions. The substitution effect of the higher real wage causes leisure to fall and hours worked to rise, while the income effect causes leisure to rise and hours worked to fall. The net effect on leisure and hours worked depends on which effect dominates.[9] If the substitution effect dominates, then a higher real wage results in a decrease in desired leisure and an increase in desired working hours. If the income effect dominates, the opposite is true and the individual's labor supply curve is "backward bending" when plotted against the real wage.

The available evidence suggests that for many workers, the income effect tends to dominate slightly. Estimates are that for men, an increase of 10 percent in the real wage results in approximately a 1.5 percent reduction in the hours worked. This reduction in hours worked reflects an income effect of approximately −2.5 percent and a substitution effect of about 1 percent. Other evidence suggests a similar pattern for working women.[10]

The choice of participation within a period

Thus far we have considered a household representative of those who are in the labor force working a positive number of hours. Yet this masks the unambiguous effect of a higher real wage on the labor supply of those households not in the labor force. To show this, we consider a corner solution with respect to labor supply, in particular a household, denoted a, that has chosen not to participate in the labor market. For such a household, let us return to the Bellman equation for period t and introduce explicitly the nonnegativity constraint for labor supply (i.e., $N_t \geq 0$). Letting μ_n denote the multiplier associated with this constraint, we have as first-order conditions for household a's consumption and labor supply:[11]

$$\partial u_{at}/\partial c_{at} - (\partial W(x_{a,t+1})/\partial x_{a,t+1})R_t = 0,$$

$$- \partial u_{at}/\partial(1 - N_{at}) + \mu_n + (\partial W(x_{a,t+1})/\partial x_{a,t+1})R_t w_t/p_t = 0,$$

$$N_{at} \geq 0, \mu_n N_{at} = 0.$$

Substituting the first equation into the second and rearranging gives

$$\frac{-\partial u_{at}/\partial(1 - N_{at})}{\partial u_{at}/\partial c_{at}} = \frac{w_t}{p_t} + \frac{\mu_n}{\partial u_{at}/\partial c_{at}}.$$

For individuals not participating in the labor force, $\mu_n \geq 0$. The "corner solution" is a case in which the marginal rate of substitution of leisure in terms of consumption is greater than the real wage. In other words, the absolute value of the indifference curve is equal to or greater than the absolute value of the budget line at the point where $N_{at}^s = 0$.

Note that at the optimal choice the corresponding indifference curve is more steeply sloped than the budget line. Thus, even when all hours are devoted to leisure and none to work, the individual's marginal rate of substitution of leisure in terms of consumption still exceeds the real wage rate. In other words, the individual's valuation of leisure exceeds the market's valuation of leisure. As a result, individual a does not find it worthwhile to participate in the labor market.

The greater the real wage, the greater is the probability that a given individual will choose to participate in the labor market. A higher real wage rotates the budget line outward. Since the individual is not working, an increase in the net real wage does not make him better off and thus has no income effect. There is only a substitution effect. Thus, if the real wage rises sufficiently, the individual can be induced to enter the labor market.

According to the above analysis, the economy-wide labor supply response to an increase in the current real wage is a combination of an ambiguous effect on the labor supply of those currently working, but an unambiguous increase in the labor supply among those not working.[12] It is the net of these two effects, the "hours" decision and the "participation" decision, that is captured by the aggregate labor supply function; it is commonly assumed that this net effect is such that the aggregate quantity of labor supplied is an increasing function of the current real wage.

The labor supply intertemporal substitution hypothesis

Our discussion has yet to consider "the labor market intertemporal substitution hypothesis (ISH) which states that labor supply responds positively to transitory increases in real wages and increases in the real interest rate, ... a central hypothesis of modern, competitive models of the business cycle" (Alogoskoufis 1987).

To do so, we simply expand our focus to the inherent intertemporal decision confronting the household. In particular, recall our expression (4.8) for the optimal allocation of labor supply over time. The view of labor supply embedded in (4.8) has life-cycle as well as business-cycle implications. With respect to life-cycle implications, the theory predicts that workers will concentrate their labor supply in years of peak earnings, consuming leisure in larger than average amounts during childhood and old age.

With respect to the business cycle, the above helps explain an apparent contradiction in the static theory of labor supply – the observed wage inelasticity of labor supply in the long run with short-run fluctuations in employment, which require an elastic labor supply if one takes a "market-clearing" approach with respect to the labor market.[13] It does so by introducing a distinction between a permanent change in the real wage and a temporary or transitory change in the real wage.

To show the intertemporal substitution effect with respect to labor supply, specify w^*/p^* as the permanent or "normal" real wage, with the anticipated real wage next period equal to this value, such that

$$w_i/p_i = w^*/p^*, \qquad i = t+1, t+2, \dots.$$

Further, we assume that:

$$R_i = R^*, \qquad i = t, t+1, t+2, \dots.$$

In this case, equation (4.8) becomes:

$$\frac{\partial u_t/\partial(1 - N_t)}{\beta \partial u_{t+1}/\partial(1 - N^*)} = R^* \frac{w_t/p_t}{w^*/p^*}, \tag{4.8$'$}$$

where N^* denotes the "long-run" supply of labor at "normal" wages. Further, let us assume that for the representative household $\beta R^* = 1$. Then equation (4.8$'$) becomes:

$$\frac{\partial u_t/\partial(1 - N_t)}{\partial u_{t+1}/\partial(1 - N^*)} = \frac{w_t/p_t}{w^*/p^*} \tag{4.8$''$}$$

Equation (4.8$''$) indicates that if the current real wage is higher than the normal real wage, then "more labor is supplied than would be implied by the long-run labor supply function." That is, this theory views suppliers of labor as reacting primarily to three variables: an anticipated "normal" or "permanent" real wage rate, which corresponds to the wage rate in the usual one-period analysis of the labor–leisure choice and has a negligible effect on labor supply; the deviation of the current real wage from this normal rate, which has a strong positive effect on labor supply; and the expected real rate of interest (Lucas and Rapping 1970: 284–285).[14]

The above theory provides the underlying microtheoretical basis for the following statement: "measured unemployment (more exactly, its nonfrictional component) is then viewed as consisting of persons who regard the wage rates at which they can currently be employed as temporarily low, and who therefore choose to wait or search for improved conditions rather than invest in moving or occupational change" (Lucas and Rapping 1970: 285).

Empirical tests seem to provide some support for this intertemporal substitution hypothesis.[15] Alogoskoufis (1987: 950) finds that for measures of the total number of employees, the real wage and interest rate elasticities are high and relatively well determined: "The elasticity of labor supply to transitory changes in real wages is around unity and is statistically significant at conventional significance levels, with one exception . . . . The real interest rate always has a significant independent influence." Note that, as suggested by equation (4.8), Alogoskoufis finds that a rise in the real interest rate increases current labor supply.

Note that equation (4.8) does not explicitly identify the initial asset holdings as a variable that affects the *relative* choice of labor supply across periods. Similarly, the condition for the optimal choice of consumption across periods did not have the initial value of assets affecting the *relative* consumption purchases across periods. This is a property of time-separable preferences.

Special topics in intertemporal choices

As we have seen, the intertemporal problem confronting the individual involves simultaneous decisions with respect to consumption versus saving and with respect to the composition of the asset portfolio. To make some sense of what is involved, we start by considering what is known as the "Fisherian" problem, which focuses on the individual's choice of consumption across time.

Fisherian analysis

The Fisherian problem typically deals with the allocation of consumption across time when there is a single means by which income can be allocated across time.[16] To restrict our analysis to such a case, we can simply omit real money holdings from the utility function. Further, we consider only interior solutions with respect to consumption (i.e., $c_{ai} > 0$, $i = t, \ldots, t + T$).[17]

Thus the maximization problem becomes:[18]

$$\max_{\substack{c_{at},\ldots,c_{a,t+T} \\ x_{a,t+1}\ldots x_{a,t+T+1}}} \sum_{i=t}^{t+T} \beta^{i-t} u^a(c_{ai})$$

subject to

$$-x_{a,t+1} + R_t[\bar{x}_{at} + \bar{c}_{at} - c_{at}] = 0,$$
$$-x_{a,t+2} + R_{t+1}[\bar{x}_{a,t+1} + \bar{c}_{a,t+1} - c_{a,t+1}] = 0,$$
$$-x_{a,t+3} + R_{t+2}[\bar{x}_{a,t+2} + \bar{c}_{a,t+2} - c_{a,t+2}] = 0,$$
$$\ldots,$$
$$-x_{a,t+T+1} + R_{t+T}[\bar{x}_{a,t+T} + \bar{c}_{a,t+T} - c_{a,t+T}] = 0,$$
$$x_{a,t+T+1} \geq 0.$$

Recall that $R_i = (1+r_i)/(1+\pi_i)$, $i = t, \ldots, t+T$, denotes the "gross real rate of return" on agent a's portfolio between the end of period i and the end of period $i+1$, and asset holdings are solely in the form of bonds, such that

$$\bar{x}_{at} \equiv (1+\bar{r})\bar{p}_b\bar{B}_a/p_t,$$

$$\bar{x}_{a,t+1} \equiv (1+\bar{r}_t)\bar{p}_{bt}\bar{B}_{at}/p_{t+1} = [(1+r_t)/(1+\pi_t)]p_{bt}B_{at}/p_t$$

$$\bar{x}_{a,t+i} \equiv (1+\bar{r}_{t+i-1})\bar{p}_{b,t+i-1}\bar{B}_{a,t+i-1}/p_{t+i}$$
$$= [(1+r_{t+i-1})/(1+\pi_{t+i-1})]p_{b,t+i-1}B_{a,t+i-1}/p_{t+i-1},$$
$$i = 2, \ldots, T+1.$$

Let λ_i, $i = t, \ldots, t+T$, denote the Lagrange multipliers for the constraints linking the total value of real asset holdings at the end of period i with the total value of real asset holdings at the end of period $i+1$. Let μ_T denote the multiplier for the nonnegativity condition that $x_{a,t+T+1} \geq 0$. Then the first-order conditions for the implied Lagrangian L include:

$$\partial L/\partial c_{ai} = \beta^{i-t} du_i^a/dc_{ai} - \lambda_i R_i = 0, \quad i = t, \ldots, t+T,$$

$$\partial L/\partial x_{a,i+1} = -\lambda_i + \lambda_{i+1}R_{i+1} = 0, \quad i = t, \ldots, t+T-1,$$

$$\partial L/\partial x_{a,t+T+1} = -\lambda_{t+T} + \mu_T = 0,$$

$$\partial L/\partial \lambda_i = -x_{a,i+1} + R_i(x_{ai} + \bar{c}_{ai} - c_{ai}) = 0, \quad i = t, \ldots, t+T,^{[19]}$$

$$\partial L/\partial \mu_T = x_{a,t+T+1} \geq 0,$$

$$\mu_T \geq 0,$$

where $u_i^a = u^a(c_{ai})$, $i = t, \ldots, t+T$.[20] Note that the above set of first-order conditions consist of $3(T+1)+1$ equations to determine $3(T+1)+1$ variables. The variables to be determined are c_{ai}, $i = t, \ldots, t+T$, x_{ai}, $i = t, \ldots, t+T+1$, and μ_T. Assuming continuity and strict concavity in $u^a(\cdot)$ and given a convex set of constraints,

$$\{x_{a,i+1}, x_{ai}, c_{ai} | -x_{a,i+1} + R_i[x_{ai} + \bar{c}_{ai} - c_{ai}] \geq 0\},$$

there is a unique solution to the problem.

There are several implications of the above first-order conditions. First, the conditions imply that the desired total real value of assets (bonds) inherited at time $t+T+1$, $x_{a,t+T+1}^d$, will equal zero if $du_{t+T}^a/dc_{a,t+T} > 0$. In particular, from the condition

$$\partial L/\partial c_{a,t+T} = \beta^T (du_{t+T}^a/dc_{a,t+T}) - \lambda_{t+T}R_{t+T} = 0,$$

we see that if $du_{t+T}^a/dc_{a,t+T} > 0$, then $\lambda_{t+T} > 0$. From the condition

$$\partial L/\partial x_{a,t+T+1} = -\lambda_{t+T} + \mu_T = 0,$$

we thus have that $\mu_T > 0$. This in turn implies, from the condition

$$\mu_T \partial L / \partial \mu_T = \mu_T x_{a,t+T+1} = 0,$$

that $x_{a,t+T+1} = 0$. This finding should not be surprising. With a time horizon of $t + T$, agent a perceives no gain (utility) from acquiring assets at time $t + T$ to finance consumption in period $t + T + 1$ and a clear loss from doing so at time $t + T$ in terms of consumption forgone given the assumption of nonsatiation ($du^a_{t+T}/dc_{a,t+T} > 0$). Second, from the first set of equations we know that between any two periods i and $i + 1$,

$$\frac{\beta^{i-t} du^a_i / dc_{ai}}{\beta^{i-t+1} du^a_{i+1} / dc_{a,i+1}} = \frac{\lambda_i R_i}{\lambda_{i+1} R_{i+1}}, \quad i = t, \ldots, t + T - 1.$$

This expression can be simplified to obtain

$$\frac{du^a_i / dc_{ai}}{\beta du^a_{i+1} / dc_{a,i+1}} = R_i, \quad i = t, \ldots, t + T - 1,$$

where R_i, the real gross return between the end of periods i and $i + 1$, is given by $(1+r_i)/(1+\pi_i)$. R_i has been called Fisher's "(gross) real interest rate" since he was one of the first to provide a lucid account of its role in determining consumption across time.

Fisher's "(net) real interest rate," denoted by m_i, is then defined by

$$1 + m_i \equiv R_i = (1 + r_i)/(1 + \pi_i).$$

Subtracting one from both sides and rearranging, we have

$$m_i = (r_i - \pi_i)/(1 + \pi_i).$$

Thus, for small expected rates of inflation we have the approximation[21]

$$m_i = r_i - \pi_i.$$

In words, the real interest rate is approximately equal to the nominal interest rate minus the rate of inflation. The expected real interest rate is then the nominal interest rate minus the expected rate of inflation.

There are several features of the above that should be noted. First, if an individual's discount factor ($\beta < 1$) equals the reciprocal of the real gross rate of interest ($[R_i]^{-1} = (1 + \pi_i)/(1 + r_i)$) between periods i and $i + 1$, so that

$$\beta R_i = 1,$$

then the above expression of the first-order conditions for c_{ai} and $c_{a,i+1}$ indicates that $du^a_i / dc_{ai} = du^a_{i+1}/dc_{a,i+1}$. Given the concavity of the single-period utility function ($u^a(\cdot)$) and our assumption of a time-invariant one-period utility function, it then follows that the individual will choose the same rate of consumption across periods i and $i + 1$ in such a case.[22] This constant path of consumption between the two periods can be said to emerge if an individual's "rate of time preference" equals the (real) interest rate.

If the expected gross return between two periods were higher (or for an individual with a higher discount factor), the fact that $\beta > (R_i)^{-1}$ or equivalently $\beta R_i > 1$ means from the first-order conditions that $du_i^a/dc_{ai} > du_{i+1}^a/dc_{a,i+1}$. Given the assumed concavity of the one-period utility function, the implication is that agent a's consumption during period i would be less than during period $i + 1$. That is, $\beta R_i > 1 \Rightarrow c_{ai}^d < c_{a,i+1}^d$. Conversely, if the expected real gross return were to be lower (or for an individual with a lower discount factor), the fact that $\beta < (R_i)^{-1}$ or equivalently $\beta R_i < 1$ means that the individual's consumption during period i would be greater than during period $i + 1$. That is, $\beta R_i < 1 \Rightarrow c_{ai}^d > c_{a,i+1}^d$.

For the two-period case (say, periods t and $t + 1$), the optimal consumption in each of the two periods can be shown graphically by the point of tangency between an indifference curve with slope $-(du_i^a/dc_{ai})/\beta(du_{i+1}^a/dc_{a,i+1})$ and a budget line with slope $-R_t$.[23] If one were to place $c_{a,t+1}$ on the vertical axis and c_{at} on the horizontal axis then it would be possible to determine whether an individual is a borrower or a lender in any period. For example, if disposable income were less than consumption in the first period t, then the individual is a lender at time t. Note that points on the same indifference curve are such that

$$d\left[u^a(c_{at}) + \beta u^a(c_{a,t+1})\right] = (du_t^a/dc_{a,t+1})dc_{at} + \beta(du_{t+1}^a/dc_{a,t+1})dc_{at+1}$$
$$= 0.$$

Rearranging, we have the slope of an indifference curve given by

$$\frac{dc_{a,t+1}}{dc_{at}} = -\frac{du_t^a/dc_{at}}{\beta du_{t+1}^a/dc_{a,t+1}}.$$

Note that points on the budget line satisfy the present value constraint:

$$c_{at} + (R_t)^{-1}c_{a,t+1} = \bar{c}_{at} + x_{at} + (R_t)^{-1}\bar{c}_{a,t+1}.$$

Rearranging, we have

$$c_{a,t+1} = R_t[\bar{c}_{at} + x_{at} - c_{at}] + \bar{c}_{a,t+1},$$

such that the slope of the budget line is given by

$$dc_{a,t+1}/dc_{at} = -R_t.$$

Thus, at the point of tangency between the budget line and an indifference curve,

$$\frac{du_t^a/dc_{at}}{\beta du_{t+1}^a/dc_{a,t+1}} = R_t$$

which is the expression we obtained previously concerning the optimal choice of consumption between periods i and $i + 1$.

Note that the above analysis is for an individual consumer. Thus, aggregate consumption need not behave as that predicted above for the individual. For instance, an aging population could lead to variations in aggregate consumption that reflect the aggregation at different times across agents with differing characteristics.

Life-cycle and permanent income hypotheses

We have seen how a household's consumption in any period is not constrained by the income it receives during that period, but rather that the discounted value of lifetime consumption is constrained by the discounted stream of income accruing to the household over its lifetime plus initial asset holdings. While income tends to rise and fall during the lifetime of an individual, through appropriate saving and borrowing the individual can maintain a smooth or constant rate of consumption over his lifetime. This smoothing of consumption across time plays a critical role in Franco Modigliani's "life-cycle hypothesis" of consumption.[24]

A stylized pattern of income and consumption expenditures over an individual's lifetime is the following: Prior to retirement, income exceeds consumption and saving is positive. During this period, saving increases household wealth. On retirement, consumption is financed by dissaving. During the retirement period, household wealth falls as people draw on their accumulated savings to finance consumption. Implied in this discussion is an inverted U-shape wealth–age profile (save during pre-retirement years and dissave in years following retirement, running down the stock of accumulated wealth). A number of studies of aggregate household consumption and saving behavior support this wealth–age pattern.[25]

To make clear the implications of consumption smoothing for the demand for the consumption good at time t, let us make the simplifying assumptions that

(a) for any period $i = t, \ldots, t + T$, $R_i = R$, and
(b) the individual's personal discount rate, β, equals the constant real "market" discount rate, R^{-1}.[26]

From the first-order conditions we thus have the result that agent a will completely smooth out consumption spending across time, so that consumption $c_{ai}^d = c_a^d$, $i = t, \ldots, t + T$. In this case, we can use the prior combined budget constraint to obtain:

$$c_{at}^d = \Omega \left\{ \bar{x}_{at} + \sum_{i=t}^{t+T} (\bar{c}_{ai}/R^{i-t}) \right\}$$

where Ω, which equals $1/\sum_{i=t}^{t+T}(1/R^{i-t})$, is what Modigliani has called the "proportionality factor" and indicates the proportion of households' total resources – consisting of initial assets, current income and anticipated future income – devoted to consumption each year.

An important implication of Modigliani's life-cycle hypothesis is that the fraction of an increase in current income ($\bar{c}_{at}$) that goes toward increased current consumption (the "marginal propensity to consume") will vary depending on whether the increase in current disposable income is accompanied by an equivalent increase in anticipated future income ($\bar{c}_{at}, i = t+1, \ldots, t+T$).[27] If a change in current income is viewed as "transitory," most of the increase in income will go to saving in order to finance increased consumption during future years.

This idea that the effect of a change in current disposable income on consumption demand depends on the degree to which the change in income is viewed as temporary or permanent lies at the heart of Milton Friedman's permanent income hypothesis. The permanent income hypothesis is like the life-cycle hypothesis in that it emphasizes the fact that consumption demand in period t depends not only on current income, but also on anticipated income in the future periods. Permanent income is that income which if received each year over a household's time horizon would yield an income stream with present value exactly equal to the present value of the household's anticipated income stream. That is, permanent income $\bar{c}_p$ is defined by the following equation:

$$\sum_{i=t}^{t+T}(\bar{c}_p/R^{i-t}) = \sum_{i=t}^{t+T}(\bar{c}_{ai}/R^{i-t}) + \bar{x}_{at}. \tag{4.9}$$

Factoring out $\bar{c}_p$ on the left-hand side of (4.9) and rearranging, we have

$$\bar{c}_p = \Omega \left\{ \bar{x}_{at} + \sum_{i=t}^{t+T}(\bar{c}_{ai}/R^{i-t}) \right\} \tag{4.10}$$

Equation (4.10) indicates that permanent income is simply a weighted average of current and future incomes, but in this case income in the more distant future is weighted less heavily since it is discounted more highly.

Comparing permanent income to agent a's consumption demand in period t, c_{at}^d, if there is complete smoothing of consumption spending across time then we obtain

$$c_{at}^d = \bar{c}_p.$$

The implication of this equation is that the marginal propensity to consume out of a change in current income that is perceived as permanent is equal to one, while the marginal propensity to consume out of a change in current disposable income that is perceived as entirely transitory (having little impact on permanent income) is small. Changes in transitory components of income are almost entirely saved if positive, or borrowed if negative.[28]

Our discussion so far of the impact of changes in income on current consumption demand has been restricted to what might be referred to as the effects of "transitory" versus "permanent" income changes. In doing so, we have assumed a deterministic world in which individuals have perfect foresight concerning future income streams. But what happens if individuals do not have perfect foresight? In particular, what if we introduce stochastic elements so that realized future income is a random variable? Then the above theories suggest a difference in the response of consumption demand to income changes that are anticipated or expected versus unanticipated changes. In particular, the life-cycle/permanent income hypothesis would predict that previously anticipated (or expected) changes in income would have no effect on consumption demand since consumption plans have already incorporated this income.[29]

Portfolio choice

Now let us consider the more general case in which agent a chooses not only consumption across time but the portfolio of assets (money and bonds). That is, consider the following problem:

$$\max_{\substack{c_{at},\ldots,c_{a,t+T} \\ x_{a,t+1},\ldots,x_{a,t+T+1} \\ M_{at}/p_t,\ldots,M_{a,t+T}/p_{t+T}}} \sum_{i=t}^{t+T} \beta^{i-t} u^a(c_{ai}, M_{ai}/p_i)$$

subject to

$$-x_{a,t+1} + R_t[\bar{x}_{at} + \bar{c}_{at} - c_{at}] - [R_t - R_{mt}]M_{at}/p_t = 0,$$

$$-x_{a,t+2} + R_{t+1}[\bar{x}_{a,t+1} + \bar{c}_{a,t+1} - c_{a,t+1}]$$
$$\quad - [R_{t+1} - R_{m,t+1}]M_{a,t+1}/p_{t+1} = 0,$$

$$-x_{a,t+3} + R_{t+2}[\bar{x}_{a,t+2} + \bar{c}_{a,t+2} - c_{a,t+2}]$$
$$\quad - [R_{t+2} - R_{m,t+2}]M_{a,t+2}/p_{t+2} = 0,$$

$$\ldots,$$

$$-x_{a,t+T+1} + R_{t+T}[\bar{x}_{a,t+T} + \bar{c}_{a,t+T} - c_{a,t+T}]$$
$$\quad - [R_{t+T} - R_{m,t+T}]M_{a,t+T}/p_{t+T} = 0,$$

$$x_{a,t+T+1} \geq 0.$$

As before, to simplify the problem we assume interior solutions, in this case not only with respect to the consumption good but also with respect to money holdings. Again, let λ_i, $i = t,\ldots,t+T$, denote the Lagrange multipliers for the constraints linking the real asset holdings at the end of period i with their real value at the end of period $i + 1$, and let μ_T denote the multiplier for the nonnegativity condition that $x_{a,t+T+1} \geq 0$. The first-order conditions are:

$$\partial L/\partial c_{ai} = \beta^{i-t} du_i^a/dc_{ai} - \lambda_i R_i = 0, \quad i = t,\ldots,t+T,$$

$$\partial L/\partial(M_{ai}/p_i) = \beta^{i-t} \partial u_i^a/\partial(M_{ai}/p_i) - \lambda_i[R_i - R_{mi}] = 0, \quad i = t,\ldots,t+T,$$

$$\partial L/\partial x_{a,i+1} = -\lambda_i + \lambda_{i+1}R_{i+1} = 0, \quad i = t, \dots, t+T-1,$$

$$\partial L/\partial x_{a,t+T+1} = -\lambda_{t+T} + \mu_T = 0,$$

$$\partial L/\partial \lambda_i = -x_{a,i+1} + R_i(x_{ai} + \bar{c}_{ai} - c_{ai})$$

$$- [R_i - R_{mi}]M_{ai}/p_i = 0, \quad i = t, \dots, t+T,^{30}$$

$$\partial L/\partial \mu_T = x_{a,t+T+1} \geq 0,$$

$$\mu_T \partial L/\partial \mu_T = \mu_T x_{a,t+T+1} = 0,$$

$$\lambda_i \geq 0, \quad i = t, \dots, t+T,$$

$$\mu_T \geq 0,$$

where $u_i^a = u^a(c_{ai}, M_{ai}/p_i)$, $i = t, \dots, t+T$. To isolate the portfolio choice, consider the portfolio choice of money and bond holdings for a given level of current consumption. That is, let us look at the optimal choice of M_{ai}/p_i given that c_{ai} is held constant. From the second set of conditions,

$$\beta^{i-t}\partial u_i^a/\partial(M_{ai}/p_i) - \lambda_i[R_i - R_{mi}] = 0.$$

Substituting the condition for the optimal choice of the total value of assets in that period,

$$\lambda_i = \lambda_{i+1}R_{i+1},$$

we obtain

$$\beta^{i-t}\partial u_i^a/\partial(M_{ai}/p_i) - \lambda_{i+1}R_{i+1}[R_i - R_{mi}] = 0.$$

Now substituting the condition for the optimal choice of consumption next period $(i+1)$, as given by

$$\beta^{i-t+1}du_{i+1}^a/dc_{a,i+1} - \lambda_{i+1}R_{i+1} = 0,$$

we obtain

$$\beta^{i-t}\partial u_i^a/\partial(M_{ai}/p_i) - \beta^{i-t+1}(du_{i+1}^a/dc_{a,i+1})[R_i - R_{mi}] = 0.$$

Rearranging gives

$$\frac{du_i^a/d(M_{ai}/p_i)}{\beta du_{i+1}^a/dc_{a,i+1}} = R_i - R_{mi}.$$

Recalling that the expected gross real return on bonds in period i, R_i, equals $(1 + r_i)/(1 + \pi_i)$, and that the expected gross real return on money, R_{mi}, equals $1/(1 + \pi_i)$, the above expression can be written as:

$$\frac{du_i^a/d(M_{ai}/p_i)}{\beta du_{i+1}^a/dc_{a,i+1}} = \frac{r_i}{1 - \pi_i}.$$

Note that in the limit (as the length of the period goes to zero) the expected rate of inflation term would vanish. The implication is that the optimal division of assets between money and bonds depends primarily on the money interest rate alone. What is essentially being shown is that an increase in money holdings with no change in current consumption means a reduction in bond holdings, and thus the loss of nominal interest income r_i, or real interest income $r_i/(1 + \pi_i)$.

Absence of money illusion, real balance effects, and real indebtedness effects

There are two aspects of agent a's demand function that should be noted. First, agent a's demand functions at time t can be shown to be homogeneous of degree 0 in the current price level p_t, initial money balances $\overline{M}_a$, and initial bond holdings $\overline{B}_a$. In this economy, this is said to reflect the "absence of money illusion." One critical reason for this is the assumption of unit elastic expectations with respect to future prices, so that changes in the current price level leave unchanged the expected rates of change in the price level in subsequent periods. Also note that the current and expected future money payments attached to bonds are being held constant, so that given the fixed money payment x on maturity, interest rates are unchanged. Alternatively, one could have money prices and the fixed future money payment attached to one-period bonds rise by the same proportion.

The above implies that individual a's demand for the consumption good and real money balances at time t can be represented by

$$c_{at}^d = c_{at}^d(r_t, r_{t+1} \ldots, r_{t+T-1}, \pi_t, \ldots, \pi_{t+T-1}, W_{at}),$$

$$M_{at}^d/p_t = M_{at}^d/p_t(r_t, r_{t+1} \ldots, r_{t+T-1}, \pi_t, \ldots, \pi_{t+T-1}, W_{at}),$$

where $\bar{x}_{at}$ is the individual's real wealth at the end of period t, as given by

$$W_{at} = \bar{x}_{at} + \bar{c}_{at} + \sum_{j=t}^{t+T-1} \left[\prod_{i=t}^{j} (R_i) \right]^{-1} (\bar{c}_{aj+1}).$$

From the budget constraint for period t, we know that the above two demand conditions imply a real demand for bonds of a similar form since:

$$p_{bt} B_{at}^d/p_t = \bar{c}_{at} + \bar{x}_{at} - \left[c_{at}^d + M_{at}^d/p_t \right].$$

Note that the above demand functions do not depend solely on wealth and the pattern of expected real (gross) rates of interest since, given the portfolio choice, a given pattern of expected real (gross) interest rates could alter demand depending on the underlying values of the money interest rate. As before, individual a's excess demand function for the consumption good and money in period t are defined by $z_{at} = c_{at}^d - \bar{c}_{at}, z_{am} = M_{at}^d/p_t - \overline{M}_a/p_t$, and $z_{ab} = p_{bt} B_{at}^d/p_t$.[31]

The "real balance effect" indicates the effect of a change in real balances $(\overline{M}_a/p_t)$ on individual demand for goods other than money. As before, there is a real balance effect that reflects a wealth effect. That is, a decrease in initial real balances leads to a reduction in real money demand, M_{at}^d/p_t, and a reduction in the real demand for bonds, $p_{bt}B_{at}^d/p_t$. There is also what might be referred to as a "real indebtedness effect" in that a change in prices alters not only real money balances but also real initial debt. If $\overline{B}_a > 0$, an increase in p_t reduces wealth, while if $\overline{B}_a < 0$, an increase in p_t increases wealth. This is why the characterization of the absence of money illusion has been expanded to include changes in $\overline{B}_a$.

It is typical in macroeconomics to adopt the convention of the "representative agent" to reduce notational clutter. Recall that the "representative agent" is essentially the average agent. For instance, if we let c_{at}^d denote the demand for the consumption good in period t by representative agent a and c_t^d market demand at the time, then $c_{at}^d = c_t^d$. Thus, depending on the context, we can interpret c_t^d as demand by the representative agent or market demand. Recall that in doing so, we essentially ignore distribution effects, such as effects on market demand of changes in the distribution of initial endowments of commodities or money balances or of changes in the distribution of future endowments. In the context of the real indebtedness effect, since in the aggregate $\overline{B} = 0$, this effect is removed from our analysis.

Intertemporal substitution: the evidence

We have focused above on the behavior of an individual with respect to the planned path of consumption across time. As Robert Hall (1988: 340) indicates:

> The essential idea ... is that consumers plan to change their consumption from one year to the next by an amount that depends on their expectations of real interest rates. Actual movements of consumption differ from planned movements by a completely unpredictable random variable that indexes all information available next year that was not incorporated in the planning process the year before. If expectations of real interest rates shift, then there should be a corresponding shift in the rate of change of consumption. The magnitude of the response of consumption to a change in real interest rate expectations measures the intertemporal elasticity of substitution.[32]

Hall (1988: 340–341) goes on to state that

> the basic model of the joint distribution of consumption and the return earned by one asset that has emerged ... is the following: The joint distribution of the log of consumption in period t, $\log c_t$, and the (real) return earned by the assets from period $t - 1$ to period t, m_{t-1}, is normal with a covariance matrix that is unchanging over time. The means obey the linear relation:

$$E(\log c_t) = k + c_{t-1} + \sigma E(m_{t-1}). \tag{4.11}$$

That is, the expected change in the log of consumption is a parameter, σ, times the expected real return plus a constant ... If the expected real interest rate $E(m_{t-1})$ is observed directly, then the key parameter σ can be estimated simply by regressing the change in the log of consumption on the expected real rate. That regression also has the property that no other variable known in period $t - 1$ belongs in the regression.

Hall proceeds to estimate the parameter using aggregate data on consumption and finds that there is "little basis for a conclusion that the behavior of aggregate consumption in the United States in the twentieth century reveals an important positive value of the intertemporal elasticity of substitution" (1988: 356).

Hall's empirical finding is of importance to macroeconomic analysis. The work by Hall and others is also of interest as an example of how theoretical macroeconomic analysis, specifically Fisherian analysis, can be tested. To see the link between the theory developed in the prior section and the proposed test (equation (4.11)), assume the following:

Assumption 4.3 The path of aggregate consumption reflects agent a's decisions concerning the optimal allocation of consumption across time. That is, we treat agent a as the "representative consumer." Thus $c_{ai}, i = t, \ldots, t+T$, which denotes consumption in period i of the representative agent a, differs only in scale from c_i, $i = t, \ldots, t+T$, which denotes the aggregate level of consumption. This assumption that an aggregate variable can be viewed as reflecting decisions of a representative agent is not innocuous. For instance, the actual path of aggregate consumption could well differ from that predicted by an analysis of individuals' optimal decisions due to changes across time in the composition of individuals in the economy.[33]

Assumption 4.4 Individuals' expectations in period $t - 1$ of future real interest rates incorporate all information available as of period $t - 1$. New information occurring in period t that alters consumption from what was planned results in the distribution of consumption being "log normal, conditional on information available last period; that is, log c_t is normal with mean $E(c_t)$" (Hall 1988: 342).

Assumption 4.5 In period $t - 1$, the representative agent's utility function takes the following form:

$$\sum_{i=t-1}^{t+T} \exp\{-\delta_i + ((\delta - 1)/\delta) \log(c_i)\},$$

where $c > 0, \sigma > 0$, and $\delta > 0$. This exponential utility function has the following desired properties:

1 It is time-separable.
2 If consumption were equal across any two periods, the individual would place greater value on an increase in consumption in the earlier period – that is, if

$c_{t-1} = c_t$, then

$$\exp\{-\delta(t-1) + ((\delta-1)/\delta)\log(c_{t-1})\}$$
$$> \exp\{-\delta t + ((\delta-1)/\delta)\log(c_t)\}.$$

3   Given $1 > \sigma \geq 0$, utility increases in any period with increased consumption but at a decreasing rate – that is,

$$du(c_{t-1}) = dc_{t-1}$$
$$= [(1-\delta)/(\delta c_{t-1})] \cdot \exp\{-\delta t(t-1)$$
$$+ ((\delta-1)/\delta)\log(c_{t-1})\}$$
$$> 0, d^2 u(c_{t-1})/dc_{t-1}^2 < 0.$$

Note that the "intertemporal elasticity of substitution" will be given by σ. As σ approaches 0, substitution of consumption across time in response to changes in the real interest rate will approach zero as well.

Assumption 4.6   Individuals' forecasts of future variables are held with subjective certainty. This last assumption is a departure from Hall's analysis that allows us for the moment to maintain the "deterministic" aspect of the prior optimization problem. That is, we continue to assume that individual's expectations of future variables such as expected rates of inflation and future interest rates are held with subjective certainty.

Given the above assumptions, we know from our prior discussion that the choice of consumption for periods $t-1$ and t must satisfy the following first-order condition:

$$\frac{du/dc_{t-1}}{du/dc_t} = R_{t-1}.$$

Substituting in the appropriate expressions for the marginal utility of consumption in periods $t-1$ and t, we obtain

$$\frac{[(1-\delta)/\delta c_{t-1}] \cdot \exp\{-\delta(t-1) + ((\delta-1)/\delta)\log(c_{t-1})\}}{[(1-\delta)/\delta c_t] \cdot \exp\{\delta + ((\delta-1)/\delta)\log(c_t)\}}$$

or

$$(c_t/c_{t-1})\exp\{\delta + ((\delta-1)/\delta)\log(c_{t-1}/c_t)\} = R_{t-1}.$$

Taking the logarithm of both sides of the above expression and rearranging, the above first-order condition becomes

$$\log(c_t/c_{t-1}) + \delta - ((\delta-1)/\delta)\log(c_{t-1}/c_t) = \log(R_{t-1}),$$

which simplifies to

$$\delta + (1/\delta) \log(c_{t-1}/c_t) = \log(R_{t-1})$$

or

$$\log c_t = -\delta\sigma + \log c_{t-1} + \sigma \log(R_{t-1}) \tag{4.12}$$

which is similar in form to (4.11). Note that the "intertemporal elasticity of substitution" is given by

$$\sigma = (dc_t/dR_{t-1})c_t/R_{t-1}.$$

The form of equation (4.2) can be made closer to that of equation (4.11) if we note that we can define the "instantaneous real rate of interest" associated with continuous compounding, m_{t-1}, by the expression

$$\exp(m_{t-1}) = R_{t-1}.$$

Then (4.12) becomes

$$\log c_t = -\delta\sigma + \log c_{t-1} + \sigma m_{t-1}.$$

Conclusion

This chapter has developed an in-depth understanding of household behavior. A good deal of the discussion has dealt with intertemporal choices and the tradeoffs inherent in consuming today versus consuming in the future. Many policy-related issues in macroeconomics are related to decisions made today that are not independent of future states or activities. This issue will arise again and again throughout this book and it is imperative that one comprehend the nature of decision-making and time.

5 Summarizing the behavior and constraints of firms and households

Introduction

In this chapter we summarize our discussion of the behavior of firms and households in the simple Walrasian model with money and production. In doing so, we consider first the nature of constraints faced by the participants in the economy with respect to decisions during period t, and then their behavior in terms of demand and/or supply. Along the way, we will try to simplify the notation and introduce various expectations and assumptions of different macroeconomic models. We start our discussion with firms.

Summarizing firms' constraints

We have seen how we can divide the general constraint facing firms that total revenues from all sources just exhausts expenditures each period into two separate constraints. One is the "firm financing constraint," which states that desired changes in the capital stock as well as any capital adjustment costs are financed by issuing new bonds or equity shares. That is, for period t,

$$I_{nt}^d + \psi(I_{nt}^d) - \text{net } A_t^s = 0, \tag{5.1}$$

where

$$\text{net } A_t^s \equiv A_t^s - \overline{A}_t,$$
$$A_t^s \equiv \left[p_{bt} B_t^s + p_{et} S_t^s \right] / p_t,$$
$$\overline{A}_t \equiv \left[p_{bt} \overline{B} + p_{et} \overline{S} \right] / p_t,$$
$$I_{nt}^d \equiv K_{t+1}^d - \overline{K}.$$

Note that we implicitly assume that firms' plans for purchasing capital during the period correctly anticipate the price of output (capital) during the period and the prices of bonds and equity shares to be issued at the end of the period to finance such purchases.

The second constraint, the "firm distribution constraint," is that all revenues from the sale of output net of that required to replace capital used up in the production process during the period be distributed to households either as wages, interest payments, or dividends. At time t, firms' anticipated distribution constraint is given by

$$d_t + (w_t/p_t)N_t^d + z\overline{B}/p_t - (y_t^s - \delta\overline{K}) = 0, \tag{5.2}$$

where z is the coupon payment and planned output supply is related to labor demand by the production function

$$y_t^s = f(N_t^d, \overline{K}). \tag{5.3}$$

Equation (5.2) implicitly assumes that firms at time t have perfect foresight with respect to the price of output during period t. Alternatively, the firm financing constraint would take the above form if we presumed there were futures markets at time t for the exchange of output during period t and financial assets at the end of period t.

The labor market at time t determines employment for the period at a level N_t^* and an associated rate of output denoted by y_t^*. At the realized price of output, the firm distribution constraint for period t will turn out to be

$$d_t + (w_t/p_t)N_t^* + z\overline{B}/p_t - (y_t^* - \delta\overline{K}) = 0. \tag{5.4}$$

As (5.4) indicates, actual real output during the period, net of that used to replace depreciated capital, will be distributed to households.[1]

Summarizing households' constraints

With respect to households, there is a single budget constraint for period t. Like that of the firm distribution constraint, its form changes depending on what is assumed concerning the correctness of expectations or the timing of markets. As we have seen, at time t, households make plans with respect to labor supply, consumption demand, and desired additions to their real holdings of financial assets and money balances based on a perceived constraint of the form

$$c_t^d + (M_t^d - \overline{M})/p_t^e + \text{net } A_t^d - (w_t/p_t)^e N_t^s - (d_t + z\overline{B}/p_t) = 0, \tag{5.5}$$

where

$$\text{net } A_t^d \equiv A_t^d - \overline{A}_t,$$

$$A_t^d \equiv \left[p_{bt}B_t^d + p_{et}S_t^d \right]/p_t,$$

$$\overline{A}_t \equiv \left[p_{bt}\overline{B} + p_{et}\overline{S} \right]/p_t.$$

We presume that households have perfect foresight at time t with respect to the real value of financial assets and the real value of dividends plus interest payments received from firms at the end of period t. We leave open the possibility of errors in expectations (held with subjective certainty) concerning the price level as it affects real money balances and the real wage. The term p_t would replace p_t^e if we presumed perfect foresight on the part of households concerning the price level or equivalently presumed that there were futures markets at time t for the exchange of output during period t.

The labor market at time t determines employment and output for the period. As before, we let N_t^* and y_t^* denote the actual rate of employment and production of output during period t. In such a case, the actual firm distribution constraint (5.4) can be substituted into the household budget constraint. Since prices will be known by households at this point, we may also replace the expected prices of output, bonds, and equity shares by their actual prices. Thus, during period t the household budget constraint for period t can then be expressed as

$$c_t^d + (M_t^d - \overline{M})/p_t + \text{net } A_t^d - (y_t^* - \delta\overline{K}) = 0. \tag{5.6}$$

As discussed below, households' behavior in the output and financial markets will be based on realized income and prices, and will differ from their plans made at time t based on expected prices and a labor supply decision unless they possess perfect foresight at time t concerning the prices that will prevail over period t and the labor market clears with actual employment equal to labor supply.[2]

Walras' law: labor market and other markets at time t

Recall that Walras' law reflects the summing up of the constraints faced by individual agents in the economy. Since our preceding analysis concerned the constraints of the "representative" firm and household, we need only sum the constraints of such representative agents to obtain Walras' law. There still remains a potential problem, however, as to which of the different versions of the constraints enumerated above for firms and households to use. The choice, as one would suspect, depends on whether the market for labor effectively occurs at the same time as the markets for output and financial assets or at different times.

One version of Walras' law essentially combines the market for labor at time t with a futures market at time t for the exchange of output during period t and financial assets at the end of period t. Equivalently, this version of Walras' law assumes limited perfect foresight at time t by both firms and households with respect to prices for the period.[3] In such a case, we would sum constraints (5.1), (5.2), and (5.5) (with p_t replacing p_t^e in (5.5)) to obtain:

$$\left[c_t^d + I_{nt}^d + \delta\overline{K} + \psi(I_{nt}^d) - y_t^s \right] + \left[\text{net } A_t^d - \text{net } A_t^s \right]$$
$$+ (w_t/p_t)\left[N_t^d - N_t^s \right] + [M_t^d - \overline{M}]/p_t = 0. \tag{5.7}$$

Thus we have that the sum of excess demand across four markets – the labor, output, financial, and money markets – must equal zero.[4] Note that one of these four markets, the money "market," reflects the equality between the demand for and supply of money. The money "market" is not, of course, like other markets of an economy – which is why the word "market" is in quotes. That is, unlike the other markets, the money "market" is not a place where the exchange of goods (e.g., labor, financial assets, or output) takes place.[5]

Walras' law: sequential markets and potential lack of perfect foresight

There is a modification to make with respect to the above that is required if markets occur sequentially and if there is not perfect foresight on the part of all agents at time t concerning prices for period t. The sequential nature of markets is clear, in that we have the labor market occurring at time t while the markets for output and financial assets occur during the period. In addition, households in particular may not correctly foresee at time t the price of output for period t. Under such circumstances, the prior version of Walras' law no longer holds, for it would then sum constraints that are only anticipated, not realized. Instead, given the sequential nature of the markets, we must break the analysis down into an analysis of the labor market and an analysis of the other three markets.

At time t, the labor market occurs. Assuming a competitive equilibrium for the labor market, we have a money wage determined at time t such that

$$N_t^s = N_t^d.$$

Underlying the supply of labor at time t are households' plans with respect to consumption demand and saving (either in the form of financial assets or money) during the period. These plans are influenced at time t by the anticipated price level for commodities, p_t^e, among other variables and as such these plans may not be feasible given realized prices during period t.

Once the labor market ends, employment and output are determined for the period at levels N_t^* and y_t^*, respectively. At that point, households make plans with respect to consumption and saving in light of the realized prices and the resulting effective household budget constraint. That realized household budget constraint is simply equation (5.6), which incorporates the actual firm distribution constraint. Adding the firm financing constraint (5.1), we obtain a modified Walras' law for the markets during period t of the form:

$$\left[c_t^d + I_{nt}^d + \delta \overline{K} + \psi(I_{nt}^d) - y_t^* \right] + \left[\text{net } A_t^d - \text{net } A_t^s \right] + [M_t^d - \overline{M}]/p_t = 0.$$

In the absence of perfect foresight, the demands for consumption, money balances, and financial assets during the period expressed in the above equation can differ from the plans made at time t.

Summarizing firm behavior with limited perfect foresight

Consider firms' optimal plans at time t. Note that at time t firms have an expectation of the price of output for the period. We shall continue to assume that firms have perfect foresight at time t with respect to the price of output over the period. With respect to labor demand, a diminishing marginal product of labor implies an inverse relationship between the real wage and labor demand:

$$N_t^s = N_t^d(w_t/p_t, \overline{K}).$$

It is typical to assume that the labor market is such that firms achieve employment equal to that demanded. In this case, given the production function and the nature of the labor demand function, we have an output supply function for period t of the form[6]

$$y_t^s = y_t^d(w_t/p_t, \overline{K})$$

An increase in the real wage reduces labor demand and thus output supply, so that we have

$$\partial N_t^d/\partial(w_t/p_t) < 0 \quad \text{and} \quad \partial y_t^s/\partial(w_t/p_t) < 0.$$

Now consider firms' behavior with respect to investment and consequent financial asset supply. Given a diminishing marginal product of capital, capital demand is inversely related to the expected real user cost of capital.[7]

Assuming labor and capital are complements in the production process $(\partial^2 f/\partial K \partial N > 0)$, capital demand will be inversely related to the expected real wage in the subsequent period as well.[8] In particular, in the absence of adjustment costs (for both capital and labor) we have the following capital demand function:

$$K_{t+1}^d = K_{t+1}^d(m_t^e + \delta, w_{t+1}^e/p_{t+1}^e) \tag{5.8}$$

with

$$\partial K_{t+1}^d/\partial(m_t^e + \delta) < 0 \quad \text{and} \quad \partial K_{t+1}^d/\partial(w_{t+1}^e/p_{t+1}^e) < 0.[9]$$

The above demand for capital stock at the end of period t (in place at time $t+1$) implies a net investment demand function for period t of the form:

$$I_{nt}^d = I_{nt}^d(m_t^e + \delta, w_{t+1}^e/p_{t+1}^e, \overline{K}),$$

where net investment demand is inversely related to the expected real user cost of capital, $m_t^e + \delta$, the anticipated real wage in the next period, w_{t+1}^e/p_{t+1}^e, and the existing capital stock at time t, $\overline{K}$.

Recall that the firm financing constraint, in the absence of capital adjustment costs, equates firms' net real financial asset supply to net investment demand. Thus given the nature of the net investment demand function, the net real financial asset supply function for firms at the end of period t (at time $t + 1$) is identical to net investment demand, or:

$$\text{net } A_t^s = \text{net } A_t^s(m_t^e + \delta, w_{t+1}^e/p_{t+1}^e, \overline{K}),$$

where net real financial asset supply for period t, like net investment demand during period t, is inversely related to the expected real user cost of capital, the anticipated real wage in the next period, and the existing capital stock at time t.

With convex adjustment costs, the optimal capital stock (as well as investment demand) depends on the entire future path of the expected real user cost of capital and real wages. That is, with adjustment costs,

$$K_{t+1}^d = K_{t+1}^d(m_t^e + \delta, m_{t+1}^e + \delta, \ldots, w_{t+1}^e/p_{t+1}^e, w_{t+2}^e/p_{t+2}^e, \ldots). \qquad (5.9)$$

We can rewrite the above demand function for capital given adjustment costs so as to collapse future periods into essentially a single subsequent period.[10] To do so, recall that the expected real rate of interest for period i, m_i^e, equals $(r_i - \pi_i^e)/(1 + \pi_i^e)$. Let us assume static expectations concerning future interest rates, so that $r_i = r_t, i = t + 1, t + 2, \ldots$. Further, let us assume static expectations concerning future expected inflation, so that $\pi_i^e = \pi_t^e, i = t + 1, t + 2, \ldots$. The result is that the expected constant real rate of interest between periods t and $t + 1$ is expected to prevail in the future, so that $m_i^e = m_t^e, i = t + 1, t + 2, \ldots$. We can then rewrite the demand function for capital accumulated at the end of period t in the simpler form

$$K_{t+1}^d = K_{t+1}^d(m_t^e + \delta, w_{t+1}^e/p_{t+1}^e, w_{t+2}^e/p_{t+2}^e, \ldots).$$

Now note that we can decompose the anticipated wage for period i and the expected price level for period i into two components, the wage or price level in period $i - 1$ and the expected rate of change in wages or prices, respectively. In particular, the anticipated money wage and price level for period $t + 2$ can be expressed by

$$w_{t+2}^e \equiv w_{t+1}^e(1 + \pi_{w,t+1}^e) \quad \text{and} \quad p_{t+2}^e \equiv p_{t+1}^e(1 + \pi_{t+1}^e).$$

Let us now assume static expectations with respect to the rate of change in wages beyond the next period, so that $\pi_{wi}^e = \pi_{w,t+1}^e, i = t + 2, t + 3, \ldots$. Recall that we have already assumed a constant rate of price inflation in subsequent periods. If we then add the assumption that, beyond the next period, the (constant) rate of inflation in wages ($\pi_{w,t+1}^e$) equals the expected rate of inflation in prices (π_{t+1}^e), we have that $w_i^e/p_i^e = w_{t+1}^e/p_{t+1}^e, i = t + 2, t + 3, \ldots$. In words, the real wage in the subsequent period, $w_{t+1}^e/p_{t+1}^e, i = t + 2, t + 3, \ldots$ is anticipated to persist indefinitely.[11] We can now rewrite the capital demand function given adjustment cost (equation (5.9)) as:

$$K_{t+1}^d = K_{t+1}^d(m_t^e + \delta, w_{t+1}^e/p_{t+1}^e). \qquad (5.10)$$

Note that, given our expectation assumptions, the capital demand function with adjustment costs (equation (5.4)) has the same form as the capital demand function in the absence of capital adjustment costs. However, the actual response to changes in the real user cost of capital or in the anticipated real wage in the subsequent period would typically be less with adjustment costs, as such costs would lead firms to only gradually move toward a new optimal capital stock.

Equation (5.10) captures the idea that the demand for capital to be in place at the end of period t (at time $t + 1$) depends inversely on the expected real user cost of capital and that, assuming capital and labor are complements, capital demand depends inversely on the anticipated future real wage. Similarly, since net investment demand during period t simply reflects the difference between capital demand at the end of the period and the initial capital stock, we have investment demand being inversely related to the expected real user (or rental) cost of capital and to the anticipated real wage for the subsequent period. Finally, from the firm financing constraint that relates firms' net real financial asset supply to net investment demand, we have firms' net financial asset supply being inversely related to the expected real user cost of capital and the expected future real wage. Thus, in summary, we have:

$$\partial K^d_{t+1}/\partial(m^e_t + \delta) < 0, \qquad \partial I^d_{nt}/\partial(m^e_t + \delta) < 0,$$

$$\partial K^d_{t+1}/\partial(w^e_{t+1}/p^e_{t+1}) < 0, \qquad \partial I^d_{nt}/\partial(w^e_{t+1}/p^e_{t+1}) < 0,$$

$$\partial \text{net } A^s_t/\partial(m^e_t + \delta) > 0, \qquad \partial \text{net } A^s_t/\partial(w^e_{t+1}/p^e_{t+1}) < 0,$$

where $m^e_i \equiv (r_t - \pi^e_t)/(1 + \pi^e_t)$. Note that gross investment demand is given by

$$I^d_t \equiv K^d_{t+1} - \overline{K} + \delta\overline{K} = I^d_{nt} + \delta\overline{K}.$$

Summarizing household behavior with limited perfect foresight

Households' plans at time t concerning the labor supply choice, the consumption/saving choice, and the portfolio choice for period t are constrained by the anticipated household budget constraint as given by equation (5.5). From our intertemporal analysis of these optimal choices, we know that in general at time t we thus have labor supply at time t,

$$N^s_t = N^s_t(w_t/p^e_t, w^e_{t+1}/p^e_{t+1}, \ldots, r_t, r_{t+1}, \ldots, \pi^e_t, \pi^e_{t+1}, \ldots, \overline{A}_t, \overline{M}/p^e_t, d_t$$
$$+ z\overline{B}/p_t),$$

consumption demand planned at time t,

$$c^d_t = c^d_t(w_t/p^e_t, w^e_{t+1}/p^e_{t+1}, \ldots, r_t, r_{t+1}, \ldots, \pi^e_t, \pi^e_{t+1}, \ldots, \overline{A}_t, \overline{M}/p^e_t, d_t$$
$$+ z\overline{B}/p_t),$$

and money demand planned at time t,

$$L_t^d = L_t^d(w_t/p_t^e, w_{t+1}^e/p_{t+1}^e, \ldots, r_t, r_{t+1}, \ldots, \pi_t^e, \pi_{t+1}^e, \ldots, \overline{A}_t, \overline{M}/p_t^e, d_t$$
$$+ z\overline{B}/p_t),$$

where for notational ease we have defined planned real money demand by the term L_t^d. From the anticipated budget constraint, as given by

$$c_t^d + (M_t^d - \overline{M})/p_t^e + \text{net } A_t^d - (w_t/p_t^e)N_t^s - (d_t + z\overline{B}/p_t) = 0,$$

we can infer net real financial asset demand planned at time t, net A_t^d, from households' plans concerning money demand, consumption demand, and labor supply.

With perfect foresight at time t concerning the prices for period t, households' plans made at time t concerning consumption, money demand, and net real financial asset demand during period t will be fulfilled. Thus, letting $\bar{x}_t = d_t + z\overline{B}/p_t + \overline{A}_t + \overline{M}_t/p_t$, we can express the above behavior conditions as follows: labor supply at time t is

$$N_t^s = N_t^s(w_t/p_t, w_{t+1}^e/p_{t+1}^e, \ldots, r_t, r_{t+1}, \ldots, \pi_t^e, \pi_{t+1}^e, \ldots, \bar{x}_t),$$

consumption demand for period t is

$$c_t^d = c_t^d(w_t/p_t, w_{t+1}^e/p_{t+1}^e, \ldots, r_t, r_{t+1}, \ldots, \pi_t^e, \pi_{t+1}^e, \ldots, \bar{x}_t),$$

and money demand for period t is

$$L_t^d = L_t^d(w_t/p_t, w_{t+1}^e/p_{t+1}^e, \ldots, r_t, r_{t+1}, \ldots, \pi_t^e, \pi_{t+1}^e, \ldots, \bar{x}_t),$$

where $L_t^d \equiv M_t^d/p_t$.

As we did with respect to firms' capital demand function given adjustment costs, we now introduce expectation assumptions that essentially collapse the entire sequence of future periods into a single future period. First, we assume static expectations concerning future interest rates, so that $r_i = r_t$, $i = t+1, t+2, \ldots$. Next, we assume static expectations with respect to future rates of inflation, such that $\pi_i^e = \pi_t^e$, $i = t+1, t+2, \ldots$. Finally, we assume that the expected rate of wage inflation beyond the next period is constant and equal to the expected rate of inflation (i.e., $\pi_{wi}^e = \pi_{w,t+1}^e$, $i = t+2, t+3, \ldots$, and $\pi_{w,t+1}^e = \pi_{t+1}^e$), so that the real wage anticipated for the next period is expected to prevail indefinitely. Given the above restrictive expectation assumptions, we can rewrite the households' behavioral functions in the following form: the labor supply at time t becomes

$$N_t^s = N_t^s(w_t/p_t, w_{t+1}^e/p_{t+1}^e, r_t, \pi_t^e, \bar{x}_t),$$

consumption demand for period t becomes

$$c_t^d = c_t^d(w_t/p_t, w_{t+1}^e/p_{t+1}^e, r_t, \pi_t^e, \bar{x}_t),$$

and money demand for period t becomes

$$L_t^d = L_t^d(w_t/p_t, w_{t+1}^e/p_{t+1}^e, r_t, \pi_t^e, \bar{x}_t),$$

where real money demand at the end of period t is given by $L_t^d \equiv M_t^d/p_t$.

Our discussion of the labor supply decision suggests that labor supply is directly related to the real wage and inversely related to the real wage next period (which reflects the real wage in all subsequent periods given our expectation assumptions). This response to changes in the real wages incorporates the intertemporal substitution hypothesis. The intertemporal substitution hypothesis also suggests that labor supply is directly related to the interest rate and inversely related to the expected rate of inflation in that either change implies a higher expected real rate of interest and thus a substitution from leisure to increased labor supply today. Finally, higher real initial holdings of financial assets, real money balances, or income in the current period from bond and equity shares holdings will reduce labor supply if leisure is a normal good. In summary, we thus have

$$\partial N_t^s/\partial(w_t/p_t) > 0, \qquad \partial N_t^s/\partial(w_{t+1}^e/p_{t+1}^e) < 0, \qquad \partial N_t^s/\partial r_t > 0,$$
$$\partial N_t^s/\partial \pi_t^e < 0, \qquad \partial N_t^s/\partial \bar{x}_t < 0.$$

Our discussion of the consumption/saving decision suggests that consumption demand is directly related to both the current and anticipated future real wage since an increase in either implies an increase in the discounted stream of income. Focusing on the Fisherian analysis of the allocation of consumption across time, consumption demand would be inversely related to the money interest rate and directly related to the expected rate of inflation, since either change implies a higher expected real rate of interest. Finally, an increase in $\bar{x}_t$ (reflecting, say, higher real initial holdings of financial assets, increased real money balances, or higher income in the current period from bond and equity share holdings) will raise consumption demand in the current period. In summary, we thus have

$$\partial c_t^d/\partial(w_t/p_t) > 0, \qquad \partial c_t^d/\partial(w_{t+1}^e/p_{t+1}^e) > 0, \qquad \partial c_t^d/\partial r_t < 0,$$
$$\partial c_t^d/\partial \pi_t^e > 0, \qquad \partial c_t^d/\partial \bar{x}_t > 0.$$

Our discussion of the portfolio decision suggests that real money demand is directly related to both the current and anticipated future real wage since an increase in either implies an increase in the discounted stream of income. Focusing on the portfolio analysis, money demand would be inversely related to the money interest rate as households shift from money to financial asset holdings. Any effect of a change in the expected rate of inflation is indirect, and will be ignored. Finally, an increase in $\bar{x}_t$ (reflecting, say, higher real initial holdings of financial assets, increased real money balances, or higher income in the current period from bond and equity share holdings) will likely raise money demand in the current period.

In summary, we thus have

$$\partial L_t^d / \partial (w_t/p_t) > 0, \qquad \partial L_t^d / \partial (w_{t+1}^e/p_{t+1}^e) > 0, \qquad \partial L_t^d / \partial r_t < 0,$$

$$\partial L_t^d / \partial \bar{x}_t > 0.$$

So far, our discussion has not included households' real net financial asset demand. To see what determines this, we can simply use the budget constraint and money, labor, and commodity demand functions. Specifically, rewriting the budget constraint for period t,

$$\text{net } A_t^d = (w_t/p_t)N_t^s + d_t + z\bar{B}/p_t - c_t^d - (M_t^d - \overline{M})/p_t.$$

An increase in the current real wage, initial real money balances, or dividend and interest payments for the current period is presumed to increase not only current consumption and money demand but also future consumption and money demand, and thus increase net financial asset demand by households. From the intertemporal substitution hypothesis, an increase in the expected future real wage will reduce current labor supply, as well as increase current consumption demand; both changes imply a fall in net real financial asset demand for households.

From the Fisherian analysis, a higher expected rate of inflation will reduce the expected real rate of interest; the above constraint indicates that the resulting increase in current consumption demand will reduce households' acquisition of financial assets. Similarly, an increase in real initial financial asset holdings, by raising both current consumption and money demand, will lead to a fall in real *net* financial asset demand. On the other hand, a higher money interest rate, due to both the Fisherian effect on current consumption demand and the portfolio effect on money demand, implies a higher net financial asset demand. In summary, we thus have

$$\partial \text{net } A_t^d / \partial (w_t/p_t) < (\text{or} > \text{or} =) 0, \qquad \partial \text{net } A_t^d / \partial (w_{t+1}^e/p_{t+1}^e) < 0,$$

$$\partial \text{net } A_t^d / \partial r_t > 0,$$

$$\partial \text{net } A_t^d / \partial \pi_t^e < 0, \qquad \partial \text{net } A_t^d / \partial \bar{A}_t < 0, \qquad \partial \text{net } A_t^d / \partial \overline{M}/p_t) > 0,$$

$$\partial \text{net } A_t^d / \partial (d_t + z\bar{B}/p_t) < (\text{or} > \text{or} =) 0,$$

where there are ambiguous effects on net financial asset demand of a change in the real wage and of a change in anticipated dividend and interest payments because an increase in either raises both consumption demand and money demand. Note that in the limit, as the length of the period goes to zero, the household budget constraint at time t becomes:

$$\text{net } A_t^d + (M_t^d - \overline{M})/p_t = 0,$$

as all the flow terms go to zero at a point in time. In this case, assuming real money demand is directly related to income, we obtain the unambiguous effect of

$$\partial \text{net } A_t^d / \partial (d_t + z\overline{B}/p_t) < 0, \qquad \partial \text{net } A_t^d / \partial (w_t/p_t) < 0.$$

However, in the period analysis net A_t^d reflects net real financial asset demand at the end of the period. Thus, assuming any increase in income is not fully reflected in an increased rate of consumption, we have an offsetting effect and thus ambiguity.

Summarizing household behavior without perfect foresight

If we presume that households learn of prices that will exist for period t after time t and they differ from what was expected, then the actual demands for output, money, and financial assets can differ from those reflecting plans made at time t. The key reason for this is that the actual constraint faced by households will differ from that anticipated. In particular, using the actual firm distribution constraint, we replace anticipated real income from wages, dividends, and interest payments from firms with the actual real income net of depreciation ($y_t^* - \delta \overline{K}$). The resulting realized household budget constraint after time t is then

$$c_t^d + (M_t^d - \overline{M})/p_t^e + \text{net } A_t^d - (y_t^* - \delta \overline{K}) = 0.$$

If anticipations by households were incorrect at time t concerning prices or dividends during the period, then revisions in plans for consumption and saving will be made in light of the actual budget constraint faced. In this case, the actual household demand functions for output and money are written as follows: consumption demand during period t is

$$c_t^d = c_t^d (w_{t+1}^e/p_{t+1}^e, r_t, \pi_t^e, \overline{A}_t, \overline{M}/p_t, y_t^*),$$

money demand during period t is

$$L_t^d = L_t^d (w_{t+1}^e/p_{t+1}^e, r_t, \pi_t^e, \overline{A}_t, \overline{M}/p_t, y_t^*),$$

and we replace $\partial c_t^d / \partial (w_t/p_t) > 0$ and $\partial c_t^d / \partial (d_t + z\overline{B}/p_t) > 0$ with

$$\partial c_t^d / \partial y_t^* > 0.$$

Note that the term $\partial c_t^d / \partial y_t^*$ is referred to as the "marginal propensity to consume."[12] Similarly, we replace $\partial L_t^d / \partial (w_t/p_t) > 0$ and $\partial L_t^d / \partial (d_t + z\overline{B}/p_t) > 0$ with

$$\partial L_t^d / \partial y_t^* > 0.$$

Money illusion and the real balance effect

Let us consider (sufficient) assumptions under which demands and supplies are homogeneous of degree 0 in current wages, prices, and the nominal stock of money – that is, there is the absence of money illusion. Note that in considering whether or not there exists money illusion, we must now look at the behavior not only of households but also of firms. Consider firms first.

Assuming perfect foresight on the part of firms, it is clear that current labor demand is homogeneous of degree 0 in current prices (the wage rate w_t and the price level p_t). Thus, so also current output supply. Assuming unit elastic expectations with respect to wages and prices in all future periods and expectations of future interest rates that are invariant to changes in current prices and wages, we have that capital demand, and thus also investment demand and firms' net real financial asset supply, are homogeneous of degree 0 in current prices.

We already assumed static expectations concerning future interest rates and unit elastic expectations with respect to prices beyond period $t + 1$ in terms of next period's price to obtain a simple form for the demand functions for investment. Thus we need only add (a) the assumption of unit elastic expectations concerning the price of output between period t and $t+1$ (implying an expected rate of inflation π_t^e and thus an expected real rate of interest that is independent of a change in the price level p_t)[13] and (b) unit elastic expectations concerning next period's wage and price level (implying an anticipated real wage next period independent of an equiproportionate change in wages and prices in the current period) to obtain the absence of money illusion with respect to firms' investment demand.[14]

To obtain the absence of money illusion with respect to households, we must show that each of the arguments in their demand and supply functions is invariant to an equiproportional change in current prices, wages, and the nominal stock of money. Given perfect foresight, the current real wage and initial real money balances meet this condition. But what about the expected real wage next period, the expected rate of inflation, current dividends and interest payments, and the real value of initial financial assets holdings? As it turns out, the assumption of unit elastic expectations with respect to all future prices and wages is again critical in showing these to be invariant, as it was in deriving a capital demand homogeneous of degree 0 in current wages and prices.

First, it is clear that the assumption of unit elastic expectations with respect to future wages and prices makes future real wages invariant to equiproportional changes in the current wages and prices. But note that in so doing we have eliminated the "intertemporal substitution hypothesis" effect on labor supply of a change in the current real wage. Similarly, the assumption of unit elastic expectations with respect to the future price level eliminates any effect of a change in the price level on the expected rate of inflation. Finally, assuming that expectations of nominal future interest rates are invariant to an equiproportionate change in current prices, wages, and the money supply, the expected real rate of interest will not be affected by equiproportionate changes in wages, prices, and the money supply. But note that the "intertemporal substitution hypothesis" impact on labor supply of a change in the expected real rate of interest initiated by a change in the current price level is now absent as well.[15]

What is left in order to obtain the absence of money illusion for households is to show that changes in current prices leave current dividend payments and the real value of initial bond and stock holdings unchanged. Once again, as we see below, the assumption of unit elastic expectations concerning next period's wages and prices will be invoked to achieve this. What we are looking for are sufficient assumptions that will result in the terms $d_t + z\overline{B}/p_t$ and $\overline{A}_t$ being homogeneous of degree 0 in w_t and p_t.

From the firm distribution constraint (5.2) and assuming firms' labor demand is satisfied (i.e., $N_t^* = N_t^d$ and thus $y_t^* = y_t^s$) we know that

$$d_t + z\overline{B}/p_t = y_t^s - \delta\overline{K} - (w_t/p_t)N_t^d.$$

Since N_t^d and y_t^s are homogeneous of degree 0 in prices, it is clear that the sum of current dividends plus interest payments is not affected by equiproportionate changes in both the current wage and price level. A higher price level does alter the composition of payments, however, as real dividends rise and real interest payments fall.

Now consider $\overline{A}_t$. To show that this can be homogeneous of degree 0 in the current wage and price level, note from the firm distribution constraint and from the assumption that firms' demand for labor is satisfied in subsequent periods that

$$d_t + z\overline{B}/p_{t+1}^e = f(N_{t+1}^d, K_{t+1}^d) - (w_{t+1}^e/p_{t+1}^e)N_{t+1}^d - \delta K_{t+1}^d.$$

A similar equation holds for future periods as well. $\overline{A}_t$ simply reflects the present value of such future real payments using the appropriate expected real interest rates for discounting. The assumption of unit elastic expectations concerning prices in all future periods, coupled with expectations of future nominal interest rates that are unaffected by an equiproportionate change in money prices and the money supply, thus means that $\overline{A}$ is homogeneous of degree 0 with regard to a change in prices (price level and wages) and the money supply in period t.[16]

A special case of the above is if we assume static expectations concerning future interest rates (i.e., $r_i = r_t$, $i = t + 1, t + 2, \ldots$) and zero adjustment costs. In this case, K_i^d, $i = t + 1, t + 2, \ldots$, would be the same in each future period. There would be a constant labor demand ($N_i^d = N_{t+1}^d$, $i = t + 2, t + 3, \ldots$) as well given the invariant real wage in conjunction with no change in their capital stock. Now recall that $\overline{A}_t$ is defined by

$$\overline{A}_t \equiv [p_{bt}\overline{B} + p_{et}\overline{S}]/p_t,$$

where $p_{bt}\overline{B}_t$ is the present value of future interest payments and $p_{et}\overline{S}$ is the present value of future dividends. Since $\overline{A}_t$ is simply the present value of the now constant future stream of dividends and interest payments discounted using an invariant expected real rate of interest, we thus have

$$\overline{A}_t = [d_{t+1} + zB_t/p^e_{t+1}]/m^e_t.$$

Since $d_{t+1} + zB_t/p^e_{t+1} = f(N^d_{t+1}, K^d_{t+1}) - (w^e_{t+1}/p^e_{t+1})N^d_{t+1} - \delta K^d_{t+1}$ from the firm distribution constraint, we can rewrite the initial real holdings of financial assets as

$$\overline{A}_t = [f(N^d_{t+1}, K^d_{t+1}) - (w^e_{t+1}/p^e_{t+1})N^d_{t+1} - \delta K^d_{t+1}]/m^e_t,$$

which is homogeneous of degree 0 in current wages and prices if we assume that the anticipated real wage next period is independent of an equiproportionate change in the current wages and prices. In other words, to obtain the absence of money illusion for households, we assume, as we did with firms, that there are unit elastic expectations concerning wages and prices in the next period.

Note that an increase in the money interest rate and the expected rate of inflation that leaves the expected real rate of interest unchanged will alter the composition of financial asset holdings, although not the total. To see this, recall that with static expectations concerning the interest rate, the price of bonds at the end of period t is given by

$$p_{bt} = \sum_{i=1}^{\infty} z/(1 + r_t)^i = z/r_t.$$

An increase in the money interest rate and expected rate of inflation such that the real rate of interest is unchanged means a fall in the price of bonds but an offsetting rise in the price of stock, as over time real dividend payments will be rising more rapidly while real interest payments will be falling more rapidly. Similarly, an increase in the current level of prices, although leaving $\overline{A}_t$ unaffected, would reduce the real value of bond holdings and lead to an exactly offsetting increase in the real value of equity share holdings.

The real balance effect is apparent from the nature of the demand and supply functions. In particular, an increase in nominal money balances or fall in prices with no change in nominal money balances will increase initial real money holdings and in general lead to an increase in consumption demand, real money demand, and real net financial asset demand. In general, labor supply would fall.

6 The simple neoclassical macroeconomic model (without government or depository institutions)

Introduction

We have now covered a substantial part of the underlying structure for a simple aggregate model of an economy with production. The specific elements of the "microeconomic foundations" of this aggregate model developed so far have dealt with the optimizing behavior of individuals ("representative" firms and households) in a setting in which individuals take prices as given. Implicit in these discussions is another part of the microeconomic foundations, the way in which individual markets operate. We have been assuming that prices adjust so that the presumption that buyers and sellers are price-takers is justified. In other words, equilibrium within individual markets entails price adjustment to equate supplies and demands. In addition, we will assume that all individuals in the economy correctly foresee period t's output prices when input supply and production decisions are made at the start of the period. As discussed below, however, there are other options.

Static macroeconomic models: the options

Grandmont (1977: 542) notes that:

> one way to look at the evolution of an economic system is to view it as a succession of temporary or short-run competitive equilibrium. That is, one postulates that at each date, prices move fast enough to match supply and demand. ... Although one assumes equilibrium in each period, the economic system displays a disequilibrium feature along a sequence of temporary competitive equilibrium ... at each date, the plans of the agents for the future are not coordinated and thus will be, in general, incompatible ... this is to be contrasted with the perfect foresight approach where, by definition, such a disequilibrium phenomenon cannot occur.

This temporary equilibrium view of the economy is characteristic of the simple, static neoclassical model, a model in which all prices adjust to maintain equilibrium.[1] The second key assumption of the neoclassical model is that agents are informed about prices within the period. In particular, when making their labor supply and demand decisions at the start of the period, households and firms are assumed to correctly anticipate the prices they will have to pay to purchase output during the period. As it turns out, this element of "perfect foresight" with respect to markets through time $t + 1$ is a critical feature of the analysis. Before examining the implications of these assumptions, however, some history on the origin of the neoclassical model might be helpful.

The phrase "neoclassical macroeconomic model" is a descendant of "classical" economic theory as reflected in the work of Sir William Petty during the 1600s. In *Das Kapital* Karl Marx (1976: 85) stated that "by classical Political Economy, I understand that economy which, since the time of W. Petty, has investigated the real relations of production in bourgeois society." As Marx suggested, early classical economists focused on the determinants of the economy's productive capacity. The neoclassical macroeconomic model shares this focus on the productive capacity of the economy as the determinant of total output. It also turns out to be the static precursor to much of the current analysis in the macroeconomic literature that falls under the heading of "real business cycle theory."

While the simple, static neoclassical model, along with its dynamic and stochastic counterparts, is one popular approach to macroeconomic analysis, there are other approaches. In fact, even though static analysis is restricted to markets in the current period, there remains enough flexibility to introduce at least four ways of characterizing macroeconomic analysis:

1 "Neoclassical model": competitive equilibria are assumed to exist in current and future markets, and limited perfect foresight is assumed for all participants.

2 "Illusion model": competitive equilibria are assumed to exist in current and future markets, but imperfect foresight is assumed on the part of some agents. The result is like the "Lucas supply function," popularized by Lucas (1973) in which output can respond directly to increases in the actual output prices.

3 "Keynesian model": a competitive equilibrium is assumed *not* to exist in the labor market, as the money wage is fixed and employment is demand-determined. However, other prices, in particular the prices of output, are presumed to reflect competitive equilibria. A rational expectation version of this model is developed by Fisher.

4 "Non-market-clearing model": a competitive equilibrium is assumed *not* to exist in the output market, as the price of output is fixed above the competitive equilibrium level. This model forms the basis of much of what appears in undergraduate macroeconomic analysis, including the IS-LM model.

The neoclassical model, with its assumptions of flexible prices and informed agents, provides a benchmark against which we can compare the predictions of other (static) macroeconomic models.[2] It also provides insight into the nature of the stationary states for dynamic macroeconomic models that presume market-clearing prices and accurate forecasts of prices.

Hicksian temporary equilibrium and Walras' law

For the market for any good, "competitive" equilibrium is defined by equality between market demand and supply.[3] A temporary competitive equilibrium for the economy during period t will be characterized by a money wage for labor (w_t^*), a money price for the consumption commodity (p_t^*), a money price for bonds (p_{bt}^*), a money price for equity shares (p_{et}^*), allocations to households in terms of employment, consumption, bond holdings, equity share holdings, and money balances $(N_t^*, c_t^*, B_t^*, S_t^*, \text{ and } M_t^*)$, and allocations to firms in terms of employment, output, investment, bond issues, and equity share issues $(N_t^*, y_t^*, I_t^*, B_t^*, S_t^*)$ such that:

- these allocations are in the demand (supply) set of each agent;
- these allocations are feasible.

Together these two conditions imply prices determined in the labor, output, bond, and equity shares markets for period t that result in zero excess aggregate demand for labor, output, bonds, equity shares, and money. Thus we may rewrite the conditions for a general equilibrium as a money wage, a price of output, a price of bonds, and a price of equity shares such that:

$$N_t^s = N_t^d,$$
$$y_t^s = c_t^d + I_{nt}^d + \delta\overline{K} + \psi(I_{nt}^d),$$
$$B_t^s = B_t^d,$$
$$S_t^s = S_t^d,$$
$$\overline{M}/p_t = M_t^d/p_t,$$

where

$$I_{nt}^d = K_{t+1}^d - \overline{K},$$
$$y_t^s = f(N_t^d, \overline{K}).$$

Given our assumption that bonds and equity shares are perfect substitutes, in general there will not be a unique equilibrium in terms of the number of bonds and equity shares supplied or demanded, although the total value of financial assets supplied or demanded will be determinant. Thus, we replace the bond and equity share markets with a single market, the financial market. The equilibrium conditions then become:

$$N_t^s = N_t^d,$$
$$y_t^s = c_t^d + I_{nt}^d + \delta\overline{K} + \psi(I_{nt}^d),$$

$$A_t^s = A_t^d,$$
$$\overline{M}/p_t = M_t^d/p_t,$$

where

$$A_t^s \equiv [p_{bt}B_t^s + p_{et}S_t^s]/p_t,$$
$$A_t^d \equiv [p_{bt}B_t^d + p_{et}S_t^d]/p_t.$$

We can view the financial market as simultaneously determining the price of bonds, p_{bt}, the price of equity shares, p_{et}, and the interest rate r_t. That is, once one of these is known, the other two are implied. For instance, from our definition of the interest rate:

$$1 + r_t \equiv [z + p_{b,t+1}]/p_t,$$

we see that, given the coupon rate and expected price of bonds in the subsequent period, the interest rate r_t implies a price of bonds p_{bt}. As perfect substitutes, bonds and equity shares must offer the identical expected gross return. Thus we have that

$$1 + r_t = 1 + r_{et} \equiv [d_{t+1} + p_{e,t+1}]/p_{et}.$$

As you can see, given expectations of future dividends and the future price of equity shares, an interest rate r_t also implies a price of equity shares p_{et}. We often talk of the financial market in terms of an equilibrium interest rate. The above should make it clear that associated with such an equilibrium interest rate are prices of bonds and equity shares. And a rise (fall) in the interest rate means a fall (rise) in the prices of bonds and equity shares.

We will make one additional change in the characterization of the financial market to put it in terms of additional demands and supplies, that is, put it in net rather than gross terms. The reason for this is that net financial asset demands and supplies are what correspond to household saving in the form of financial assets and firm investment. Thus, the equilibrium conditions become:

$$N_t^s = N_t^d,$$
$$y_t^s = c_t^d + I_{nt}^d + \delta\overline{K} + \psi(I_{nt}^d),$$
$$\text{net } A_t^s = \text{net } A_t^d,$$
$$\overline{M}/p_t = M_t^d/p_t,$$

where

$$\text{net } A_t^s \equiv A_t^s - \overline{A}_t,$$
$$\text{net } A_t^d \equiv A_t^d - \overline{A}_t,$$
$$\overline{A}_t \equiv [p_{bt}\overline{B} + p_{et}\overline{S}]/p_t.$$

According to the above, we have four equilibrium conditions but only three prices – the money wage rate, the level of output prices, and the interest rate – to be determined. As usual, Walras' law is invoked to show that only $n - 1$ of the n equilibrium conditions are independent. However, the nature of Walras' law depends on whether we assume limited perfect foresight or not.

Walras' law for limited perfect foresight sums up the constraints faced by the individual agents in the economy at time t to obtain:

$$[c_t^d + I_{nt}^d + \delta \overline{K} + \psi(I_{nt}^d) - y_t^s] + [\text{net } A_t^d - \text{net } A_t^s]$$
$$+ (w_t/p_t)[N_t^d - N_t^s] + M_t^d/p_t - \overline{M}/p_t = 0.$$

Thus the sum of excess demands for output, financial assets, labor, and money must equal zero.

When there is not perfect foresight at time t concerning prices for period t in the output and financial markets, we have the equilibrium condition for the labor market,

$$N_t^s - N_t^d = 0,$$

and the modified Walras' law based on the resulting employment and output of the form:

$$[c_t^d + I_{nt}^d + \delta \overline{K} + \psi(I_{nt}^d) - y_t^*] + [\text{net } A_t^d - \text{net } A_t^s] + M_t^d/p_t - \overline{M}/p_t = 0.$$

In this case, the money wage, employment, and thus output are determined in the labor market, and the modified Walras' law indicates that the price level and interest rate are determined by any two of the remaining three markets.

As it turns out, most macroeconomic analysis takes this second approach to solving for equilibrium. That is, the analysis focuses on the labor (and other input) markets and determines the effect of changes in output price (and potentially other variables such as the interest rate) on equilibrium employment and thus output. This generates an "aggregate supply equation," which is then combined with two of the remaining three equilibrium equations – typically the commodity and money market equilibrium conditions – to determine the equilibrium price level, interest rate, and output. The modified Walras' law is invoked to ensure equilibrium in the financial market at this point. Working backward, one can infer from the aggregate supply equation the equilibrium money wage and employment implied by the analysis.

The advantage of the above approach is that it can be used whether or not there exists limited perfect foresight at time t with respect to the price level and whether or not prices adjust to clear markets. A disadvantage of the analysis is that, in the case of the neoclassical model with limited perfect foresight and competitive equilibrium, it arbitrarily breaks up the analysis of markets. In doing so, it requires that demand functions for such goods as money and commodities be specified with income as an argument. This form of the demand functions obscures the fact that, as we have seen, in standard general equilibrium analysis demand functions depend on prices (including the real wage), and income is a variable determined by the choice of labor supply.

With these qualifications in mind, we take the standard approach of macroeconomics and separate out the analysis of the labor (and other input) markets (the "aggregate supply" part) from the other markets (the "aggregate demand" part). The next section considers the labor market at time t.

Labor market equilibrium

At the start of period t the labor market takes place and a rate of production of output is determined. From our analysis of firm behavior at time t, we know that behind labor demand is an expected price of output over the period and associated expected real wage, an existing capital stock, and existing technology as incorporated in the production function. We shall assume that firms correctly anticipate at time t the price of output for the period, so that firms confront the actual real wage: w_t/p_t.

From our analysis of household decision-making at time t, we know that behind labor supply at time t is not only the expected price of output and implied expected real wage, but also such factors as the relationship of the anticipated current real wage to anticipated future real wages, the expected real rate of interest, anticipated wealth in the form of financial asset and real money holdings, and anticipated current nonlabor income. Like firms, we will assume households have limited perfect foresight in that at time t they correctly foresee the price level for period t. Assuming a Walrasian or "competitive equilibrium" view of the labor markets, the money wage w_t adjusts to achieve equilibrium in the labor market under these circumstances.

We have already seen how static expectations concerning future rates of wage and price inflation, along with the assumption of unit elastic expectations concerning wages and prices next period, simplify the labor supply function by removing expected future real wages as explicit arguments. Patinkin (1965), among others, goes several steps beyond these simplifying assumptions and assumes that all other variables excepting the real wage do not have a significant impact on labor supply.[4] Thus, equilibrium in the labor market is given by a level of employment N_t and money wage w_t such that

$$N_t = N_t^d(w_t/p_t, \overline{K}) \quad \text{and} \quad N_t = N_t^s(w_t/p_t).$$

As Patinkin (1965: 264) notes:

> it will immediately be recognized that we have greatly oversimplified the analysis of this market. Both the demand and supply functions for labor should actually be presented as dependent on the real value of bond and money holdings as well as on the real wage rate.[5] Further, if we were to permit the firm to vary its input of capital, its demand for labor would depend also on the rate of interest. Finally, a full utility analysis of individual behavior would show the supply of labor also to depend on this rate.[6]

Besides a competitive labor market and the above simplified labor supply function, the neoclassical model assumes that suppliers correctly anticipate the aggregate price level. As we will see, the assumption of the neoclassical model that suppliers, like firms, have perfect foresight at time *t* with respect to the price of output for the period means that changes in the price of output have no effect on output supply. This characteristic of the neoclassical model implies an underlying "block recursive" nature to the analysis, as described below.

At the start of the period, the labor market occurs, with employment and thus output and the money wage being determined for the period. Employment and output are determined based on individuals' expectations of subsequent variables such as the price of output. And the level of employment and output influence the remaining variables to be determined. But in the neoclassical model the level of employment and output are not influenced by the remaining variables to be determined. We can thus solve the equilibrium sequentially, looking first at the labor market and the determination of employment and output, then looking at the output, financial, and money markets and the determination of the price level and interest rate.

Financial market equilibrium

With regard to the financial market, Patinkin (1965: 215) states:

> a decrease in the price of bonds (and equity shares) decreases the amount demanded of consumption commodities; it will also be assumed that it decreases the amount demanded of money balances; hence, by the household's budget constraint, their total expenditures on [net] bond holdings must increase.

Thus Patinkin invokes a "Fisherian effect" and a "portfolio effect" of a change in the interest rate to obtain

$$\partial(\text{net } A_t^d)/\partial p_{bt} < 0.$$

From the firm financing constraint and the fact that a firm's net investment demand is inversely related to the interest rate, we have

$$\partial(\text{net } A_t^s)/\partial p_{bt} > 0.$$

The above analysis differs slightly from that found in Patinkin (1965: 214). For instance, Patinkin uses the assumption of static expectations concerning interest rates and a coupon rate, *z*, equal to 1 to express the price of bonds as the reciprocal of the interest rate, that is,

$$p_{bt} = 1/r_t.$$

Further, Patinkin assumes no equity shares, so his financial market consists only of bonds. Finally, Patinkin does not graph net real bond demand and supply. Rather, he graphs the total number of bonds demanded and supplied. Thus, Patinkin has demands and supplies of bonds of the form

$$B^s = r_t p_t A_t^s \equiv B_t^s,$$
$$B^d = r_t p_t A_t^d \equiv B_t^d.$$

As might be expected, Patinkin's bond demand and supply curves differ in nature from net real financial asset demand and supply curves. For instance, it is clear from the analysis of investment demand that a rise in the interest rate (a fall in the price of bonds) will lead to reduced investment demand and thus reduced net real financial asset supply. This relationship between investment and firms' net real financial asset supply follows directly from the firm financing constraint, which, given $p_{bt} = 1/r_t$, is of the form

$$\text{net } A_t \equiv 1/p_t r_t [B_t^s - \overline{B}] = I_{nt}^d + \psi(I_{bt}^d).$$

Naturally, if net investment were initially zero and there were zero adjustment costs (so that $B_t^s = \overline{B}$), the fall in investment that results from a rise in the interest rate would imply a similar decrease in the number of bonds supplied (B_t^s). However, if initially $B_t^s > \overline{B}$, then a higher interest rate, even though it decreases investment, could at the same time increase the number of bonds supplied. As Patinkin (1965: 217) observes:

> consider the effect of an increase in the rate of interest (fall in $1/r_t$). The internal consistency of our model requires that this decrease the amount of real bonds supplied.

However, this need not reduce the number of bonds supplied. As Patinkin (1965: 217) continues:

> a rise in the interest rate (p_{bt} falls) has lowered the price received for bonds and so may increase the number of bonds necessary to finance the firm's expenditures on investment commodities ($B_t^s > \overline{B}$ initially), even though these expenditures have decreased.

A similar analysis would apply to a comparison of households' demand for bonds in terms of numbers with household net real financial asset demand.

Money "market" equilibrium

As we know from Walras' law, having depicted equilibrium in the labor and financial markets, we need only look at one of the other two remaining markets, the output market or the money "market." Consider a money market in which nominal money supply, $\overline{M}$, and nominal money demand, $M_t^d \equiv p_t L_t^d$, are plotted against the reciprocal of the price level, which indicates the "relative" price of one unit of money in terms of output. If there is no real balance effect with respect to real money holdings, then the money demand curve is invariant to a change in the price level (elasticity of demand equals 1). If there is a real balance effect with respect to money demand, then a fall in the price level (a rise in the relative price of money $(1/p_t)$) would lead to a less than proportionate decrease in nominal money demand (elasticity of demand less than 1).

Aggregate supply and demand: an introduction

Temporary equilibrium for the economy can be characterized in several ways. As we alluded to above, one way common in journal articles and textbooks is to divide the analysis under the headings of "aggregate supply" and "aggregate demand."

Under the heading of "aggregate supply" is an analysis of the input markets, in particular the labor market. One aim is to determine input prices (in particular the money wage), the employment of inputs, and the implied production of output that occur at different levels of output prices (and potentially different levels of interest rates). The term "aggregate supply" is applied to this analysis for the simple reason that it determines the "supply" of total output at different prices.

Under the heading of "aggregate demand" is an analysis of the other markets in the economy during period t, in particular the output, financial, and money markets. The aim is to determine the level of output prices and the interest rate that occur at different levels of output. The term "aggregate demand" attached to this analysis reflects the fact that the analysis determines how the price level and interest rate adjust to equate the "demand" for total output to different levels of production.

Combining the aggregate supply and demand analysis, we can determine the output, price level, and interest rate associated with temporary equilibrium, as well as the underlying equilibrium money wage, real wage, employment, consumption, investment, and real money balances. To understand more clearly what is involved in aggregate supply and demand analysis and how they can be combined, we consider below the specific case of the neoclassical model, starting with the aggregate supply.

Equilibrium and aggregate supply

As we have said, behind aggregate supply is an analysis of various input markets to determine the response of total output to changes in such variables as the price level.[7] In the neoclassical model changes in prices lead to equiproportionate changes in money wages with no change in the equilibrium level of employment and thus no change in aggregate supply. To formally show this, let us start with the following statement of equilibrium in the labor market in terms of a money wage w_t and level of employment N_t such that

$$N_t^d(w_t/p_t, \overline{K}) - N_t = 0,$$
$$N_t^s(w_t/p_t) - N_t = 0$$

A critical aspect of the above is the fact that suppliers, in particular suppliers of labor, correctly anticipate the price level that will exist with respect to output, so that w_t/p_t replaces w_t/p_t^e in the labor supply function.

Totally differentiating the above two equations with respect to w_t, N_t, and p_t, one obtains

$$\begin{bmatrix} (\partial N_t^d/\partial(w_t/p_t))(1/p_t)-1 & \\ (\partial N_t^s/\partial(w_t/p_t))(1/p_t)-1 & \end{bmatrix} \begin{bmatrix} dw_t \\ dN_t \end{bmatrix} = \begin{bmatrix} (\partial N_t^d/\partial(w_t/p_t))(w_t dp_t/(p_t)^2) \\ (\partial N_t^s/\partial(w_t/p_t))(w_t dp_t/(p_t)^2) \end{bmatrix}.$$

Applying Cramer's rule, one obtains:

$$dw_t/dp_t = w_t/p_t \quad \text{and} \quad dN_t/dp_t = 0.$$

Thus in the neoclassical model, the real wage and employment level determined in the labor market are independent of changes in the price level.[8]

The "aggregate supply equation" combines the analysis of the labor market (and other input markets) and resulting determination of employment of various inputs with the production function to determine the resulting output supplied. For the neoclassical model, the aggregate supply equation is of the form:

$$y_t^* = y_t^*(\overline{K}, \ldots). \tag{6.1}$$

What is important about this equation is that the price level and interest rate are not arguments in the supply equation. Of course, changes in the capital stock, changes in technology, or changes in the supply of other inputs (e.g., changes in the oil supply) can affect output. Similarly, a change in the composition of the labor force or government policies that affect labor supply can affect equilibrium employment and thus output.[9]

We may summarize the above findings graphically. Consider an increase in p_t. Given perfect foresight, both firms and households at time t would anticipate this higher price level. In the labor market, the result would be an increase in the equilibrium money wage in the same proportion as the increase in the expected price level, so that the anticipated real wage would remain the same, as would employment and output. This outcome for the labor market is shown in Figure 6.1. Note that the result of no change in employment or output in light of a higher output price simply requires that both labor demand and supply curves shift vertically by the same amount. Such equal shifts reflect the fact that the same increase in the money wage leaves both firms and households anticipating the same real wage as before.

In undergraduate textbooks, the fact that changes in the price of output leave employment and real output unaffected in the neoclassical model is often shown

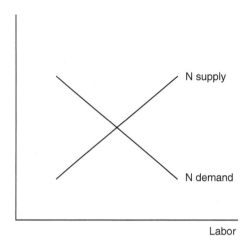

Figure 6.1 Labor market equilibrium.

in (p_t, y_t) space by a vertical "aggregate supply curve." Such a curve summarizes the underlying behavior for the economy-wide labor market. Later we will see that under other assumptions, such as embedded in Lucas's model ("money illusion") and the Keynesian model (fixed nominal wage), the aggregate supply curve will be upward sloping.

It is important to realize that the aggregate supply shown in Figure 6.2 is *not* the typical market supply curve of microeconomics. In microeconomics, a higher price of good x, and consequent increase in the demand for inputs by firms producing that good, draws inputs away from the production of other goods, so that the higher price of good x induces increased output of that good and associated increased employment of inputs (such as labor) in the production of the good. Implicit in this analysis is that there is reduced production of other goods in the economy. However, as the above analysis makes clear, if the focus is on the aggregation of all commodity markets, a higher price level no longer induces increased aggregate output unless the quantity of total inputs supplies rises, which will not be the case under neoclassical assumptions.[10]

The natural rate of unemployment

The key feature of the above analysis of aggregate supply is the assumption that prices adjust to continuously maintain equilibrium in the various markets and that individuals are perfectly informed concerning prices. The result is a level of real output sometimes called the "full employment level." So far missing from the analysis, however, is any mention of unemployment. If one expands the model to introduce unemployment, the rate of unemployment is called the "natural" rate.[11] By "natural" is meant that it is the rate of unemployment that the economy will

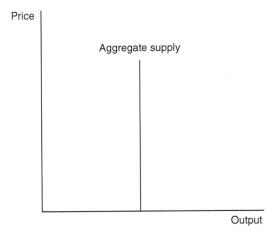

Figure 6.2 Aggregate supply.

gravitate to as prices adjust to clear markets and individuals become fully informed concerning prices (i.e., under the assumptions of the neoclassical model).

To introduce unemployment into the analysis when the labor market is in equilibrium at full employment requires recognition of two facts. First, the labor market is in a constant state of flux. Not only do individuals enter and leave the labor force continually, but labor demand varies continuously across firms as they experience variations in the relative demand for their output. This instability of jobs themselves has been estimated to account for roughly one-quarter of the average unemployment rate, as in an average year one in every nine jobs disappears and one in every eight is newly created (Leonard 1988). Second, information is costly. It takes time for new workers entering the labor force and for workers who have been laid off or have quit previous jobs to discover which employers have vacancies and how wages vary across employers.

When we take into account the continuous flows to unemployment together with workers' imperfect information about job vacancies, we see that unemployment is no longer inconsistent with the neoclassical model. At any moment, there exist new entrants into the labor market who are spending time searching for acceptable jobs. There also exist laid-off workers who are either searching for alternative jobs or awaiting recall. And there are workers who have quit their jobs and are searching for other jobs. This kind of unemployment is generally referred to as frictional unemployment.

Sometimes part of frictional unemployment is called structural unemployment, with structural unemployment occurring because of a change in the composition or "structure" of aggregate output across firms. For example, the replacement of steel with plastic in automobiles led to a shift in employment from steel factories to firms making plastic. During this transition, some steel workers experienced structural unemployment.

To summarize, when the labor market is in equilibrium, there exists a positive unemployment rate because workers continuously move into and out of the labor force and between jobs.[12] To signify that this unemployment rate is "natural," or consistent with equilibrium in the labor market, it is generally called the natural rate of unemployment.[13] The corresponding level of employment is then often referred to as the full employment level.

Like equilibrium output and employment in the neoclassical model, "supply factors" determine the natural rate of unemployment as well.[14] Among these is the demographic composition of the labor force, but also unemployment insurance and minimum wage legislation. In recent years a large body of literature has analyzed labor markets and the sources of unemployment with the focus on search and labor contracts. Note that an understanding of the natural rate of unemployment is important in determining the effects of government policies aimed at the unemployed.

Equilibrium and aggregate demand

The aggregate demand side of macroeconomic models considers the equilibrium conditions of two of the remaining three markets, in particular the output market (reflected by an "IS" equation) and the money market (reflected by an "LM" or "portfolio" equation). The "IS" equation, since it is simply the expression for equilibrium during period t with respect to the output market, is given by[15]

$$c_t^d + I_{nt}^d + \delta \overline{K} + \psi(I_{nt}^d) - y_t^* = 0. \tag{6.2}$$

Note that the equation is termed the "IS" equation because we can rewrite it to obtain

$$I_{nt}^d + \delta \overline{K} + \psi(I_{nt}^d) = y_t^* - c_t^d,$$

indicating that equilibrium in the output market is equivalent to the equality between *I*nvestment expenditures (the left-hand side of the equation) and household *S*aving (the right-hand side of the equation).[16]

The assumption of unit elastic expectations concerning wages and prices gives the following simple form for households' consumption demand and firms' investment demand functions during period t:[17]

$$c_t^d = c_t^d(r_t, \pi_t^e, \overline{A}_t, \overline{M}/p_t, y_t^*)$$

and

$$I_{nt}^d = I_{nt}^d(m_t^e + \delta, \overline{K}).$$

The "LM" equation, since it is simply the expression for equilibrium in period t with respect to the "money" market, is given by

$$L_t^d = \overline{M}/p_t \tag{6.3}$$

This equation is termed the "LM" equation for it reflects the equality between *L*iquidity preference or demand and the *M*oney supply. We have seen that our assumption of unit elastic expectations concerning wages and prices gives us the following simple form for the real money demand function:

$$L_t^d = L_t^d(r_t, \pi_t^e, \overline{A}_t, \overline{M}/p_t, y_t^*).$$

From the modified Walras' law it follows that a price level and interest rate that satisfy the "IS" equation and "LM" equation for a given level of output y_t^* will also result in equilibrium in the financial market.

We thus have three equations (the aggregate supply equation (6.1), the "IS" equation (6.2), and the "LM" equation (6.3)) that can be solved for the equilibrium levels of output, price, and interest rate. Looking at what underlies these three equations, we can then infer the changes in money wages and employment (the labor market) as well as changes in the components of output demand (investment and consumption demand). Equilibrium can be depicted in terms of a price level and interest rate (Patinkin's CC–LL–BB curves) or in terms of a price level and output (i.e., aggregate demand and supply curves). We start with Patinkin's depiction of equilibrium.

Depiction of equilibrium: the Patinkin analysis

The neoclassical model aggregate supply is independent of changes in the price level and interest rate.[18] This means that for any given level of output, we can focus on equations (6.2) and (6.3) to determine the equilibrium interest rate and price level. This is a reflection of the "block recursive" nature of the solution to the neoclassical model mentioned earlier.

Patinkin (1965) suggests a graphical way of showing such an equilibrium combination of price level and interest rate using any two of three curves denoted the CC, LL and BB curves. The CC curve depicts combinations of the price level and interest rate that satisfy the equilibrium condition for output (6.2); the LL curve depicts combinations that satisfy the equilibrium condition for money (6.3). Where these two lines so constructed intersect, it must then be the case that this price combination satisfies two of the three equilibrium conditions simultaneously. It follows from the modified Walras' law that the curve indicating various combinations of the price level and interest rate that satisfy the equilibrium condition with respect to the financial market (the BB curve) goes through this point as well.[19]

For the market for output, equilibrium in period *t* is characterized by (6.2). Recall that real output y_t^* denotes that output reflecting the capital stock $\overline{K}$, technology, and the employment of labor determined in the labor market at time *t*. From the neoclassical assumptions with respect to labor demand and supply, equilibrium employment and thus output are unchanged for any change in the price level or interest rate.

Let us presume that the pair (p_t^*, r_t^*) is associated with equilibrium in the output market. In (price, interest rate) space, this combination is identified by a unique point on the CC curve that identifies combinations of p_t and r_t associated with equilibrium in the commodity market (Figure 6.3).

To understand what lies behind the shape of the CC curve depicted above, totally differentiate the market-clearing condition for the commodity market with respect to p_t and r_t. Doing so, we obtain[20]

$$[\partial c_t^d / \partial(\overline{M}/p_t)] - [\overline{M}/p_t^2]dp_t + [\partial c_t^d / \partial r_t + (1 + \psi')\partial I_{nt}^d / \partial r_t]dr_t = 0.$$

Rearranging, we have that the slope of the CC curve is given by

$$\{dr_t/dp_t | y_t^d - y_t^* = 0\}$$
$$= [\partial c_t^d / \partial(\overline{M}/p_t)][\overline{M}/p_t^2]/[\partial c_t^d / \partial r_t + (1 + \psi')\partial I_{nt}^d / \partial r_t] < 0.$$

The negative slope of the CC curve can be explained in the following way. The positive numerator of the expression for the slope reflects the real balance effect with respect to commodities; this term indicates the fall in consumption demand that would accompany a rise in the price level, for such a rise reduces agents' wealth in the form of initial real money balances.[21] The negative denominator indicates the effect of a change in the interest rate on consumption and investment demand.

Now let us consider the money market. As before, there is a unique point that indicates an interest rate and a price of output at which there is equilibrium in the economy, and this point on the LL curve identifies combinations of p_t and r_t associated with equilibrium in the money market (Figure 6.4). Recall that the LL curve identifies combinations of p_t and r_t associated with equilibrium in the money "market" as given by (6.3).

The slope of the LL curve is given by totally differentiating the zero excess demand condition with respect to money. Doing so, and rearranging, one obtains

$$\{dr_t/dp_t | L_t^d - \overline{M}/p_t = 0\} = [1 - \partial L_t^d / \partial(\overline{M}/p_t)][\overline{M}/p_t^2]/[-\partial L_t^d / \partial r_t] > 0.$$

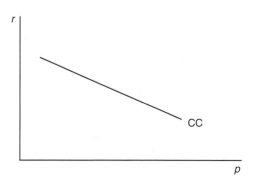

Figure 6.3 Commodity market.

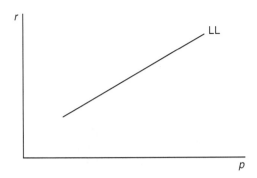

Figure 6.4 Money market.

Note that the numerator of this term is positive. The change in real money balances will be greater than the consequent change in real money demand given real balance effects with respect to financial assets and/or commodities. The denominator is positive as well, reflecting the fact that an increase in the interest causes households to shift their portfolio out of money holdings into bonds.

Putting together the CC and LL curves, we have equilibrium in the economy at the point where these two curves intersect. From the modified Walras' law, we know that at this point demand for financial assets equals supply as well. In fact, there is a corresponding BB curve that goes through this same intersection.

As with the CC curve, to understand what lies behind the shape of the BB curve, we can totally differentiate the market-clearing condition for the financial market with respect to p_t and r_t. That market-clearing condition is

$$\text{net } A_t^d = \text{net } A_t^s = 0,$$

where, in simplest form,

$$\text{net } A_t^s = \text{net } A_t^s(m_t^e + \delta, \overline{K}),$$
$$\text{net } A_t^d = \text{net } A_t^d(r_t, \pi_t^e, \overline{A}_t, \overline{M}/p_t, y_t^*).$$

Differentiating, we obtain:

$$[\partial \text{net } A_t^d / \partial(\overline{M}/p_t)] - [\overline{M}/p_t^2]dp_t + [\partial \text{net } A_t^d / \partial r_t - \partial \text{net } A_t^s / \partial r_t]dr_t = 0$$

Rearranging, we have that the slope of the BB curve is given by

$$\{dr_t/dp_t | \text{net } A_t^d - \text{net } A_t^s = 0\}$$
$$= [\partial \text{net } A_t^d / \partial(\overline{M}/p_t)][\overline{M}/p_t^2]/[\partial \text{net } A_t^d / r_t - \partial \text{net } A_t^s / \partial r_t] > 0.$$

The positive slope of the BB curve can be explained in the following way. The positive numerator of the slope expression reflects the real balance effect with respect to financial assets. The term indicates the fall in net real financial asset demand (and planned decrease in future consumption) that would accompany a rise in the price level, for such a rise reduces agents' wealth in the form of initial real money balances. The positive denominator indicates the effect of a change in the interest rate on household lending and firm borrowing. A rise in the interest rate would tend to decrease current consumption demand ("Fisherian" effect) and money demand ("portfolio" effect), and thus increase household net financial asset demand. On the other hand, a rise in the interest rate would tend to reduce firm investment demand by raising the expected real user cost of capital, and thus reduce firm net real financial asset supply.

While both the slope of the BB curve and the LL curve are positive, it is the case that the LL curve is steeper.

A depiction of equilibrium: aggregate demand and supply curves

Using Patinkin's analysis, a higher output would require a lower price level to maintain equilibrium in the output, financial, and money markets. Alternatively, one can show the effect of a change in y_t^* on p_t and r_t by totally differentiating equations (6.2) and (6.3) with respect to p_t, r_t, and y_t^*.

The aggregate demand curve summarizes this inverse relationship between the price level and output arising from an analysis of the output, financial, and money markets. Specifically, such a curve depicts combinations of output and price level associated with equilibrium in the output, financial, and money markets. It is downward sloping, indicating that an increase in output requires a lower price level to clear the output, financial, and money markets. Behind a movement down the aggregate demand curve are larger real balances that stimulate output demand either directly (through a real balance effect on consumption demand) or indirectly (the resulting increase in real money balances leads to an increase in net real financial asset demand by households and thus a lower interest rate).[22]

It is important to realize that the phrase "equilibrium in the output market" in this context abstracts from supply-side considerations. At each price level, the aggregate demand curve indicates the output that, if produced, would equal output demand (along with satisfying the equilibrium conditions with respect to the financial and money markets). Production of output equal to that demanded would occur if firms sought simply to produce to meet market demand and if workers were readily available for employment so that firms could hire to achieve production equal to what was demanded. The term "equilibrium in the output market" does not imply equality between output demand and the output that our analysis of the labor market suggests would be supplied.

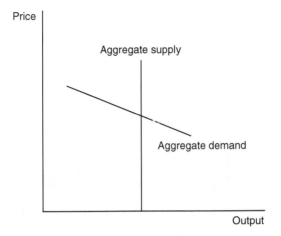

Figure 6.5 Macroeconomic equilibrium.

Figure 6.5 combines the aggregate demand and aggregate supply curves. Where they intersect we know by construction that the resulting price level $(p_t)_0$ and output $(y_t)_0$ are such that

- the labor market is in equilibrium (the economy is at a point on the aggregate supply curve) and
- the output, financial, and money markets are in equilibrium (the economy is at a point on the aggregate demand curve).

Conclusion

Using a very simple framework, this chapter has developed a powerful macroeconomic model of the economy. This model is grounded in the general equilibrium theory set forth in earlier chapters. Moreover, this model highlights that degree of connectedness that exists among the output, labor, financial, and money markets. The microfoundations of macroeconomics have been emphasized, and it has been shown how market forces work in such a way as to lead to aggregate supply and demand, two key elements in any macroeconomic model.

7 Empirical macroeconomics

Traditional approaches and time series models

Introduction

Quantitative approaches to analyzing economic data provide meaningful and useful insight for understanding how variables interact and how they might be expected to behave in a variety of circumstances, including the future. This chapter outlines the traditional econometric-based method and the relatively simple, but often more elegant, time series method for analyzing economic data in the time domain. The stochastic nature of economic data is discussed and the now common ARIMA model found in much of the empirical macroeconomic literature is developed in parts. The chapter provides a solid background for understanding "macroeconometrics" and time series analysis.

Traditional approaches

Empirical macroeconomics can be roughly divided into two approaches – a traditional approach that draws heavily on macroeconomic theory and a more recent approach advocated for forecasting that does not rely to any great extent on theory. To consider the former, we start by presenting a simple theoretical model of the macroeconomy. The model is used to illustrate traditional empirical analyses reflecting (a) tests of behavioral hypotheses, (b) tests of reduced-form expressions for various economic aggregates, and (c) the construction of econometric models for policy simulations and forecasting. The more recent empirical macroeconomics approach of using time series models for forecasting aggregate variables, which places less reliance on macroeconomic theory, is then briefly considered.

A simple theoretical macroeconomic model

Consider the following linear approximation of the simple, static classical model (closed economy), such as that popularized by Sargent (1987a: 20).[1] The economy is divided into four markets: a labor market (where wages, w, and total employment, n, are determined), an output market (where total output, y, and the price level, p, are determined), a financial market (where the interest rate, r, is determined), and a money "market." Our goal is to construct a model that will determine such endogenous variables as the level of employment, wages, output, prices, and the interest rate.

From Walras' law (as we will see more clearly later on), we need only explicitly consider three of the above four markets in the analysis. For the labor market, let us assume the following linear approximations for the key behavioral relations:[2]

$$n^d = f - g(w/p),$$ (7.1)

$$n^s = h + j(w/p).$$ (7.2)

These two linear equations indicate that firms' labor demand n^d is inversely related to the real wage (w/p) and households' labor supply n^s is directly related to the real wage.[3]

For the output market, the key underlying behavioral and technological relations are, in linear form

$$c^d = a + b(y - T) - cr,$$ (7.3)

$$i^d = d - er,$$ (7.4)

$$y^s = f(n, K).$$ (7.5)

Equation (7.3) indicates that households' consumption demand, c^d, is directly related to real disposable income (income, y, minus lump-sum taxes, T) and inversely related to the interest rate, r.[4] Equation (7.4) indicates that firms' investment demand, i^d, is inversely related to the interest rate, r. Equation (7.5) is the aggregate production function, relating employment, n, and capital stock, k, to total output supplied, y^s.

For the money "market," the key underlying behavioral relation is

$$L^d = l \cdot y - m \cdot r.$$ (7.6)

Equation (7.6) indicates that households' real money demand, L^d, is directly related to real income and inversely related to the interest rate. Nominal money supply, M^s, is exogenous.

General equilibrium in this economy means an equilibrium level of employment n^*, wage w^*, price level p^*, output y^*, and interest rate r^* such that the labor market is in equilibrium,

$$n^s - n = 0,$$ (7.7)

$$n^d - n = 0,$$ (7.8)

the output market is in equilibrium,

$$y^s - y = 0,$$ (7.9)

$$c^d + i^d + g^d - y = 0;$$ (7.10)

and the money "market" is in equilibrium,

$$L^d - M^s/p = 0. \tag{7.11}$$

Note that the component of output demand g^d in (7.10) reflects exogenous real government demand for output.

The above macroeconomic model consists of 11 equations. Macroeconomic models often can be represented by a system of equations. This system of equations is sometimes said to be a "structural model" because the form is given from the underlying theory. As we will see below, we can solve this system of equations for each of the "endogenous" variables as a function solely of the predetermined or "exogenous" variables.[5] Such solutions can be called the "reduced-form" solutions.

By substituting the behavioral equations (7.1)–(7.6) into the equilibrium conditions, we obtain the following set of five equilibrium conditions that can be solved for the five variables n^*, w^*, p^*, y^*, and r^*:[6]

$$f - g(w/p) - n = 0,$$
$$h + j(w/p) - n = 0,$$
$$f(n, K) - y = 0, \tag{7.12}$$
$$a + by - bT - cr + d - er + g^d - y = 0,$$
$$ly - mr - M^s/p = 0.$$

Note that the first three equations in the system (7.12) can be solved to obtain w^*, n^*, and y^* as a function of the price level p^*. In particular, we obtain:[7]

$$w^* = [(f - h)/(g + j)]p^*, \tag{7.13}$$
$$n^* = [1(j + g)][jf + gh], \tag{7.14}$$
$$y^* = f(n^*, K) = f([1/(j + g)][jf + gh], K). \tag{7.15}$$

Equation (7.15) is an example of a reduced-form expression for output, for it expresses output solely in terms of the exogenous variables. It is a special case of what is called the "aggregate supply equation" in which the price level does not affect the level of output produced.[8] Note that equation (7.13) indicates that changes in the price level lead to equiproportionate changes in the equilibrium money wage, so that changes in the price level do not lead to changes in the equilibrium real wage.

To obtain a reduced-form expression for the price level, we can use the reduced-form expression for output in conjunction with the last two equations in the system (7.12). These last two equations are sometimes termed the "IS equation" and the "LM equation," respectively.[9] Solving the LM equation (the last equation of the system (7.12)) for r and substituting both this expression for r and the prior expression for equilibrium output y^* (7.15) into the IS equation (the penultimate equation of the system (7.12)), we obtain the reduced-form expression for the equilibrium price level:

$$p^* = \frac{M^s c'/m}{[1 - b + c'/m]f([1/(j+g)][jf + gh], K) - a'},$$ (7.16)

where $a' = a + d + g^d - b \cdot T$ and $c' = c + e$.

Changes in the variable a' indicate changes in the autonomous component of consumption (the term a in (7.3)), autonomous investment demand (d in (7.4)), and government spending or taxing (g^d or T, respectively). By "autonomous," we mean that part of households' and firms' output demand that is independent of the variables to be determined by the analysis, particularly income and the interest rate. The variable c' indicates the combined response of consumption demand (c in (7.3)) and investment demand (d in (7.4)) to a unit change in the interest rate.

Note that the procedure to obtain equation (7.16) could be alternatively described as follows. First combine the last two equations in the system (7.12) to eliminate the interest rate r. The result is termed the "aggregate demand equation." This relates the price level to the level of output at which the money and output markets (and thus, by a modified version of Walras' law, the financial market) are in equilibrium. In this context, equilibrium in the output market is defined as the level of production that, if produced, would equal output demand. This aggregate demand equation would then be combined with the aggregate supply equation (7.15) to determine the equilibrium price level or output.[10]

Tests of behavioral hypotheses

Theoretical macroeconomic models embody predictions concerning factors that influence the behavior of various groups in the economy. For instance, consider the behavioral equations (7.1)–(7.6) in the prior simple macroeconomic model. We could test the prediction that investment is inversely related to the interest rate (see (7.4)) or that money demand depends inversely on the interest rate (see (7.6)). Or we could expand our theory of consumption behavior (equation (7.3)) to test a particular behavioral relationship between aggregate household consumption and permanent income.[11] Or we could expand our view of labor supply behavior (equation (7.2)), as Stuart (1981) did in an examination of Swedish data, to test the prediction that sufficiently high marginal tax rates will reduce the economy-wide labor supply.

Tests of reduced-form hypotheses

Theoretical macroeconomic models also generate predictions concerning the reasons for fluctuations in such aggregate variables as real output, unemployment, and the level of prices. These predictions typically reflect the reduced-form solutions of macroeconomic models. Examples of reduced forms in our simple macroeconomic model are equations (7.15) for output and (7.16) for price.

One example of an empirical test of macroeconomic theory that focuses on testing the reduced-form predictions is Taylor (1979). Specifically, Taylor tests the reduced-form relationships between the money supply and the logarithm of income from trend and between the money supply and the rate of inflation using quarterly US data from 1953 to 1975.[12] Similarly, Christopher Sims (1972) uses quarterly US data on nominal output and the money supply to test whether changes in the money supply lead to changes in the current dollar value of national income (see Ewing 2001).

Large-scale econometric models and forecasting

Besides testing macroeconomic theories, empirical macroeconomic analysis often seeks to forecast the future paths of economic aggregates. Interest in forecasting stems not only from an obvious curiosity about the future path of aggregate variables such as real output and prices but also from the fact that many, if not all, macroeconomic theories suggest that expectations of future events influence current activity. In this context, forecasts can be used to proxy individuals' expectations of future events in tests of various aspects of macroeconomic models.

One approach to making forecasts of future aggregate variables is to rely on theoretical macroeconomics as a guide in the construction of large-scale econometric models. Behavioral equations that are more detailed, disaggregated versions of equations (7.1)–(7.6) are estimated, and coefficients are checked to make sure they agree with theory. These models reflect attempts to produce large systems that faithfully represent the interrelationships in a complex national economy. Given postulated paths of the exogenous variables, the actual estimated equations are then used to generate forecasts of the various aggregate variables such as output and its components (e.g., consumption and investment), prices, and interest rates.

While large-scale econometric models as forecasting devices have their advocates (and many individuals reveal they have a positive value by willingly paying for their forecasts), Granger and Newbold (1986: 292–293), among others, question the value of such a forecasting approach. They note that "teams of macroeconomists have constructed forecasting models involving hundreds of simultaneous equations fitted to data that time series analysts would view as neither plentiful nor of especially high quality."

An alternative to the large-scale macroeconomic models that is suggested are "time series models." As summarized by Granger and Newbold (1986), "in their anxiety econometricians have failed to touch some very important bases" that include:

- the fact that there are many areas in which "economic theory is not terribly well developed";
- the fact that even where the theory is satisfactory, it is "almost invariably insufficiently precise about dynamic specifications in the sense that it is clear that one structure must be appropriate";

- the fact that even after appeal to economic theory, there will be error terms since "no theory provides a completely accurate description of the behavior of economic agents, so that any postulated equation necessarily includes a stochastic error term."

Given these problems, many macroeconomists suggest that the appropriate starting point to forecasting future macroeconomic variables is the use of time series models. One result is that such time series modelling terms as AR, ARMA, and ARIMA now abound in the macroeconomic literature. It is thus useful to briefly review the nature of time series models. However, at the outset it should be made clear that the discussion below is *not* complete, but rather is provided simply as an introduction to some terms and concepts. Proofs of various propositions and rigorous definitions of various properties of time series models can be found in time series texts such as Enders (2004) and Mills (1999).

Time series models

Let us take as our premise the idea that the actual observed time series of some variable $y_t, t = 0, 1, \ldots, T$ (e.g., the logarithm of economy-wide output for the last 30 years), is the realization of some theoretical process which can be called a "stochastic process." As phrased by Harvey (1993), "each observation in a stochastic process is a random variable, and the observations evolve in time according to certain probabilistic laws. Thus a stochastic process may be defined as a collection of random variables which are ordered in time." To forecast future values of y_t, one needs a model that defines the mechanisms by which the observations are generated.

A distinguishing feature of a pure, univariate time series model is that movements in y_t are "explained" solely in terms of its own past, or by its position in relation to time.[13] That is, time series models look for patterns in the past movements of a particular variable and use that information to predict future movements of the variable. In general, a time series model's forecast of y based on known values $\bar{y}_{T+1}$ is given by:

$$\bar{y}_{T+1} = E(y_{T+1}|y_0, \ldots, y_T).$$

As Pindyck and Rubinfeld (1991) suggest, "in a sense a time-series model is just a sophisticated method of extrapolation ... yet ... it may often provide a very effective tool for forecasting." In this sense, time series models are more along the lines of empirical analyses that "let the data speak for themselves" rather than empirical analyses that (strictly speaking) "test economic theories." As Harvey (1993) states, "an essential feature of time series models is that they do not involve behavioural relationships." Time series models reflect a "statistical" approach to forecasting. However, the patterns in the data discovered by time series models do influence theoretical discussions of the macroeconomy, and tests of macroeconomic theories concerning behavior have incorporated time series models.[14] An example of

how time series analysis has influenced theoretical macroeconomic discussions is
given at the end of this section.

Some properties of stochastic processes

There are several key properties of stochastic processes for time series that we
can introduce. One is "stationarity." For a stochastic process to be stationary, the
following conditions must be satisfied for all t:

$$E(y_t) = \mu,$$

$$E[(y_t - \mu)^2] = \sigma_y^2,$$

$$E[(y_t - \mu)(y_{t-k} - \mu)] = \gamma_k.$$

Note that $\gamma_0 = \sigma_y^2$. In words, if a series is stationary, the mean of the series is
invariant to time, the variance of the series is invariant to time, and the covariance
of the series is invariant to time. As Pindyck and Rubinfeld (1991) note, "if a
stochastic process is stationary, the probability distribution $p(y_t)$ is the same for
all time t and its shape (or at least some of its properties) can be inferred by looking
at a histogram of the observations $y_1, \ldots, y_T$ that make up the observed series."[15]
Also, an estimate of the mean μ of the process can be obtained from the *sample
mean* of the series

$$\bar{y} = \frac{1}{T} \sum_{j=0}^{T} y_t$$

and an estimate of the variance σ_y^2 can be obtained from the sample variance[16]

$$\sigma_y^2 = \frac{1}{T} \sum_{j=0}^{T} (y_t - \bar{y})^2.$$

As Granger and Newbold (1986: 4) phrase it, "a stationarity assumption is equivalent to saying that the generating mechanism of the process is time-invariant,
so that neither the form nor the parameter values of the generation procedure
change through time." The simplest example of a stationary stochastic process is
a sequence of uncorrelated random variables with constant mean and variance.

A second property of a stochastic process is the "autocorrelation function." The
autocorrelation function provides us with a measure of how much correlation there
is (and by implication how much interdependency there is) between neighboring
data points in the series y_t. For stationary processes, the autocorrelation with lag
k is given by[17]

$$\rho_k = \gamma_k / \gamma_0$$

$$= E[(y_t - \mu)(y_{t-k} - \mu)] / \sigma_y^2.$$

For any stochastic process, $\rho_0 = 1$. If the stochastic process is simple "white noise" (i.e., $y_t = \varepsilon_t$, where ε_t is an independently distributed random variable with zero mean and finite variance), then the autocorrelation function for this process is given by:

$$\rho_0 = 1, \rho_k = 0 \text{ for } k > 0.\text{[18]}$$

A simple example of a stochastic process is the "random walk" process, in which each successive change in y_t is drawn independently from a probability distribution with zero mean.[19] Thus y_t is determined by:

$$y_t = y_{t-1} + \varepsilon_t, \tag{7.17}$$

where ε_t is a sequence of uncorrelated random variables ($E(\varepsilon_t \varepsilon_s) = 0$ for $t \neq s$) with mean zero ($E(\varepsilon_t) = 0$) and constant variance ($E(\varepsilon_t^2) = \sigma_e^2$ for all t). Recall that a sequence ε_t of this kind is typically called "white noise." If the stochastic process is a random walk, the one-period-ahead forecast of y_{t+1} is simply y_t.

A simple extension of the random walk process is to incorporate a trend in the series y_t. We then obtain the following stochastic process known as a random walk with drift:[20]

$$y_t = y_{t-1} + d + \varepsilon_t. \tag{7.18}$$

The one-period-ahead forecast of y_{t+1} is now $y_t + d$. By repeatedly substituting for past values of y_t into (7.18), we obtain

$$y_t = \sum_{j=0}^{t-1} \varepsilon_{t-j} + td + y_0. \tag{7.19}$$

For the random walk process without drift ($d = 0$), we see from (7.19) that the first requirement for stationarity, namely that the mean be constant over time, is satisfied if y_0 is fixed.[21] That is, $E(y_t) = E(y_0)$. Nevertheless, the process is not stationary since $\text{Var}(y_t) = t\sigma_e^2$. The random walk process tends to meander away from its starting value, but exhibits no particular trend in doing so.[22]

Autoregressive processes

A process similar to the random walk that is stationary is called the "first-order autoregressive process," or AR(1).[23]

The AR(1) process is given by:

$$y_t = \phi y_{t-1} + (1 - \phi)\mu + \varepsilon_t. \tag{7.20}$$

A necessary condition for stationarity is that $|\phi| < 1$, in which case $E(y_t)$ equals the constant term μ in (7.20).[24]

One possible example of an autoregressive process is the total number unemployed each month (Granger and Newbold 1986). Let the total number unemployed in one month be y_t. This number might be thought to consist of a fixed proportion ϕ of those unemployed in the previous month (the others having found employment) plus a new group of workers seeking jobs. If the new additions are considered to form a white noise series with positive mean $\mu(1 - \phi)$, then the unemployment series is a first-order autoregressive process expressed by equation (7.20).

For convenience only it is often assumed that the process has a zero mean, i.e., $\mu = 0$. Note that we can always define a new variable, $y_t' \equiv y_t - \mu$, such that y_t' has a zero mean and is given by the AR(1) process:

$$y_t' = \phi y_{t-1}' + \varepsilon_t, \tag{7.21}$$

with $|\phi| < 1$. Setting $\mu = 0$ thus simply means that the variable y_t (e.g., employment, real output, etc.) is measured in terms of deviations from its mean.

By successive substitution for y_t in (7.20), we obtain (assuming $\mu = 0$)

$$y_t = \sum_{j=0}^{t-1} \phi^j \varepsilon_{t-j} + \phi^t y_0. \tag{7.22}$$

If the process is regarded as having started at some point in the remote past and $|\phi| < 1$, then we can write:

$$y_t = \sum_{j=0}^{\infty} \phi^j \varepsilon_{t-j}. \tag{7.23}$$

Given that ε_t is white noise, we thus have that $E(y_t) = \mu = 0$. Assuming stationarity ($|\phi| < 1$), we know that the variance and covariances are constant. Recall that ε_t is white noise, such that $E(\varepsilon_t \varepsilon_s) = 0$ for $s \neq t$. We thus have[25]

$$\gamma_0 = \sigma_y^2 = E[(y_t - \mu)^2] = E\left[\left[\sum_{j=0}^{\infty} \phi^j (\varepsilon_{t-j})\right]^2\right] = \sigma_e^2/(1 - \phi^2),$$

$$\gamma_1 = E[(y_t - \mu)(y_{t+1} - \mu)] = \phi \sigma_e^2/(1 - \phi^2),$$

$$\gamma_2 = E[(y_t - \mu)(y_{t+2} - \mu)] = \phi^2 \sigma_e^2/(1 - \phi^2), \text{ etc.}$$

The autocorrelation function for AR(1) is thus particularly simple – it begins at $\rho_0 = 1$ and then declines geometrically: $\rho_k = \phi^k$. Note that this process has an infinite memory. The current value of the process depends on all past values, although the magnitude of this dependence declines with time.

In general, an autoregressive process of order p is generated by a weighted average of past observations going back p periods, together with a random disturbance in the current period. The AR(p) process is thus given by[26]

$$y_t = \phi_1 y_{t-1} + \phi_2 y_{t-2} + \phi_3 y_{t-3} + \cdots + \phi_p y_{t-p}$$
$$+ (1 - \phi_1 - \phi_2 - \cdots - \phi_p)\mu + \varepsilon_t \tag{7.24}$$
$$= \mu + \varepsilon_t + \sum_{j=1}^{p} \phi_j (y_{t-j} - \mu),$$

with a necessary condition for stationarity being that $\phi_1 + \phi_2 + \cdots + \phi_p < 1$.[27]
The next section discusses necessary and sufficient conditions for stationarity.

A brief digression on necessary and sufficient conditions for stationarity

To get some idea of what are necessary and sufficient conditions for stationarity, let us consider two specific cases, AR(1) and AR(2). In the AR(1) case,

$$y'_t - \phi y'_{t-1} = \varepsilon_t,$$

where $y'_t \equiv y_t - \mu$. Note that ε_t can be termed the "stochastic" component of the expression and the remainder the "deterministic" component.[28]

Focusing on the deterministic component, and assuming for convenience that $\mu = 0$, we have a homogeneous first-order difference equation of the form[29]

$$y_t - \phi y_{t-1} = 0. \tag{7.25}$$

To solve this equation, let us try the general solution

$$y_t = Ab^t, \tag{7.26}$$

which naturally implies $y_{t-1} = Ab^{t-1}$.[30] The problem, then, is to find the values of A and b. Substituting the trial solution into the above difference equation, we obtain

$$Ab^t - \phi Ab^{t-1} = 0,$$

which, by multiplying through by b^{1-t}/A, can be rewritten as

$$b - \phi = 0. \tag{7.27}$$

Equation (7.27) is called the "auxiliary" or characteristic equation of (7.25). This equation provides us with the solution for b, which is simply that $b = \phi$. This solution value is sometimes referred to as the "root" of the characteristic equation.

Using (7.27) to substitute for b in (7.26), we thus have as the solution to the first-order difference equation (7.25) the expression

$$y_t = A\phi^t. \tag{7.28}$$

The "equilibrium" solution for y_t given a homogeneous difference equation such as (7.25) is $y_t = 0$. That is, if $y_t \equiv 0$, then y_t will not change over time. This equilibrium solution is "stable" if, as $t \rightarrow \infty$, $y_t \rightarrow 0$. That is, deviations from the equilibrium y_t will return toward that equilibrium value. Obviously, given our solution (7.28), a necessary and sufficient condition for stability is that $|\phi| < 1$.

In the context of an AR(1) process, the notion of "stationarity" corresponds to the notion of stability for the first-order homogeneous difference equation (7.25) that is the deterministic component of y_t for an AR(1) process. The condition of stationarity is thus that $|\phi| < 1$. The effect of a given shock will mitigate over time if this stationarity condition is met. A special nonstationary case is the "unit root" case of the random walk process in which $\phi = 1$. In that case, the effect of a given shock will not dampen with the passage of time.

Now let us consider the AR(2) case where

$$y'_t - \phi_1 y'_{t-1} - \phi_2 y'_{t-2} = \varepsilon_t,$$

in which $y'_t \equiv y_t - \mu$. As before, ε_t can be termed the "stochastic" component of the expression. Assuming again for convenience that $\mu = 0$, we can express the deterministic component as a homogeneous second-order difference equation of the form

$$y_t - \phi_1 y_{t-1} - \phi_2 y_{t-2} = 0. \tag{7.29}$$

To solve this equation, let us try $y_t = Ab^t$, which naturally implies $y_{t-1} = Ab^{t-1}$ and $y_{t-2} = Ab^{t-2}$. The problem, then, is to find the values of A and b. Substituting the trial solution into the above difference equation, we obtain

$$Ab^t - \phi_1 Ab^{t-1} - \phi_2 Ab^{t-2} = 0,$$

which, by multiplying through by b^{2-t}/A, can be rewritten as:

$$b^2 - \phi_1 b - \phi_2 = 0. \tag{7.30}$$

The quadratic equation (7.30) is called the "auxiliary" or "characteristic equation" of the second-order difference equation (7.29). The roots of this equation will be the solutions of (7.30).[31] The two "characteristic" roots m_1 and m_2 may be found in the usual way from the formula:[32]

$$m_1, m_2 = [\phi_1 \pm (\phi_1^2 + 4\phi_2)^{1/2}]/2, \tag{7.31}$$

each of which is acceptable in the solution Ab^t. Note that for the quadratic equation (7.30) the roots m_1 and m_2 satisfy

$$(b - m_1)(b - m_2) = 0,$$

where $\phi_1 = m_1 + m_2$ and $\phi_2 = -m_1 m_2$.

Expression (7.31) provides us with two values for b and thus two potential solutions for y_t:

$$y_t = A_1 m_1^t \quad \text{and} \quad y_t = A_2 m_2^t.$$

The general solution to a second-order difference equation combines these two by taking the sum. Thus the general solution of the second-order homogeneous difference equation (7.29) is:[33]

$$y_t = A_1 m_1^t + A_2 m_2^t. \tag{7.32}$$

Inspection of (7.32) suggests that stability for the linear second-order homogeneous difference equation (7.29) requires that both roots of the characteristic equation have an absolute value less than one. This reflects the fact that the general solution of the second-order homogeneous difference equation includes both roots m_1 and m_2. The root with the higher absolute value is sometimes termed the "dominant root." If both m_1 and m_2 are less than unity in absolute value, y_t will be close to zero if t is large. Equivalently, if the dominant root is less than one in absolute value, convergence will occur.

In the context of an AR(2) process, the notion of "stationarity" corresponds to the notion of stability for the second-order homogeneous difference equation (7.29) that is the deterministic component of the process. The condition of stationarity is thus that $|m_1| < 1$ and $|m_2 < 1|$. That is, for the AR(2) process, stationarity requires that the roots of the characteristic equation (7.30) are less than one in absolute value – that is, that they all lie *inside* the unit circle.[34]

In terms of ϕ_1 and ϕ_2, the conditions for stationarity may thus be defined as follows:[35]

$$\phi_1 + \phi_2 < 1, \qquad -\phi_1 + \phi_2 < 1, \qquad \phi_2 > -1.$$

As you can see, the prior necessary condition that $\phi_1 + \phi_2 < 1$ is augmented with two other conditions.

We have seen that stability for the second-order homogeneous difference equation requires that the maximum of $(|m_1|, |m_2|)$ – that is, the dominant root – be less than 1. To see how one obtains the three necessary conditions listed above for stability, we assume this is the case and determine the resulting restrictions placed on the coefficients ϕ_1 and ϕ_2.[36] Recall that

$$m_1, m_2 = [\phi_1 \pm (\phi_1^2 \pm 4\phi_2)^{1/2}]/2.$$

Suppose $\phi_1^2 + 4\phi_2 > 0$, so that the roots are real. A maximum of $(|m_1|, |m_2|)$ less than one means that

$$2 - \phi_1 > (\phi_1^2 + 4\phi_2)^{1/2} > -2 - \phi_1$$

and

$$2 - \phi_1 > -(\phi_1^2 + 4\phi_2)^{1/2} > -2 - \phi_1.$$

The sum of the roots is ϕ_1, and since we are assuming each root is between -1 and 1, it must be the case that $2 > \phi_1 > -2$ or $0 > -2 - \phi_1$ and $2 - \phi_1 > 0$. Thus the second and third inequalities are always true and hence place no restrictions on ϕ_1 and ϕ_2.

The first and fourth inequalities squared read

$$(2 - \phi_1)^2 > \phi_1^2 + 4\phi_2 \quad \text{and} \quad \phi_1^2 + 4\phi_2 < (-2 - \phi_1)^2,$$

respectively. These two expressions can be rewritten to obtain:

$$\phi_1 + \phi_2 < 1 \quad \text{and} \quad -\phi_1 + \phi_2 < 1,$$

which are the first two conditions for stability. The third condition for stability ($\phi_2 > -1$) is obtained from the case of complex conjugate roots.[37] The three necessary conditions for the dominant root being less than one in absolute value are also sufficient conditions. This can be verified by showing, using these inequalities, that it is possible to reverse the steps in the above calculations and arrive at the maximum of $(|m_1|, |m_2|)$ being less than one.

In general, a necessary and sufficient condition for stationarity of an AR(p) process is if the roots of the characteristic equation

$$b^p - \phi_1 b^{p-1} - \cdots - \phi_p = 0 \qquad (7.33)$$

are less than one in absolute value.

Note that for the AR(2) case, there are three possible situations. If $\phi_1^2 + 4\phi_2 > 0$, the square root in (7.31) is a real number, and m_1 and m_2 will be real and distinct. In this case, the solution to (7.29) is given by

$$y_t = A_1 m_1^t + A_2 m_2^t,$$

where A_1 and A_2 are constants which depend on the starting values y_0 and y_{-1}.

The second situation is that of repeated roots, where $\phi_1^2 + 4\phi_2 = 0$ such that $m_1 = m_2 = m$. In this case, the solution to (7.29) takes the form

$$y_t = A_3 m^t + A_4 t m^t.$$

If $|m| < 1$, the damping force of m^t will dominate both terms.

The third situation for the AR(2) process is when $\phi_1^2 + 4\phi_2 < 0$, in which case the roots are a pair of complex conjugates (i.e., $m_1, m_2 = h \pm vi$ where $h = \phi_1/2$, $v = (4\phi_2 + \phi_1^2)^{1/2}/2$, and i is the imaginary number $(-1)^{1/2}$). Thus, the solution to (7.29) is given by

$$y_t = A_5 (h + vi)^t + A_6 (h - vi)^t.$$

Appealing to De Moivre's theorem, this expression can be transformed into trigonometric terms. The general form of the solution is

$$y_t = p^t(A_7 \cos \lambda t + A_8 \sin \lambda t),$$

where p is the modulus of the roots $= (-\phi_2)^{1/2})$ and λ satisfies the two conditions $\cos \lambda = h/p$ and $\sin \lambda = v/p$. As in the other two cases, if the absolute value of the conjugate complex roots, $|h \pm vi| < 1$, is less than one, the process is stable. The time path followed by y_t in response to a shock is cyclical, but the periodic fluctuation will mitigate as time passes ("sinusoidal decay") if the process is stationary.

Moving average processes

In a moving average process, the process y_t is described completely by a weighted sum of current and lagged random variables. The simplest moving average process, the moving average process of order 1 or MA(1), takes the form

$$y_t = \mu + \varepsilon_t + \theta\varepsilon_{t-1}. \tag{7.34}$$

The term "moving average" reflects the fact that a series so characterized will be smoother than the original white noise series ε_t. In general, such a moving average process of order q, MA(q), is written as:[38]

$$y_t = \mu + \varepsilon_t + \theta_1\varepsilon_{t-1} + \theta_2\varepsilon_{t-2} + \cdots + \theta_q\varepsilon_{t-q}$$

$$= \mu + \varepsilon_t + \sum_{j=1}^{q} \theta_j\varepsilon_{t-j}. \tag{7.35}$$

As before, if y_t has nonzero mean, we can focus with no loss of generality on the transformed series $y'_t = y_t - \mu$ which has zero mean.

One possible example of a moving average process is economy-wide output (Granger and Newbold 1986). Output y_t could be in equilibrium (at mean μ) but is potentially moved from its equilibrium position each period by a series of unpredictable events, such as periods of exceptional weather or strikes. If the system is such that the effects of such events are not immediately assimilated, but exert an influence on output for q periods, then a moving average model can arise.

Note that by repeatedly substituting for lagged valued of ε_t into an MA(1) process (equation (7.34)), one obtains[39]

$$y_t = \sum_{j=1}^{\infty} (-\theta)^j y_{t-j} + \varepsilon_t. \tag{7.36}$$

If y_t is not to depend on a shock to the system arising at some point in the remote past, θ must be less than one in absolute value. Comparing (7.36) to (7.24), we see that assuming what was previously denoted the stationarity condition but what in this context is called the "invertibility condition," namely that $|\theta| < 1$, then an MA(1) process can be represented by an AR(∞) process.[40] The weights on past values of y_t for this AR(∞) process decline exponentially.

In general, if similar invertibility conditions are met, then any finite-order moving average process has an equivalent autoregressive process of infinite order. Likewise, we have already shown (see (7.23)) that if the AR(1) process is stationary, it is equivalent to a moving average process of infinite order, MA(∞). In fact, for any stationary autoregressive process of any order there exists an equivalent moving average process of infinite order, so that the autoregressive process is "invertible" into a moving average process.

Mixed autoregressive moving average processes

An obvious generalization of the above discussion is to combine an AR(p) process (i.e. (7.24)) and an MA(q) process (i.e. (7.35)). An autoregressive moving average process of order (p, q), or ARMA(p, q), can be written as[41]

$$
y_t = \mu + \varepsilon_t + \sum_{j=1}^{p} \phi_j(y_{t-j} - \mu) + \sum_{j=1}^{q} \theta_j \varepsilon_{t-j}
\tag{7.37}
$$

where, as before, ε_t is a zero-mean white noise. For simplicity, consider the case where $\mu = 0$.

Whether or not a mixed process is stationary depends solely on its autoregressive part. If the ARMA process is stationary, then there is an equivalent MA(q') process. Similarly, provided invertibility conditions hold, there is an AR(p') process equivalent to the above ARMA(p, q) process. It thus follows that a stationary ARMA process can always be well approximated by a high-order MA process and that if the process obeys the invertibility condition, it can also be well approximated by a high-order AR process. However, an ARMA process has the advantage of "parsimony" in that the mixed model ARMA(p, q) often can achieve as good a fit as, say, an AR(p'), but uses fewer parameters (i.e., $p + q < p'$).

As an example of an ARMA(p, q) process, we need only consider a case where the variable y_t is the sum of a "true series", that is, AR(p) plus a white noise observation error. Thus, an ARMA(p, q) series results.[42]

Integrated processes

In series arising in economics, the assumption of stationarity is often very restrictive. That is, often the characteristics of the underlying stochastic process generating a time series appear to change over time. With economic data, sometimes a transformation (such as taking the logarithm of the variable) can result in a stationary series. In other cases, we can obtain a stationary series by differencing one or more times. We say that y_t is a "homogeneous nonstationary process of order d" if

$$w_t = \Delta^d y_t$$

is a stationary series. Here Δ denotes differencing, that is,

$$\Delta y_t = y_t - y_{t-1}, \qquad \Delta^2 y_t = \Delta y_t - \Delta y_{t-1} = y_t - 2y_{t-1} + y_{t-2}, \ldots.$$

The process y_t is an "integrated" process if after a series y_t has been differenced to produce a stationary series w_t, the series w_t can be modelled as an ARMA process. If $w_t = \Delta^d y_t$ and w_t is an ARMA(p, q) process, then we say that y_t is an "integrated autoregressive moving average process of order (p, d, q)," or simply ARIMA (p, d, q).

An application of time series models

To gain a better understanding of how time series models are used in macroeconomic empirical work, let us consider the time series for the logarithm of the level of real output, to be denoted by y_t. As we stated above, theoretical macroeconomic models typically postulate shocks or "impulses" to the economy (e.g., shocks to technology, money supply, and government policy) that, in conjunction with a prediction of how various markets in the economy adjust to these shocks, offers an explanation of the actual fluctuations in aggregate variables. One important question that can arise is whether such shocks are "transitory," in that their effects do not persist, or "permanent," where the economy moves to a new level of real output.

The "traditional" answer to the above question of transitory versus permanent effects of shocks has been, according to Campbell and Mankiw (1987a: 111), that fluctuations in real output "primarily reflect temporary deviations of production from trend." That is, the traditional view has been that quarterly real output could be represented by

$$y_t = T_t + S_t + X_t \tag{7.38}$$

where T_t is a deterministic component representing trend, S_t is a deterministic seasonal component, and X_t is a stationary autoregressive process with no deterministic component.[43]

Trend and seasonal components were typically estimated in various fashions and then eliminated. The focus of empirical work had then been on examining variations in the detrended, seasonally adjusted real output series. For example, Blanchard (1981) estimated the following second-order autoregressive process for deviations of the log of seasonally adjusted real output from its estimated trend, y_t^*, and obtained the equation:

$$y_t^* = 1.34 y_{t-1}^* - 0.42 y_{t-2}^* + \varepsilon_t. \tag{7.39}$$

Note that the necessary conditions for stationarity with respect to the series y_t^* (namely, $\phi_1 + \phi_2 < 1$, $-\phi_1 + \phi_2 < 1$, and $\phi_2 > -1$) are met.

The traditional view is embodied in (7.39). A shock to output increases for a few quarters, but the effect ultimately dies out. In fact, only 8 percent of a shock remains after 20 quarters. Assuming an ARMA(2,2) process, Blanchard and Fischer (1989: 9) obtain a similar result:

$$y_t^* = 1.31y_{t-1}^* - 0.42y_{t-2}^* + \varepsilon_t - 0.06\varepsilon_{t-1} + 0.25\varepsilon_{t-2}, \tag{7.40}$$

where, by construction, ε_t is that part of the deviation of current output from trend that cannot be predicted from past output. As Blanchard and Fischer note:

> A shock has an effect on GNP that increases initially and then decreases over time. After 10 quarters, the effect is still 40% of the initial impact; after 20 quarters, all but 3% of the effect has disappeared. The view that reversible cyclical fluctuations account for most of the short-term movements of real GNP and unemployment has been dominant for most of the last century.

However, as Granger and Newbold (1986: 37) note, "the more modern view is that, as far as possible, the trend, seasonal, and 'irregular' components should be handled simultaneously in a single model aimed at depicting as faithfully as possible the behavior of a given time series." Seasonality can be treated through a generalization of ARMA models.[44] More importantly for the question at hand, trend is generally treated by differencing, leading to the consideration of the "integrated processes" suggested above. In fact, Campbell and Mankiw (1987b) indicate that the answer to the question of the importance of temporary versus permanent shocks to output is biased if detrended data are used.[45] Campbell and Mankiw go on to point out that examining the differences in the logarithm of real output does not prejudge the issue of whether shocks to the economy are transitory or permanent. For instance, suppose that y_t follows an IMA(1,1) process, so that

$$y_t - y_{t-1} = d + \varepsilon_t - \theta\varepsilon_{t-1}.$$

Then a unit impulse in y_t changes the forecast of y_{t+n} by $1 - \theta$ regardless of n. "Hence, depending on the value of θ, news about current GNP could have a large or small effect on one's forecast of GNP in ten years" (Campbell and Mankiw 1987b: 860).[46]

Campbell and Mankiw consider ARMA(p, q) processes for the difference in the log of real output for $p = 0, 1, 2, 3$ and for $q = 0, 1, 2, 3$.[47] Interestingly, they find a high level of persistence in shocks. One intriguing suggestion of Campbell and Mankiw (1987b: 868) is that "when we examine postwar annual data, we cannot reject the hypothesis that the log of real GNP is a random walk with drift. In this case, the impulse response is unity at all horizons." Recall that the random walk process with drift (7.18) is an example of a nonstationary process that is first-order homogeneous nonstationary. To see this, simply consider the series w_t that results from differencing the random walk – that is, the series

$$w_t = \Delta y_t - y_{t-1} = d + \varepsilon_t. \tag{7.41}$$

Since ε_t are assumed independent over time, w_t is clearly a stationary process. The term $d + \varepsilon_t$ is a white noise process. In this example, y_t is an ARIMA(0,1,0), and Δy_t is an ARMA(0,0). The impulse response to a shock is unity in such a case.

As we will see later, one way to interpret the above finding of persistence is to place weight on "aggregate supply" shocks such as technological disturbances rather than on "aggregate demand" shocks such as changes in the money supply in explaining fluctuations in real output. That is, the finding gives credence to the view of Nelson and Plosser (1982), among others, that real (i.e., permanent) shocks dominate as a source of output fluctuations.[48]

However, as pointed out by Campbell and Mankiw (1987b: 877), the Nelson and Plosser conclusion is an extreme:

> one can attribute a major role to supply shocks without completely abandoning a role for demand shocks. For example, suppose that output $Y(= \log y)$ is the sum of two components, a supply-driven "trend" Y^T and demand-drive "cycle" Y^c, that are uncorrelated at all leads and lags. Suppose further that ΔY^T is a first-order autoregressive process with parameter ϕ and that Y^c is some stationary process. . . . If trend output is approximately a random walk, so that ϕ is small, then the finding of great persistence implies that fluctuations in the cycle are small relative to fluctuations in the trend. If the change in the trend is highly serially correlated (ϕ is large), however, the finding of persistence is consistent with a substantial cyclical component.

Campbell and Mankiw (1987b: 877) go on to suggest that

> a second way to interpret the finding of persistence is to abandon the . . . natural rate hypothesis . . . Models of multiple equilibria might explain a long-lasting effect of aggregate demand shocks if shocks to aggregate demand can move the economy between equilibria. Shocks to aggregate demand could have permanent effects if technological innovation is affected by the business cycle.

Note that so far we have considered only a single or univariate time series. The concepts involved, however, can be extended to multivariate series. For instance, a simple vector autoregression model (VAR) could take the form

$$y_t = \Phi y_{t-1} + \varepsilon_t,$$

where now y_t is considered an $N \times 1$ vector reflecting N variables, the random disturbance term ε_t is also an $N \times 1$ vector, and Φ is an $N \times N$ matrix of parameters. The disturbances are uncorrelated over time, but may be contemporaneously correlated. As in the univariate case, such a model is usually only fitted to variables which are stationary (possibly obtained by logarithmic transformations or by taking first or second differences). As in the univariate case, the objective would be to find a model that transforms a vector of time series into a white noise vector. As Harvey (1993) notes, "although a model of (this) form is often used for forecasting in econometrics, economic theory will typically place *a priori* restrictions on elements of Φ." There are also questions concerning the correlation between innovations across different series of data, for example, the link between innovations in money supply and output. But given that our aim is to review basic macroeconomic theory, we will not pursue such topics.

Conclusion

This chapter has emphasized the empirical nature of macroeconomics. In particular, time series analysis and econometric methods have been shown to be useful tools for analyzing macroeconomic data. Many of the policy conclusions that will be developed in the remainder of the book can be tested using these methods. The results obtained from a thorough understanding of the time series properties of important macroeconomic variables such as interest rates, employment numbers, real output measures, and the like, together with the underlying theory, may be used to provide policy recommendations. Moreover, more and more businesses are relying on empirical macroeconomics when making operating decisions.

Appendix: translation of higher-order difference equations into lower order

Any higher-order difference equation can be interpreted in terms of an equivalent system of first-order difference equations. To see this, consider equation (7.29):

$$y_t - \phi_1 y_{t-1} - \phi_2 y_{t-2} = 0.$$

To facilitate matters, we start by shifting the origin of this second-order, homogeneous difference equation from $t = -2$ to $t = -1$, such that we may rewrite (7.29) as

$$y_{t+1} - \phi_1 y_t - \phi_2 y_{t-1} = 0. \tag{7A.1}$$

Now let us introduce the new variable x_t defined as

$$x_t = y_{t-1},$$

which means that $x_{t+1} = y_t$. We may then express the second-order difference equation (7A.1) by means of two first-order simultaneous equations:

$$\begin{aligned} y_{t+1} - \phi_1 y_t - \phi_2 x_t &= 0, \\ x_{t+1} - y_t &= 0. \end{aligned} \tag{7A.2}$$

In matrix notation, (7A.2) becomes

$$\begin{bmatrix} y_{t+1} \\ x_{t+1} \end{bmatrix} = A \begin{bmatrix} y_t \\ x_t \end{bmatrix},$$

where A is the square, nonsingular matrix defined as

$$A = \begin{bmatrix} \phi_1 & \phi_2 \\ 1 & 0 \end{bmatrix}.$$

The "characteristic equation of a square matrix" is defined by the determinant

$$|A - \lambda I| = 0,$$

where I is the unit matrix $\begin{bmatrix} 1 & 0 \\ 0 & 1 \end{bmatrix}$ and λ is a scalar variable.

Letting $b = \lambda$, the "characteristic equation of matrix A,"

$$|A - \lambda I| = \begin{vmatrix} \phi_1 - b & \phi_2 \\ 1 & -b \end{vmatrix} = b^2 - \phi_1 b - \phi_2 = 0,$$

is identical to equation (7.30) which was termed the "characteristic equation of the second-order homogeneous difference equation." The values for the λs (or bs) are the roots of the characteristic equation. One reason for restating the higher-order difference equation in matrix form is that necessary and sufficient conditions for stability can be expressed in terms of conditions on the matrix A.

8   The neoclassical model

Introduction

This chapter turns our attention to one of the most popular and sometimes controversial models used by macroeconomists, the neoclassical model. The model, in its purest form, is often used as a benchmark or starting point for adding "realism" to the structure of the economy. However one views the neoclassical model, there is no denying that it is a powerful tool for generating predictions about movements in economic aggregates. As such, this chapter works through the comparative static exercise of a change in the money supply. This exercise provides a great deal of insight into how the monetary authority might influence the economy or whether it can influence the economy at all. A number of important issues are raised, for example money neutrality and money illusion. Additionally, the chapter formally derives the aggregate supply curve in the neoclassical context. The model has serious implications for the existence of a natural rate and also for the formation of expectations.

Comparative statics for the neoclassical model

We can use our previous method of analysis, known as "comparative static" analysis, to examine the effects of various shocks on the equilibrium level of prices. As the name suggests, comparative static analysis is concerned with the comparison of different equilibrium states associated with different sets of values of parameters and exogenous variables. In the current context of the neoclassical model, the labor market can be isolated from the other markets (i.e., there is a "block recursive" character to the equilibrium solution). In such a context, we can distinguish two types of exogenous variables.

One type, "supply-side" variables, alter the level of output at any given price level. Such variables could include changes in technology and the existing capital stock in the current version of the model, or we could expand the analysis to include changes in the supply of other inputs (such as oil), changes in government policies that affect incentives to supply labor, and changes in government policies that affect the incentives to invest and thus affect the productive capacity of the economy over time.

The second type of exogenous variables, "demand-side" variables, do not alter the current supply of output at prevailing prices but instead impact equilibrium prices and interest rates as determined in the output, financial, and money markets. Below we consider the impact of demand-side "shocks" such as changes in initial money balances and the expected inflation rate.

The macroeconomic approach to general equilibrium: how it can obscure

The neoclassical model can be viewed as a special case of a Walrasian general equilibrium system distinguished by the existence of money.[1] As Clower (1965) notes:

> income magnitudes do not appear as independent variables in demand and supply functions of the (Walrasian) general equilibrium model, for incomes are defined in terms of quantities as well as prices and quantity variables never appear explicitly in the market excess demand functions of traditional theory. To be sure, income variables could be introduced by taking factor supplies as given parameters, but this would preclude the formulation of a general equilibrium model containing supply functions of all marketable factor services.

Referring to Chapter 9 of Patinkin (1965), Clower goes on to note that this point

> was apparently overlooked by Patinkin when he formulated his "general theory" of macroeconomics . . . . It is instructive to notice that this chapter is not supplemented by a mathematical appendix . . . I do not mean to suggest that authors may not put such variables as they please into their models. My point is that such variables that can be shown to be fundamentally dependent on others should not then be manipulated independently.

What Clower is referring to is the fact that the neoclassical model with limited perfect foresight effectively determines at time t the money wage for the labor market and the (futures) price of output and interest rate. Given perfect foresight, individual optimizing behavior will generate planned consumption and money demand functions at time t for period t that include the real wage rather than income. That is, since labor supply is a choice variable at time t, labor income (the product of the real wage times labor supply) should not appear as an argument in households' demand and supply functions. (Note that labor income, along with dividend and interest payments, equals output minus depreciation.)

Formally, we can discover how a "small" change in one (or more) of the exogenous variables affects equilibrium values by totally differentiating the equilibrium conditions with respect to the prices to be determined and the exogenous variable, and then solving for the implied change in equilibrium prices required to maintain equilibrium.[2] The resulting changes in equilibrium prices then imply changes in the equilibrium levels of employment, output, consumption, investment, and real money holdings.

However, we choose instead the standard macroeconomic approach of arbitrarily separating the analysis into an analysis of the labor market and the resulting employment and output (the "aggregate supply equation") and then an analysis of the other markets and the detemination of the price level and the interest rate (the "IS" and "LM" equations). While Clower is right in that this obscures the traditional "general equilibrium" nature of the neoclassical model, the approach is useful in that it allows us to more easily extend the analysis to situations in which prices are not market-clearing or to situations in which there is not limited perfect foresight.

Given the assumption of perfect foresight on the part of both firms and workers concerning the price level p_t, we have seen that the aggregate supply equation is independent of the price level or the interest rate. We know from the modified Walras' law that any two of the three excess demand conditions with respect to money, financial assets, and output can be used in the comparative static analysis. Using the equilibrium conditions with respect to output and money (the "IS" and "LM" equations), we thus have the three equations

$$y_t = y_t(\overline{K}, \ldots), \tag{8.1}$$

$$c_t^d(r_t, \pi_t^e, \overline{A}_t, \overline{M}/p_t, y_t) + I_{nt}^d(m_t^e + \delta, \overline{K}) + \delta\overline{K} + \psi(I_{nt}^d) - y_t = 0, \tag{8.2}$$

$$L_t^d(r_t, \pi_t^e, \overline{A}_t, \overline{M}/p_t, y_t) - \overline{M}/p_t = 0 \tag{8.3}$$

to determine equilibrium output y_t, price level p_t, and interest rate r_t. Recall that from the modified Walras' law we know that there is a fourth equation, the equilibrium condition for the financial market that is implied by (8.2) and (8.3). This fourth equilibrium condition is

$$\text{net } A_t^d(r_t, \pi_t^e, \overline{A}_t, \overline{M}/p_t, y_t) - \text{net } A_t^s(m_t^e + \delta, \overline{K}) = 0. \tag{8.4}$$

A change in the money supply: the comparative statics

It is clear from the above that the neoclassical aggregate supply equation (8.1) determines output, while the IS and LM equations (8.2) and (8.3) determine the price level and interest rate given the equilibrium level of output. Focusing on the latter two equations and the determination of the price level and interest rate for a given level of output, total differentiation with respect to the equilibrium prices (p_t and r_t) and the money supply change gives the following system of linear equations in matrix form:[3]

$$\begin{bmatrix} -(\partial c^d/\partial(M/P))M/p^2 & \partial y^d/\partial r \\ (1 - \partial L^d/\partial(M/p))M/p^2 & \partial L^d/\partial r \end{bmatrix} \begin{bmatrix} dp \\ dr \end{bmatrix} = \begin{bmatrix} -(\partial c^d/\partial(M/p))dM/p \\ (1 - \partial L^d/\partial(M/p))dM/p \end{bmatrix},$$

where $\partial y^d/\partial r = \partial c^d/\partial r + (1+\psi')\partial I^d/\partial m$.[4] Solving the above linear-equation system for dp and dr using Cramer's rule, we obtain:

$$\frac{dp}{dM} = \frac{-(\partial c^d/\partial(M/p))(1/p)\partial L^d/\partial r - (1 - \partial L^d/\partial(M/p))(1/p)\partial y^d/\partial r}{-(\partial c^d/\partial(M/p))(M/p^2)\partial L^d/\partial r - (1 - \partial L^d/\partial(M/p))(M/p^2)\partial y^d/\partial r}$$

$$= \frac{p}{M},$$

$$\frac{dr}{dM} =$$

$$\frac{-[(\partial c^d/\partial(M/p))(M/p^2)(\partial L^d/\partial(M/p)-1)-(\partial c^d/\partial(M/p))(M/p^2)(\partial L^d/\partial(M/p)-1)](1/p)}{-(\partial c^d/\partial(M/p))(M/p^2)\partial L^d/\partial r - (1-\partial L^d/\partial(M/p))(M/p^2)\partial y^d/\partial r}$$

$$= 0.$$

As you can see, $dp/p = dM/M$ and $dr/dM = 0$. That is, a change in the money supply leads to the same proportional change in the price of the consumption good and no change in the interest rate. With regard to the latter result, the interest rate does not change as the only thing that changes the interest rate is the rate of change in prices. Since the price level adjusts there is no change in the interest rate and the LM curve does not change. Note that from the labor market equilibrium condition that underlies the aggregate supply equation, we know that the change in the price level results in an equiproportionate change in the money wage. The result is that we have "neutrality of money." In other words, if individuals correctly anticipate the effect of a change in the money supply on the price level, as is the case in the deterministic model under the assumption of limited perfect foresight, then monetary changes have no "real" effects. Real output, the real wage, the expected real rate of interest, real consumption, real investment, and the real money supply are all unaffected by the monetary change.

The basic reason why changes in the money supply are "neutral" is the absence of money illusion on the part of both firms and households. In particular, household demand and supply functions indicate that if a change in money balances is accompanied by an equiproportionate change in the price of output, then there is no change in any demands. That is, household demand and supply functions are homogeneous of degree zero in money balances and prices. This absence of "money illusion" occurs assuming:

- perfect foresight at time t for price during period t, so that a change in price results in no change in the real wage or employment (when coupled with the similar assumption of limited perfect foresight on the part of firms);
- "neutral distribution effects," such that the shift in wealth from prior creditors to debtors that would accompany a rise in the price level leaves aggregate demands unchanged;
- unit elastic expectations so that changes in the current price level can be viewed as leaving unaffected the expected rates of change in the price level.

As we will see later, this money neutrality result of the neoclassical model forms the basis of what has become known as the "policy ineffectiveness proposition" (see McCallum 1979).

The "dynamics" of the system and the neutrality of money: a review

As we discussed earlier, the "story" often told with respect to the dynamics of the above situation is a "loanable funds theory" of interest rate determination, in which the interest rate moves to clear the financial market.[5] In this case, the "tatonnement process" or movement toward equilibrium involves

$$dp_t = f(y_t^d - y_t), \qquad f(0) = 0, \qquad df/d(y_t^d - y_t) > 0,$$

$$dp_{bt} = f_b(\text{net } A_t^d - A_t^s), \qquad f_b(0) = 0, \qquad df_b/d(\text{net } A_t^d - \text{net } A_t^s) > 0.$$

Note that we put "story" in quotes since the analysis itself simply identifies various equilibrium points, with adjustments in prices to reach a different equilibrium point given a shock essentially occurring without any passage of time. Nevertheless, consider the following story with respect to a rise in the money supply.

In the Patinkin analysis described earlier, if the money supply were to double from $\overline{M}$ to $2\overline{M}$, the LL, BB, and CC curves would shift to the right so that the new equilibrium would occur at the original interest rate but at a price level double the original one. Such a once-and-for-all change in the initial money balances leaves the money interest rate and real demands unchanged (the neutrality of money).

Superneutrality: an informal review

Superneutrality of money occurs when changes in the *rate of growth* of the money supply leave the paths of capital and real output unaffected. Although the above analysis is static in nature, it does provide some insight into the issue of the superneutrality of money. To see how, suppose each period the economy can be replicated in every way. That is, the money supply, equilibrium price level, and interest rate are identical each period. If expectations of price changes are correct, expected inflation would equal zero. For the economy to replicate itself, it must also be the case that the initial capital stock is optimal, such that the capital stock and thus output does not change over time. With zero adjustment costs, such a situation would imply a marginal product of capital equal to the expected real user cost of capital ($m_t^e + \delta$, where $m_t^e \equiv (r_t - \pi_t^e)/(1 + \pi_t^e)$), net investment demand equal to zero each period, and gross investment demand equal to $\delta \overline{K}$.

Now let us compare this situation to an alternative sequence of temporary equilibrium in which the economy is identical in every way except one: the money supply is increased each period by a constant percentage from its level in the prior period. Other things being equal, the above analysis would suggest that one difference across periods would be a rise in prices due to the positive growth in the money supply. Let us further assume that expectations of inflation adjust to reflect what Sargent and Wallace (1975) would characterize as a new "systematic money supply rule."

Without fully developing the appropriate dynamic analysis, it is easy to see that one obvious adjustment of the static analysis given a growing money supply (as opposed to one that does not change across periods) is thus a higher expected inflation rate (positive as opposed to zero). In fact, the analysis of the static model can mimic to some extent the effects of a higher rate of growth in the money supply by considering the impact of an increase in exogenous inflationary expectations.

Following Sargent and Wallace (1975), among others, assume that consumption demand depends on the expected real rate of interest, $r - \pi$, not separately on its components (the money interest rate and the expected rate of inflation).[6] Further, assume that changes in expected inflation do not affect real money demand.[7] The comparative static results are then:

$$
\begin{bmatrix} -(\partial c^d/\partial (M/P))M/p^2 & \partial y^d/\partial (r - \pi) \\ (1 - \partial L^d/\partial (M/p))M/p^2 & \partial L^d/\partial r \end{bmatrix} \begin{bmatrix} dp \\ dr \end{bmatrix} = \begin{bmatrix} -(\partial y^d/\partial (r - \pi))d\pi \\ 0 d\pi \end{bmatrix},
$$

where $\partial y^d/\partial (r - \pi) = \partial c^d/\partial (r - \pi) + (1 + \psi')\partial I^d/\partial (r - \pi)$. Solving the above linear equation system for dp and dr using Cramer's rule, we obtain

$$
\frac{dp}{d\pi} =
$$

$$
\frac{-(\partial y^d/\partial (r - \pi))\partial L^d/\partial r}{-(\partial c^d/\partial (M/p))(M/p^2)\partial L^d/\partial r - (1 - \partial L^d/\partial (M/p))(M/p^2)\partial y^d/\partial (r - \pi)}
$$

$$
> 0,
$$

$$
\frac{dr}{d\pi} =
$$

$$
\frac{-(\partial L^d/\partial (M/p))(M/p^2)\partial y^d/\partial (r - \pi)}{-(\partial c^d/\partial (M/p))(M/p^2)\partial L^d/\partial r - (1 - \partial L^d/\partial (M/p))(M/p^2)\partial y^d/\partial (r - \pi)}
$$

$$
> 0.
$$

As we have discussed before, if there is no real balance effect with respect to consumption demand ($\partial c^d/\partial (M/p) = 0$) or if real money demand does not respond to changes in the interest rate ($\partial L^d/\partial r = 0$), then we can see from the above that

$$
dr = \frac{-(1 - \partial L^d/\partial (M/p))(M/p^2)\partial y^d/\partial (r - \pi)d\pi}{-(1 - \partial L^d/\partial (M/p))(M/p^2)\partial y^d/\partial (r - \pi)} = d\pi,
$$

so that the change in the expected rate of inflation results in no change in the expected real rate of interest ($r - \pi$). In this case, money is superneutral in that a change in the growth of the money supply (although it alters inflation and thus, given perfect foresight, expected inflation) leaves the expected real rate of interest unchanged and thus does not affect investment and the future size of the capital stock, which depend inversely on the expected real interest rate.

Recall that Sargent and Wallace (1975) have argued for superneutrality of money. In contrast, Begg (1980) has noted that steady-state analyses of growth models with money, like the analysis above, do find that different rates of growth in the money supply have real effects (through changes in the expected real gross interest rate).[8] As the above analysis makes clear, there are two conditions, either of which is sufficient, that will result in money being superneutral. Begg (1980: 293) describes them as follows: "The first condition is that the level of real money balances is not an argument in the consumption function, and it is this condition which distinguishes the rational expectations model of Sargent and Wallace from the analysis of growth models with money. The second condition is that the demand for money is independent of the nominal interest rate" (as well as π). Otherwise, a higher expected inflation will result in a fall in the expected real rate of interest and a higher price level.

In the Patinkin framework, with consumption demand and investment demand depending on the expected real interest rate, at a given price level and higher expected inflation the CC curve must shift up vertically by the amount of the increase in expected inflation so as to maintain the same expected real rate of interest. But the LL curve does not shift with a change in expected inflation. Thus given a downward-sloping CC curve and an upward-sloping LL curve, the new equilibrium money interest rate does not rise by the extent of the increase in expected inflation. Superneutrality of money seems not to hold.

In such a case, the static analysis thus predicts a lower real stock of money each period, higher investment, and a greater capital stock next period. This suggests a new steady state in which the capital stock is greater. In fact, a complete dynamic analysis confirms these predictions; a higher steady-state capital stock is associated with an increase in the rate of growth of the money supply and consequent increased expected inflation.

The role of the key assumptions of the neoclassical model

At this point, it might be useful to review the role played by the two key assumptions of the neoclassical model, namely price flexibility and complete information on prices. In most cases, and this is no exception, one can gain an understanding of the role of a particular assumption by exploring how the analysis would proceed if the assumption were not made. Consider first the implications of dropping the neoclassical model's assumption that prices are perfectly flexible.

Suppose that the demand for output decreases and firms cannot sell all they desire at prevailing prices. With flexible prices, output prices will fall, and the falling price level restores output demand to its previous level. However, if output prices are inflexible and do not adjust downward in response to a reduced demand for output, firms will respond by reducing production. Reduced production will lead to a lower level of labor demand and thus a fall in employment. Further, labor demand will no longer depend upon the real wage, but will be determined by what can be sold in the output market. In short, if output prices are inflexible, then the overall level of demand for goods and services is paramount in determining the level of employment.

A second modification of the neoclassical model is to assume that output prices are flexible, but money wages are not. If wages are "sticky" relative to output prices, then changes in the price level will alter the real wage. For instance, in the late 1970s high inflation rates led workers and employers in certain industries to bargain for long-term contracts with a high rate of growth of the money wage. The high expected inflation did not materialize in the early 1980s. The lower rate of inflation, with no change in the rate of increase in wages, meant a rise in the real wage. The resulting fall in the demand for labor led to lower employment and output. Given that wages are not perfectly flexible (e.g., "multiperiod labor contracts without complete indexation"), output prices below that anticipated when labor contracts are signed lead to a fall in output and employment. With inflexible money wages, the aggregate supply equation includes the price level of output as a determinant of output supply.

Let us consider one more modification of the neoclassical model. Suppose that workers have incomplete information on output prices and the real wage. A firm determines its relevant real wage by dividing the money wage it pays its workers by the price it anticipates for the particular product its workers produce. On the other hand, workers must anticipate prices for a variety of different goods to be purchased in order to determine their relevant real wage. Thus, firms may more accurately anticipate changes in prices and thus real wages than workers.

Now, suppose that there is an increase in output prices. Given our current assumption of incomplete information, this will not only lead to an increase in firms' demand for labor and to higher wages, as firms anticipate the fall in real wages, but may also lead to an increase in the quantity of labor supplied for the following reason. Workers, who have not anticipated the rise in output prices, will perceive the higher money wages as implying a rise in the real wage and will increase their supply of labor accordingly. As a result, equilibrium employment will rise with an increase in output prices. Once again, the aggregate supply equation will incorporate the current price level as a potential determinant.

The illusion model: one modification of the neoclassical model

Our first departure from the neoclassical model is to introduce the potential for "imperfect" foresight on the part of suppliers at time *t* concerning the price level for period *t*. As a consequence, the "notional" or planned demands made at time *t* based on anticipated prices for the period can differ from "effective" or realized demands and/or supplies at the actual prevailing prices. Further, realized or effective demands now depend on the quantity constraints experienced in other markets as well as prices. That is, realized output now becomes a determinant of actual consumption and money demand on the part of households.

Real wage illusion, the labor market, and aggregate supply

As we have seen, equilibrium employment is determined at the start of each period in the labor market. To formally show this, let us start with the following statement of equilibrium in the labor market in terms of a money wage w_t and level of employment N_t such that:

$$N_t^d(w_t/p_t, \overline{K}) - N_t = 0,$$
$$N_t^s(w_t/p_t^e) - N_t = 0.$$

A critical aspect of the above is the fact that suppliers – in particular, suppliers of labor – may not correctly anticipate the price level that will exist with respect to output. In particular, we let p_t^e denote suppliers' expectation formed at the start of period t of the price level for period t. We assume this expectation is held with subjective certainty so that we may express the real wage expected by suppliers simply by w_t/p_t^e. It is this anticipated real wage, not the realized real wage w_t/p_t, that appears in the labor supply function.

Firms, on the other hand, are presumed to correctly forecast the actual real wage.[9] Note that we retain the presumption that the money wage adjusts to clear the labor market. Similarly, we implicitly have assumed that the price level adjusts to clear the output market, such that firms are price-takers in the output market and thus labor demand depends on the real wage rather than on a sales constraint.

Initially, let us assume that households' anticipated level of prices is correct. That is, we start with a money wage and level of employment consistent with the neoclassical model. But, we now assume that any change in the price level will not be fully anticipated. In particular, we assume that

$$p_t^e = g(p_t), \qquad 1 > g' \geq 0.$$

The fact that $g' < 1$ implies imperfect foresight at time t on the part of households concerning the price of output for period t. If $g' > 0$, it indicates that households to some extent, but not completely ($g' < 1$), anticipate changes in the equilibrium level of prices that will prevail for period t.

Totally differentiating the above two equations representing equilibrium in the labor market with respect to w_t, N_t, p_t, and noting our prior assumption that $p_t^e = p_t$ initially, one obtains

$$\begin{bmatrix} -(\partial N_t^d/\partial(w_t/p_t))/p_t - 1 \\ (\partial N_t^s/\partial(w_t/p_t^e))/p_t \quad -1 \end{bmatrix} \begin{bmatrix} dw_t \\ dN_t \end{bmatrix} = \begin{bmatrix} (\partial N_t^d/\partial(w_t/p_t))w_t dp_t/(p_t)^2 \\ (\partial N_t^s/\partial(w_t/p_t^e))w_t g' dp_t/(p_t)^2 \end{bmatrix}.$$

Applying Cramer's rule gives

$$\frac{dN_t}{dp_t} = \frac{(\partial N_t^d/\partial(w_t/p_t))(\partial N_t^s/\partial(w_t/p_t^e))(w_t/(p_t)^2)(g'-1)}{-(\partial N_t^d/\partial(w_t/p_t))/p_t + (\partial N_t^s/\partial(w_t/p_t^e))/p_t^e} > 0,$$

$$\frac{dw_t}{dp_t} = \frac{-\partial N_t^d/\partial(w_t/p_t) + (\partial N_t^s/\partial(w_t/p_t^e))g'}{-\partial N_t^d/\partial(w_t/p_t) + \partial N_t^s/\partial(w_t/p_t^e)} \frac{w_t}{p_t} > 0.$$

Note that if $g' = 1$, then we have the standard neoclassical result that $dN_t/dp_t = 0$, and $dw_t/w_t = dp_t/p_t$ so that a change in the price level results in no change in either employment or the real wage. However, with $g' < 1$, we have that an increase in the price level leads to a rise in employment and an increase in the money wage less than proportional to the increase in the price level, such that the real wage falls (i.e., $dp_t/p_t > dw_t/w_t > 0$). Given the aggregate production function $y_t = f(N_t, \overline{K})$, we thus have an "aggregate supply function" of the form

$$y_t = y_t(p_t - p_t^e, \overline{K}, \ldots), \tag{8.1'}$$

so that aggregate supply depends directly on the difference between the price level for period t and the price level anticipated by suppliers at time t.

Consider the above findings with respect to the labor market and suppose that there is an increase in p_t. Given perfect foresight on the part of firms at time t, the labor demand curve shifts up vertically, so that at the higher money wage associated with the same real wage, demand would be the same. However, given $1 > g' \geq 0$, the vertical shift upward in the supply curve is less than this, with the result that equilibrium employment rises as the money wage rises by proportionately less than the rise in prices.

In undergraduate textbooks, the fact that changes in the price of output can now affect real output is shown in (p_t, y_t) by an upward-sloping "aggregate supply curve" as in Figure 8.1. Recall that in the neoclassical model the aggregate supply curve is vertical. In either model, such a curve summarizes the underlying events in the labor market.

The above character of the money illusion model is sometimes said to reflect the "natural rate hypothesis." The natural rate hypothesis posits that fully anticipated increases in prices have no effect on the rate of real economic activity – specifically real output, employment, and thus unemployment. Thus we will refer to the above model as a static version of a "natural rate model."

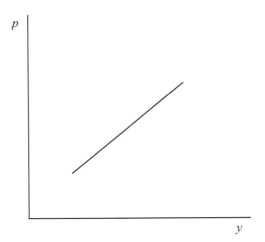

Figure 8.1 Upward-sloping aggregate supply.

Equilibrium: aggregate supply and demand

An important feature of macroeconomic theories is that to a large extent they are distinguished by their different treatment of labor markets. What this means is that the aggregate demand side is typical of macroeconomic models. Recall that the aggregate demand side of macroeconomic models considers the equilibrium conditions of two of the remaining three markets, in particular the output market (reflected by an "IS" equation) and the money market (reflected by an "LM" or "portfolio" equation). Thus, the equilibrium output, price level, and interest rate are given by equations (8.1'), (8.2), and (8.3). Equation (8.1') is the aggregate supply equation of a natural rate model, (8.2) is the "IS" equation depicting equilibrium between output demand and production, and (8.3) is the portfolio or "LM" equation expressing equilibrium with respect to the money market.

At this point, we will simplify equations (8.2) and (8.3) by removing the real balance effect, representing them as follows:

$$c_t^d(r_t, \pi_t^e, \overline{A}_t, y_t) + I_{nt}^d(m_t^e + \delta, \overline{K}) + \delta\overline{K} + \psi(I_t^d) - y_t = 0, \tag{8.2'}$$

$$L_t^d(r_t, \pi_t^e, \overline{A}_t, y_t) - \overline{M}/p_t = 0. \tag{8.3'}$$

In our model, this implies that:

$$\partial \text{net } A_t^d / \partial(\overline{M}/p_t) = 1.$$

As we will see, one justification for this form is if real money balances are not part of household wealth, which can be the case when we introduce depository institutions into the analysis. In the meantime, the above assumption makes the analysis not only simpler but also more in line with traditional macroeconomic analysis.

Graphically, the equilibrium price level and output can be shown using the aggregate demand and supply curves. In Figure 8.2, the equilibrium output and price level are thus given by p_t^* and y_t^*. Looking at what underlies these curves, we can then infer the changes in money wages and employment (specifically from an analysis of the labor market that underlies the aggregate supply curve) as well as changes in the interest rate and the components of investment and consumption components of output demand (specifically from an analysis of the output and money markets that underlie the aggregate demand curve).

Money supply change: comparative statics for a natural rate model

Collecting the aggregate supply, IS, and LM equations for the natural rate model under consideration, we have (8.1'), (8.2'), and (8.3').

These three equations determine the equilibrium output, the price level and the interest rate. Substituting (8.1') into (8.2') and (8.3') in order to focus on the

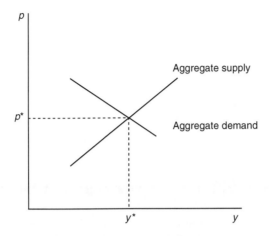

Figure 8.2 Macroeconomic equilibrium with upward-sloping supply.

determination of the price level and interest rate and totally differentiating with respect to the equilibrium prices (p_t and r_t) and the money supply change gives us the following system of linear equations in matrix form:[10]

$$\begin{bmatrix} -(\partial c^d/\partial y - 1)\partial y/p & \partial y^d/\partial r \\ (\partial L^d/\partial y)\partial y/\partial p + M/p^2 & \partial L^d/\partial r \end{bmatrix} \begin{bmatrix} dp \\ dr \end{bmatrix} = \begin{bmatrix} 0 \\ dM/p \end{bmatrix},$$

where $\partial y^d/\partial r = \partial c^d/\partial r + c1 + \psi')\partial I^d/\partial m$.[11] The term $\partial y/\partial p > 0$ reflects the direct effect of the price level on output as implied by the aggregate supply equation (8.1').[12] It is important to note that the equilibrium condition with respect to the labor market is incorporated into the above analysis in the form of this aggregate supply equation.

Solving the above linear equation system for dp and dr using Cramer's rule, we obtain

$$\frac{dp}{dM} = \frac{p/M}{1 + (p^2/M)(\partial y/\partial p)[(1 - \partial c^d/\partial y)(\partial L^d/\partial r)/(\partial y^d/\partial r) + \partial L^d/\partial y]}$$
$$> 0,$$

$$\frac{dr}{dM} = \frac{((\partial c^d/\partial y - 1)(\partial y/\partial p) - 1)(1/p)}{(\partial c^d/\partial y - 1)\partial y/\partial p(\partial L^d/\partial r) - ((\partial L^d/\partial y)(\partial y/\partial p) + M/p^2)(\partial y^d/\partial r)}$$
$$< 0.$$

As you can see, we no longer have $dr/dM = 0$. Further, letting x denote the denominator for the expression for dp, we have

$$\frac{dp}{p} = \frac{dM}{M}\frac{1}{x}.$$

Since $x > 1$, $1/x < 1$ and we now have that:

$$\frac{dp}{p} < \frac{dM}{M}.$$

Thus, the increase in the money supply leads to a less than proportionate increase in the price level, so that the real money supply is greater.[13]

Let us now consider the effect of the money supply shock on other variables. From our analysis of the labor market, we know that

$$\frac{dp}{p} > \frac{dw}{w} > 0,$$

so that while the money wage rises, the real wage falls. We also know from the labor market that the rise in the price level leads to higher employment, and thus an increase in output. From the demand functions, we can derive the effects of the change in the money supply on consumption and investment as equal to

$$\frac{dc^d}{dM} = \frac{dc^d}{dy}\frac{dy}{dp}\frac{dp}{dM} + \frac{dc^d}{dr}\frac{dr}{dM} > 0,$$

$$\frac{dI^d}{dM} = \frac{dI^d}{dm}\frac{dm}{dr}\frac{dr}{dM} > 0.$$

Graphically, one can show the effect of the money supply shock in terms of the aggregate demand and aggregate supply curves. Note that this exercise simply involves a shift out of the aggregate demand curve.

The natural rate hypothesis and expectation formation: a preview

An important feature of the above analysis, one already noted, is that real activity – in particular, employment, output, and unemployment – changes only to the extent that price changes are not fully anticipated. As we have just seen, this "natural rate hypothesis" introduces the logical foundations for a monetary change to have real effects.

However, note that monetary changes have real effects only to the extent that the resulting changes in the price level are not fully anticipated. To understand when this might occur, we first have to indicate why individuals may err in their formation of expectations concerning the price level. The Lucas model suggests one way of explaining errors in forecasts such that suppliers only partially anticipate a change in the price level (i.e., $1 > g' \geq 0$). This model introduces the assumption of rational expectations.

Combining rational expectations with the natural rate hypothesis results in a very powerful statement concerning monetary policy which has so far not been made clear. If the actions of monetary authorities are predictable, under the presumption of rational expectations individuals will correctly predict the consequences on prices. The result in the context of a natural rate model is that such predictable monetary changes will have no real effects. In the deterministic world, we are back to the neoclassical model. The analysis above then refers only to an "unexpected" increase in the money supply, or to monetary "surprises." Only such random shocks to the money supply will have real effects.

Conclusion

A formal neoclassical model of the macroeconomy has been introduced and fully developed. The issues of money neutrality and money illusion have been discussed and it has been seen that money supply changes have no effect on real economic activity when the assumptions of the neoclassical model hold. However, a number of issues have been raised, namely, the existence of a natural rate and the potential effect of unanticipated money supply changes on economic activity.

9 The "Keynesian model" with fixed money wage

Modifying the neoclassical model

Introduction

The first modification of the neoclassical model is presented in this chapter. To begin we introduce the very realistic assumption that nominal wages are fixed, at least for a period of time. The ramifications of this change in the model are developed in the context of the aggregate supply and demand model. As with the neoclassical model, we perform a comparative statics exercise in which the monetary authority changes the money supply and we trace out the effects of this action on the economic aggregates in the model. The model is then made slightly more complete, and issues associated with sticky wages and the natural rate hypothesis are discussed. We introduce the concept of rational expectations and the first "overlapping" model, and show that the Keynesian model has important implications for the conduct of monetary policy.

The "Keynesian model" with fixed money wage: modifying the neoclassical model

In the standard neoclassical model it is assumed that prices adjust in all markets to equate demand and supply. With respect to the labor market, this implies a spot market at the start of each period in which one-period labor contracts are entered into and an associated one-period wage set. Yet, employment contracts are likely to be multiperiod in the presence of hiring and training costs. That is, to minimize hiring and training costs, firms seek long-term relationships with their employees.

Firms promote long-term relationships with their employees by offering higher wages to their experienced workers. As a consequence, long-time employees become attached or "loyal" to their employers since the wages they receive are greater than those that other firms would offer them. In essence, employers are sharing the returns to their hiring and training investment with their workers in order to reduce the number who quit. A long-term attachment of workers to particular firms could also stem from the high cost to workers of finding alternative employment, as obtaining such employment means that workers must generally interview various employers, visit employment agencies, and spend valuable time simply waiting for decisions on job applications to be made.

Given long-term employment contracts between firms and their workers, wages are typically specified for extended periods of time. These long-term wage agreements are sometimes explicit, as with many labor union contracts.[1] In other cases, only an implicit understanding exists on the wages that a firm will pay its employees over some extended period of time. If these contracts or understandings specify wages in money terms, and if modifying these agreements is costly, then there exists an inherent inflexibility in money wages – that is, there are "sticky" wages.[2] This assumption of "sticky" nominal wages is often viewed as the critical aspect of what has been termed the "Keynesian" macroeconomic model.

If money wages are "sticky" relative to prices, then changes in the price level will alter the real wage. For instance, in the late 1970s high inflation rates led workers and employers in certain industries to bargain for long-term contracts with a high rate of growth of the money wage. The high expected inflation did not materialize in the early 1980s. The lower rate of inflation, with no change in the rate of increase in wages, meant a rise in the real wage. The resulting fall in the demand for labor led to lower employment and output. In this section, we formally develop these results in the context of a static neoclassical macroeconomic model with the additional assumption of a fixed money wage. The subsequent section then develops a linear, rational expectations version of this model in which overlapping, multiperiod employment contracts introduce an element of nominal wage rigidity.

Fixed money wage, the labor market, and aggregate supply

As we have seen, in the competitive (spot) labor market of the neoclassical model (or in the Lucas-type macroeconomic model) the money wage and employment are determined at the start of each period in the labor market. If we accept the neoclassical model's assumption of limited perfect foresight on the part of both labor suppliers and firms, we have equilibrium in the labor market in terms of a money wage w_t and level of employment N_t determined such that:

$$N_t^d(w_t/p_t, \overline{K}) - N_t = 0, \tag{9.1}$$

$$N_t^s(w_t/p_t) - N_t = 0. \tag{9.2}$$

In this case, a change in the price level p_t leads to an equiproportionate change in the money wage w_t and no change in employment N_t.

We now seek to modify this analysis by assuming a fixed money wage $w_t = \overline{w}$ for period t. As Sargent (1987a: 21) states:

the essential difference between the classical model and the Keynesian model is the absence from the latter of the classical labor supply curve combined with the labor market equilibrium condition. Since there is one fewer equation in the Keynesian model, it can determine only six endogenous variables instead of the seven determined in the classical model.[3] ... To close the Keynesian model, the money wage is regarded as an exogenous variable, one that at any point in time can be regarded as being given from outside the model, perhaps from the past behavior of itself and other endogenous or exogenous variables. ... It bears emphasizing that the equation that we have deleted in moving from the classical to the Keynesian model [equation (9.2)] is a combination of ... a supply schedule (and) an equilibrium condition. Note that we continue to require that employment satisfy the labor demand schedule [equation (9.1)].

Sargent goes on to say that

we shall think of the labor supply schedule as being satisfied and helping to determine the unemployment rate. ... Usually, the model is assumed to reach equilibrium in a position satisfying $N_t < N_t^s$, so that there is an excess supply of labor.

Totally differentiating the labor demand condition (9.1) that determines the level of employment with respect to the price level and employment, we have

$$-(\partial N_t^d/(\partial \overline{w}/p_t))(\overline{w}/p_t^2)dp_t - dN_t = 0, \tag{9.3}$$

which can be rearranged to give

$$dN_t/dp_t = -(\partial N_t^d/\partial(\overline{w}/p_t))(\overline{w}/p_t^2) > 0, \tag{9.4}$$

where the sign reflects the presumption that $\partial N_t^d/\partial(w_t/p_t) < 0$.

In the simple case of no labor adjustment costs, labor demand is defined by the equality between the marginal product of labor and the real wage, that is, $\partial f(N_t, \overline{K})/\partial N_t = \overline{w}/p_t$.[4] Differentiating, this implies that

$$[\partial^2 f_t/\partial N_t^2]dN_t = -(\overline{w}/p_t^2)dp_t$$

or, rearranging,

$$dN_t/dp_t = -(\overline{w}/p_t^2)/[\partial^2 f_t/\partial N_t^2] > 0, \tag{9.5}$$

given diminishing returns to the labor input (i.e., $\partial^2 f_t/\partial N_t^2 < 0$).

Combining the above analysis with the aggregate production function $y_t = f(N_t, \overline{K})$, we thus have the "aggregate supply equation"

$$y_t = y_t(p_t/\overline{w}, \overline{K}, \ldots), \qquad \text{with } \partial y_t/\partial(p_t/\overline{w}) > 0. \tag{9.6}$$

Thus (as in a Lucas-type model), we have an aggregate supply that can depend directly on the price level for period t.

The above findings can be understood with respect to the labor market. Consider a decrease in p_t. Given limited perfect foresight on the part of both firms and households *at time t*, there is a downward (vertical) shift in labor demand so that at the lower money wage w_t^* associated with the same real wage, demand would be the same. Similarly, the labor supply curve shifts down vertically, so that at this lower money wage w_t^* labor supply would be the same as well. However, multiperiod labor contracts fix the money wage at $\overline{w}$, so that the lower price level (and implied higher real wage) results in a fall in employment (which is now demand-determined) and an excess supply of labor.

In the opposite case of a rise in the price level that can lead to an excess demand in the labor market at the fixed money wage, the presumption remains that employment is demand-determined. This presumption reflects the view that, at least temporarily, firms can direct workers with whom they have long-term employment contracts to work overtime or extra shifts which the workers would otherwise not volunteer for.

The above story provides a rationale for an upward-sloping "aggregate supply curve." Both contrast with the neoclassical model in which the aggregate supply curve is vertical, as a fall in the price level results in an equiproportionate fall in the money wage, so that the real wage and employment remain unchanged. In the fixed wage model, the underlying events in the labor market summarized by the aggregate supply curve are the change in the real wage and thus labor demand and employment that accompany a price change when the money wage is fixed. Such an aggregate supply curve is upward-sloping.

Equilibrium: aggregate supply and demand

As we have noted before, an important feature of macroeconomic theories is that to a large extent they are distinguished by their different treatment of labor markets. What this means is that the aggregate demand side is similar across macroeconomic models. Recall that the aggregate demand side of macroeconomic models typically considers the equilibrium conditions of two of the remaining three markets, in particular the output market (reflected by an "IS" equation) and the money market (reflected by an "LM" or "portfolio" equation). Thus, for the Keynesian model with fixed money wage, the equilibrium output, price level, and interest rate are given by the following three equations:

$$y_t = y_t(p_t/\overline{w}, \overline{K}, \ldots), \tag{9.6}$$

$$c_t^d(r_t, \pi_{t+1}^e, \overline{A}_t, y_t) + I_{nt}^d(m_t^e + \delta, \overline{K}) + \delta\overline{K} + \psi(I_{nt}^d) - y_t = 0, \tag{9.7}$$

$$L_t^d(r_t, \pi_{t+1}^e, \overline{A}_t, y_t) - \overline{M}/p_t = 0. \tag{9.8}$$

Equation (9.6) is the aggregate supply equation of a Keynesian model with fixed money wage, (9.7) is the "IS" equation depicting equilibrium between output demand and production, and equation (9.8) is the portfolio or "LM" equation expressing equilibrium with respect to the money market. Note that we have simplified the IS and LM equations by removing the real balance effect for consumption demand and money demand.[5] Equations (9.7) and (9.8) can be combined to eliminate the interest rate. The resulting equation is referred to as the "aggregate demand equation."

The equilibrium price level and output (p_t^* and y_t^*) can be shown graphically using aggregate demand and supply curves. Looking at what underlies these curves, we can then infer the change in employment (specifically from an analysis of the labor market that underlies the aggregate supply curve) as well as changes in the interest rate and the investment and consumption components of output demand (specifically from an analysis of the output and money markets that underlie the aggregate demand curve).

A change in the money supply: the comparative statics for the Keynesian model

The aggregate supply, IS, and LM equations (9.6)–(9.8) for the static Keynesian model under consideration determine the equilibrium output, the price level and the interest rate. Substituting (9.6) into (9.7) and (9.8) in order to focus on the determination of the price level and interest rate and totally differentiating with respect to the equilibrium prices (p_t and r_t) and the money supply change gives us the following system of linear equations in matrix form:[6]

$$\begin{bmatrix} -(\partial c^d/\partial y - 1)\partial y/\partial p & \partial y^d/\partial r \\ (\partial L^d/\partial y)(\partial y/\partial p) + M/p^2 & \partial L^d/\partial r \end{bmatrix} \begin{bmatrix} dp \\ dr \end{bmatrix} = \begin{bmatrix} 0 \\ dM/p \end{bmatrix},$$

where $\partial y^d/\partial r = \partial c^d/\partial r + (1 + \psi')\partial I^d/\partial m$.[7] The term $\partial y/\partial p > 0$ reflects the direct effect on the price level as implied by the aggregate supply equation (9.6).[8] Note that the equilibrium condition with respect to the labor market is incorporated into the analysis in the form of this aggregate supply equation.

Solving the above linear equation system for dp and dr using Cramer's rule, we obtain

$$\frac{dp}{dM} = \frac{p/M}{1 + (p^2/M)(\partial y/\partial p)[(1 - \partial c^d/\partial y)(\partial L^d/\partial r)/(\partial y^d/\partial r) + \partial L^d/\partial y]}$$
$$> 0,$$

$$\frac{dr}{dM} = \frac{((\partial c^d/\partial y - 1)(\partial y/\partial p) - 1)/p}{(\partial c^d/\partial y - 1)\partial y/\partial p(\partial L^d/\partial r) - (\partial L^d/\partial y)(\partial y/\partial p) + (M/p^2)(\partial y^d/\partial r)}$$
$$< 0.$$

In contrast to the neoclassical model, we no longer have $dr/dM = 0$. Further, letting x denote the denominator for the expression for dp, we have

$$\frac{dp}{p} = \frac{dM}{M}\frac{1}{x}.$$

Since $x > 1$, $1/x < 1$ and we now have that

$$\frac{dp}{p} < \frac{dM}{M}.$$

Thus, the increase in the money supply leads to a less than proportionate increase in the price level, so that the real money supply is greater.

Consider now the effect of the money supply shock on other variables. From our analysis of the labor market, we know that $\overline{w}$ is fixed so that the increase in the price level means a fall in the real wage, and thus increased labor demand, employment, and thus an increase in output. From the demand functions for consumption and investment, we can derive the effects of the change in the money supply on consumption and investment as equal to

$$\frac{dc^d}{dM} = \frac{dc^d}{dy}\frac{dy}{dp}\frac{dp}{dM} + \frac{dc^d}{dr}\frac{dr}{dM} > 0$$

and

$$\frac{dI^d}{dM} = \frac{dI^d}{dm}\frac{dm}{dr}\frac{dr}{dM} > 0.$$

Note that the effect of the money supply shock is to increase the aggregate demand while not affecting aggregate supply.

Sticky wages and the natural rate hypothesis

Expectations play an important role in the two modifications of the neoclassical model. In the modification with fixed wages, the level at which negotiators fix future money wages depends on the expectation formed when wages were set concerning future prices. The higher the expectation of future prices, the higher the level of wages set in the labor agreements between workers and firms. The presumption is that workers and firms attempt to set future wages at their anticipated market-clearing levels. Associated with these anticipated market-clearing wages is a particular real wage, a natural rate of unemployment, and a full employment or natural rate of output.

If price expectations turn out to be incorrect, then output will vary from its natural rate. For instance, a shock that causes actual output prices to fall below those expected means that the money wage is fixed at a level that is too high for full employment. Consequently, employment and output fall below the full employment level.

In the typical Lucas-type model, firms and workers set wages for the current period based on incomplete information as well. As we saw, if suppliers' expectations are incorrect, then output will deviate from the full employment level. For example, a shock that causes actual output prices to fall below those expected means lower employment and output, as workers mistake lower money wages for lower real wages. In fact, higher real wages accompany the lower price level, and this is the source of the reduced demand for labor and employment.

The two modifications of the neoclassical model have a second common element. Both predict that a macroeconomic demand shock *ultimately* affects only the level of prices. Even though money wages in the Keynesian model are fixed for the current period, we know that money wages are not fixed forever. Over time, labor agreements are renegotiated, and money wages change to once again equate the "expected" future demand for and supply of labor. Over time, in the absence of further shocks, the economy would thus tend to behave as neoclassical analysis predicts; money wages and output prices would adjust to restore equilibrium to the various markets in the economy.

While the Keynesian model with fixed money wage admits the tendency for output to approach its natural level over time, it does introduce a potential role for monetary policy to play in dampening fluctuations in output. In so doing, it challenges the policy ineffectiveness view of Sargent and Wallace. The best-known examples employing the Keynesian model to demonstrate the potential stabilizing powers of monetary policy under rational expectations are the dual papers by Fischer (1977) and Phelps and Taylor (1977).

A linear, rational expectations version of the Keynesian model

Counting the above discussion, we have so far considered three different models that can be used to assess monetary policy. One model is along the lines of the neoclassical model with limited perfect foresight. Since this view of the economy predicts the neutrality of money, a role for monetary policy either as an instigator of output fluctuations or as an instrument to dampen output fluctuations is missing. As Mankiw (1987) suggests, people who adopt this model "view economic fluctuations through the lens of real business cycle theory," in which output fluctuations are traced to "supply-side" disturbances.

As Mankiw goes on to note, however, "there are surely readers who believe that monetary policy has real short-run effects because of temporary misperceptions or nominal rigidities." Mankiw is referring to individuals who adopt either the Lucas-type model or the "Keynesian" fixed money wage model.[9] Either one, as we have seen, introduces a role for monetary policy as an instigator of output fluctuations. However, these two models do differ as to whether monetary policy can be an instrument to dampen output fluctuations in the context of rational expectations.

A Lucas-type model built on "temporary misperceptions," when coupled with rational expectations, leaves little if any room for countercyclical monetary policy. In fact, following the analysis of Sargent and Wallace, it can be shown that while random monetary shocks can impact output, deterministic monetary policy based on a set of policy rules is ineffective in counteracting fluctuations in output given rational expectation.[10] Further, attempts at discretionary monetary policy in this context only result in a suboptimal ("too high") rate of inflation (Barro and Gordon 1983). Thus, in this model there remains a "stochastic" neutrality of money.

As the analysis in the previous section suggests, however, a "Keynesian-type" model built on "nominal rigidities" might introduce a role for monetary policy in stabilizing output even in the context of rational expectations. The reasoning for this is that wages (or, as we will see later, prices) can be set prior to the receipt of information by the monetary authority that enters into the money supply rule. In this context, as Phelps and Taylor (1977) state, "even systematic and correctly anticipated policy can make a difference for the stability of output in a rational expectations model with sticky prices and wages."[11] Below we consider one example of such a model that counters the Sargent and Wallace ineffectiveness proposition, a model proposed by Fischer that assumes "sticky" wages.

The supply equation with overlapping, two-period labor contracts

The Lucas aggregate supply equation with adjustment costs can be expressed as

$$Y_t = \gamma\theta(P_t - E_{t-1}P_t) + \lambda Y_{t-1}, \tag{9.9}$$

where $Y_t = \ln y_t - \ln y_n$ denotes difference between the logarithm of output for period t and the logarithm of the natural rate of output (which we have normalized to equal zero), $P_t = \ln P_t$ is the logarithm of the price level for period t, $E_{t-1}P_t$ is the expectation of the logarithm of the price level for period t using all information available up to the end of period $t - 1$ (at time t), and $\gamma\theta$ is a positive constant.[12]

The supply of output as expressed by equation (9.9) satisfies the condition that employment equals labor demand (9.2). The fact that a higher price level P_t induces firms to increase employment and thus output reflects the underlying lower equilibrium real wage that accompanies the higher price level when suppliers do not anticipate the higher price level. Thus we could express (9.9) in the form:[13]

$$Y_t = (P_t - W_t + \phi) + \lambda Y_{t-1}, \tag{9.9'}$$

where W_t is the logarithm of the equilibrium nominal wage for period t. The term ϕ in (9.9') is defined such that if $E_{t-1}P_t = P_t$, then the resulting log of the equilibrium real wage (i.e., $\ln(w_t/p_t)$) equals ϕ. Ignoring the lagged output term in equation (9.9'), this equilibrium real wage is the one associated with the natural level of output and employment.[14] We will follow others and assume for convenience that $\phi = 0$, implying an equilibrium real wage with no surprises equal to one.

According to (9.9'), if an increase in the price level is accompanied by a less than proportionate increase in the equilibrium money wage, $P_t - W_t$ rises (the real wage falls), and employment and output increase. In the Lucas-type model, such an event occurs if suppliers do not forecast the price increase. However, Sargent and Wallace's ineffectiveness proposition eliminates deterministic monetary policy rules as a source of such a price rise not matched by a similar rise in wages if (a) wages are set each period to equate labor demand and supply and (b) rational expectations are assumed. In this case, individuals and the monetary authorities are assumed to have a common set of information based on events up to the end of period $t - 1$ (at time t). Individuals are also privy to the monetary policy rule and they know the structure of the economy. Thus they have knowledge of the deterministic monetary policy to be followed during period t and its effect on the price level for period t as predicted by the model. Assuming flexible wages, this predicted effect of monetary policy on prices will be factored into the setting of the money wage for period t. As a consequence, such deterministic monetary policy cannot change the real wage, and thus leaves employment and output unaffected as well.

Obviously, this chain of reasoning breaks down if money wages for period t were set prior to time t. For example, this policy ineffectiveness doctrine disappears if some wages are set at the end of period $t - 2$ for period t. In this case, new information that arrives during period $t - 1$ can be incorporated by the monetary authorities into their money supply rule. Even with rational expectations, the implications of this cannot be used by individuals to adjust the money wage for period t since by assumption the money wage is fixed. Thus, deterministic monetary policy based on information revealed during period $t - 1$ can alter the real wage, employment, and output.

To formally develop this potential stabilizing role of monetary policy in a more "elegant" fashion, let us consider Fischer's model. The model disaggregates the economy into two sectors and assumes that the sectors alternate in setting multi-period employment contracts that fix nominal wages. In particular, "suppose that all labor contracts run for two periods and that the contract drawn up at the end of period $t - 2$ specifies nominal wages for periods $t - 1$ and t. [Assume] that contracts are drawn up to maintain constancy of the real wage" (Fischer 1977: 198). In other words,

$$_{t-i}W_t = E_{t-i}P_t, \qquad i = 1, 2, \tag{9.10}$$

where $_{t-i}W_t$ is the logarithm of the wage set at the end of period $t - i$ for period t.[15]

The idea embodied in (9.10) that wages are set for more than one period is critical to Fischer's finding. It essentially means that in any period half of the labor contracts have fixed money wages.[16] Given that the wage is predetermined for each firm, the aggregate supply equation is given by

$$Y_t = \tfrac{1}{2}(P_t - E_{t-1}P_t) + \tfrac{1}{2}(P_t - E_{t-2}P_t) + u_t \tag{9.11}$$

where u_t is a stochastic "real" disturbance or "supply shock" that impinges on production in each period.[17] Substituting (9.10) into (9.11) we can rewrite the aggregate supply equation as

$$Y_t = \tfrac{1}{2}(P_t - E_{t-1}P_t) + \tfrac{1}{2}(P_t - E_{t-2}P_t) + u_t. \tag{9.11'}$$

A complete model except for specifying the source of expectations

Equation (9.11′) provides us with one part of the standard macroeconomic model, the "aggregate supply equation." To close the model, we require LM and IS equations. The explicit derivation of these is left to the next chapter, but let us assume for the time being that the LM equation is given by

$$\overline{m}_t - P_t = \alpha_1 Y_t - \alpha_2 \cdot r_t - \varepsilon_t,$$

and the IS equation by

$$Y_t = X_t - \beta_1(r_t - \pi_{t+1}^e) + u_t.$$

Here $m_t = \ln M_t$, $m_t = \overline{m}_t + \varepsilon_t$, such that the deterministic component, $\overline{m}_t$, is set by government authorities (i.e., the monetary authority) according to a monetary rule. Further, $r_t - \pi_{t+1}^e$ represents the expected real rate of interest, X_t denotes a vector of exogenous variables that affect output demand, ε_t and u_t are random terms associated with output demand and money supply, respectively, and assumed independent (i.e., $E(\varepsilon_t u_t) = 0$) and well behaved.

Combining the LM and IS equations to eliminate the interest rate r_t, we obtain

$$Y_t = X_t + u_t - (\beta_1/\alpha_2)(-\overline{m}_t - \varepsilon_t + P_t - \alpha_1 Y_t) + \beta_1 \pi_{t+1}^e,$$

which on rearranging becomes an "aggregate demand equation" of the form

$$Y_t = [\alpha_2/(\alpha_2 + \alpha_1\beta_1)][X_t + u_t + (\beta_1/\alpha_2)(\overline{m}_t + \varepsilon_t - P_t) + \beta_1 \pi_{t+1}^e]. \quad (9.12)$$

Note that if $\alpha_2 = 0$ (changes in the interest rate do not affect money demand) and $\alpha_1 = 1$ (the income elasticity of real money demand is one) then this simplifies to what Fischer refers to as a "velocity equation":

$$Y_t = \overline{m}_t - P_t + v_t, \quad (9.13)$$

where $v_t = \varepsilon_t$ is now to be interpreted as a money demand disturbance term affecting the "velocity" of money.[18]

To see why (9.13) is called a "velocity equation," note that the assumption of money demand being independent of the interest rate allows us to capture the relationship between income and the price level summarized by the aggregate demand equation by looking solely at the LM equation (i.e., neglecting the IS equation). In particular, if we assume that real money demand can be expressed by the equation

$$L_t^d = y_t(\exp(-v_t)),$$

then equating real money demand to real money supply (M_t/p_t) gives us

$$y_t(\exp(-v_t)) = M_t/p_t. \quad (9.14)$$

Taking the logarithm of the equilibrium condition with respect to the money market (9.14), we obtain

$$\ln y_t - v_t = \ln M_t - \ln p_t.$$

Given $P_t = \ln p_t$, $Y_t = \ln y_t$, and $\overline{m}_t = \ln(M_t)$, this is simply equation (9.13).

Note that equilibrium velocity is defined as the ratio of nominal output to the money supply. Thus, rearranging (9.14), we have that:

$$\text{Equilibrium velocity} \equiv \frac{p_t y_t}{M_t} = \exp(v_t),$$

which explains the interpretation of v_t as a "velocity" disturbance. Fischer assumes that v_t has a zero mean, so that expected velocity is one. A v_t above zero means a decrease in real money demand relative to real output, and thus an increase in equilibrium velocity. As (9.14) makes clear, for a given M_t, a higher v_t implies a higher p_t and/or a higher y_t to maintain equilibrium with respect to the demand for and supply of money.

As Fischer states, (9.13) is "the simplest way ... of taking demand considerations into account." In sum, then, the macroeconomics model considered by Fischer is given by the aggregate supply equation (9.11′) and the aggregate demand equation (9.13).

Combining (9.11′) and (9.13) to eliminate Y_t, we have

$$\tfrac{1}{2}(P_t - E_{t-1}P_t) + \tfrac{1}{2}(P_t - E_{t-2}P_t) + u_t = \overline{m}_t - P_t + v_t.$$

This can be solved to give the reduced-form equation for the price level P_t:

$$P_t = \tfrac{1}{2}\left[\left(\tfrac{1}{2}E_{t-1}P_t + \tfrac{1}{2}E_{t-2}P_t\right) - u_t + \overline{m}_t + v_t\right]. \tag{9.15}$$

Combining (9.11′) and (9.13) to eliminate P_t, we have

$$Y_t = \tfrac{1}{2}(\overline{m}_t - Y_t + v_t - E_{t-1}P_t) + \tfrac{1}{2}(\overline{m}_t - Y_t + v_t - E_{t-2}P_t) + u_t.$$

This can be solved for the reduced-form equation for output Y_t:

$$Y_t = \tfrac{1}{2}\left[\overline{m}_t + v_t + u_t - \tfrac{1}{2}E_{t-1}P_t - \tfrac{1}{2}E_{t-2}P_t\right]. \tag{9.16}$$

According to equations (9.15) and (9.16), an increase in the "real" disturbance term u_t leads to higher equilibrium output and a reduced price level. Intuitively, this corresponds to a shift to the right in the "aggregate supply curve." On the other hand, an increase in the "velocity" disturbance term v_t corresponds to a shift to the right in the "aggregate demand curve" and thus leads to a higher output and price level given an upward-sloping aggregate supply curve. Note that an increase in v_t means a lower real money demand at each level of income. The shift in the aggregate demand curve reflects the fact that a higher price level and/or higher output is required to restore equilibrium in the money, commodity, and financial markets.

If expectations can be taken as exogenous with respect to money supply changes, then (9.16) indicates that money supply changes can affect output. But this was also the case for a Lucas-type model. The next step is thus to see what happens when we assume rational expectations. As will become clear, even with rational expectations, expectations formed at the end of period $t - 2$ can be viewed as exogenous with respect to monetary changes planned for period t based on information obtained during period $t - 1$. Thus, monetary policy has the potential to offset the persistent effect of disturbances that originate during period $t - 1$.

Introducing rational expectations

Let us now assume that individuals form their expectations $E_{t-1}P_t$ and $E_{t-2}P_t$ "rationally" in that

$$E_{t-2}P_t = E(P_t|\Omega_{t-2}), \tag{9.17}$$

$$E_{t-1}P_t = E(P_t|\Omega_{t-1}), \tag{9.18}$$

indicating that $E_{t-i}P_t$ is the mathematical expectation of P_t conditional on the information set Ω_{t-i}, which is all information available at the end of period $t - i$, $i = 1, 2$. Taking the expectation of (9.15) at the end of period $t - 2$, we thus have

$$E_{t-2}P_t = E_{t-2}\left\{\frac{1}{2}\left[\frac{1}{2}E_{t-1}P_t + \frac{1}{2}E_{t-2}P_t - u_t + v_t + \overline{m}_t\right]\right\}. \tag{9.19}$$

Note that $E_{t-2}\{E_{t-1}P_t\} = E_{t-2}P_t$. Thus (9.19) becomes:

$$E_{t-2}P_t = E_{t-2}\{-u_t + v_t + \overline{m}_t\}. \tag{9.20}$$

Taking the expectation of (9.15) at the end of period $t - 1$ (at time t), we then have

$$E_{t-1}P_t = E_{t-1}\left\{\frac{1}{2}\left[\frac{1}{2}E_{t-1}P_t + \frac{1}{2}E_{t-2}P_t - u_t + v_t + \overline{m}_t\right]\right\}. \tag{9.21}$$

Substituting (9.20) into (9.21) gives

$$E_{t-1}P_t = E_{t-1}\left\{\frac{1}{2}\left[\frac{1}{2}E_{t-1}P_t + \frac{1}{2}E_{t-2}\{-u_t + v_t + \overline{m}_t\} - u_t + v_t + \overline{m}_t\right]\right\}. \tag{9.22}$$

Rearranging,

$$\tfrac{3}{4}E_{t-1}P_t = \tfrac{1}{4}E_{t-2}\{-u_t + v_t + \overline{m}_t\} + \tfrac{1}{2}E_{t-1}\{-u_t + v_t + \overline{m}_t\}$$

or

$$E_{t-1}P_t = \tfrac{1}{3}E_{t-2}\{-u_t + v_t + \overline{m}_t\} + \tfrac{2}{3}E_{t-1}\{-u_t + v_t + \overline{m}_t\}, \tag{9.23}$$

which is Fischer's (1977) equation (16).[19]

Let the money supply be determined by the simple linear rule

$$\overline{m}_t = a_1 u_{t-1} + b_1 v_{t-1}.$$

Since $\overline{m}_t$ is a function only of information available up to the end of period $t-1$ (at time t), $E_{t-1}\{\overline{m}_t\} = \overline{m}_t$. Accordingly, (9.23) can be written as

$$E_{t-1}P_t = \tfrac{1}{3}E_{t-2}\{-u_t + v_t + \overline{m}_t\} + \tfrac{2}{3}E_{t-1}\{-u_t + v_t\} + \tfrac{2}{3}\overline{m}_t \tag{9.24}$$

Substituting (9.20) and (9.24) into the reduced-form equation for output (9.16), we obtain

$$\begin{aligned} Y_t = {}& \tfrac{1}{2}[u_t + v_t + \overline{m}_t] - \tfrac{1}{4}\left[\tfrac{1}{3}E_{t-2}\{-u_t + v_t + \overline{m}_t\} \right. \\ & \left. + \tfrac{2}{3}E_{t-1}\{-u_t + v_t\} + \tfrac{2}{3}\overline{m}_t\right] - \tfrac{1}{4}[E_{t-2}\{-u_t + v_t + \overline{m}_t\}]. \end{aligned} \tag{9.25}$$

Equation (9.25) simplifies to

$$\begin{aligned} Y_t = {}& \tfrac{1}{3}(\overline{m}_t - E_{t-2}\{\overline{m}_t\}) + \tfrac{1}{2}(u_t + v_t) + \tfrac{1}{6}E_{t-1}\{u_t - v_t\} \\ & + \tfrac{1}{3}E_{t-2}\{u_t - v_t\}, \end{aligned} \tag{9.26}$$

which is Fischer's (1977) equation (18).
As Fischer (1977: 196) notes,

> disturbances aside, this very simple macro model would be assumed in equilibrium to have the real wage set at its full employment level, would imply the neutrality of money, and would obviously have no role for monetary policy in affecting the level of output. A potential role for monetary policy is created by the presence of the disturbances u_t and v_t that are assumed to affect the level of output each period. Each of the disturbances is assumed to follow a first-order autoregressive scheme:

$$u_t = \rho_1 \cdot u_{t-1} + \varepsilon_t \qquad \text{where } |\rho_1| < 1 \tag{9.27}$$
$$v_t = \rho_2 \cdot v_{t-1} + \eta_t \qquad \text{where } |\rho_2| < 1 \tag{9.28}$$

where ε_t and η_t are mutually and serially uncorrelated stochastic terms with expectation zero and finite variances σ_e^2 and σ_n^2, respectively.

Given equations (9.27) and (9.28) and the money supply rule,

$$\overline{m}_t = a_1 u_{t-1} + b_1 v_{t-1}, \tag{9.29}$$
$$E_{t-2}\{\overline{m}_t\} = a_1 \rho_1 u_{t-2} + b_1 \rho_2 v_{t-2}, \tag{9.30}$$

so that

$$\bar{m}_t - E_{t-2}\{\bar{m}_t\} = a_1 u_{t-1} + b_1 v_{t-1} - [a_1 \rho_1 u_{t-2} + b_1 \rho_2 v_{t-2}]$$
$$= a_1 \varepsilon_{t-1} + b_1 \eta_{t-1}.$$
(9.31)

According to (9.31)

> the difference between the actual money stock in period t and that stock
> as predicted two periods earlier arises from the reactions of the monetary
> authority to the disturbances ε_{t-1} and η_{t-1} occurring in the interim. It is
> precisely these disturbances that cannot influence the nominal wage for the
> second period of wage contracts entered into at time $t-2$.
>
> (Fischer 1977: 199)

Substituting (9.31) into (9.26),

$$Y_t = \tfrac{1}{3}(a_1 \varepsilon_{t-1} + b_1 \eta_{t-1}) + \tfrac{1}{2}(u_t + v_t) + \tfrac{1}{6}E_{t-1}\{u_t - v_t\}$$
$$+ \tfrac{1}{3}E_{t-2}\{u_t - v_t\}.$$
(9.32)

From (9.27) and (9.28) we know that

$$u_t + v_t = (\rho_1 u_{t-1} + \varepsilon_t) + (\rho_2 v_{t-1} + \eta_t)$$
$$= (\rho_1 u_{t-1} + \varepsilon_t) + (\rho_2^2 v_{t-2} + \rho_2 \eta_{t-1} + \eta_t),$$

since by substitution $v_t = \rho_2^2 v_{t-2} + \rho_2 \eta_{t-1} + \eta_t$; we also have that

$$E_{t-1}\{u_t - v_t\} = \rho_1 u_{t-1} - \rho_2 v_{t-1} = \rho_1 u_{t-1} - \rho_2^2 v_{t-2} - \rho_2 \eta_{t-1}$$

and

$$E_{t-2}\{u_t - v_t\} = \rho_1^2 u_{t-2} - \rho_2^2 v_{t-2}.$$

Thus we can rewrite (9.32) as:

$$Y_t = \tfrac{1}{2}(\varepsilon_{t-1} + \eta_{t-1}) + \tfrac{1}{3}[\varepsilon_{t-1}(a_1 + 2\rho_1) + \eta_{t-1}(b_1 + \rho_2)] + \rho_1^2 u_{t-2}$$
(9.33)

which is Fischer's (1977) equation (21).[20]
Fischer (1977: 199) notes that:

> before we examine the variance of output as a function of the parameters a_1
> and b_1, it is worth explaining why the values of those parameters affect the
> behavior of output, even when the parameters are fully known. The essential

reason is that between the time the two-year contract is drawn up and the last year of operation of that contract, there is time for the monetary authority to react to new information about recent economic disturbances. Given the negotiated second-period nominal wage, the way the monetary authority reacts to disturbances will affect the real wage for the second period of the contract and thus output.

Optimal monetary policy rules: the effectiveness of policy

As in our discussion of Sargent and Wallace, let us presume that the goal of the monetary authority focuses solely on output. In particular, suppose that the monetary authority desires to set the money supply in order to minimize the fluctuation in the log of output around some desired level. Then the objective can be expressed as to

$$\min E_{t-1}(Y_t - Y^*)^2.$$

Let us assume that $Y^* = Y_n = 0$, so that the objective becomes to

$$\min E_{t-1}(Y_t)^2. \tag{9.34}$$

From (9.33), we have that

$$(Y_t)^2 = \left[\tfrac{1}{2}(\varepsilon_t + \eta_t) + \tfrac{1}{3}[\varepsilon_{t-1}(a_1 + 2\rho_1) + \eta_{t-1}(b_1 + \rho_2)] + \rho_1^2 u_{t-2}\right]$$
$$\times \left[\tfrac{1}{2}(\varepsilon_t + \eta_t) + \tfrac{1}{3}[\varepsilon_{t-1}(a_1 + 2\rho_1) + \eta_{t-1}(b_1 + \rho_2)] + \rho_1^2 u_{t-2}\right]. \tag{9.35}$$

Note that $E(\varepsilon_i) = E(\eta_i) = 0, E(\varepsilon_i^2) = \sigma_\varepsilon^2, E(\eta_i^2) = \sigma_n^2$, and that our independence assumptions imply that $E(\varepsilon_i\eta_i) = 0$ and, for $i \neq s$, $E(\varepsilon_i\varepsilon_s) = 0$ and $E(\varepsilon_i\eta_s) = 0$. Thus substituting (9.35) into (9.34), we have the following explicit form for the objective:

$$\min E_{t-1}(Y_t)^2 = \sigma_\varepsilon^2 \left[\tfrac{1}{4} + \tfrac{1}{9}(a_1 + 2\rho_1)^2\right] + (\rho_1^2 u_{t-2})^2$$
$$+ \sigma_n^2 \left[\tfrac{1}{4} + \tfrac{1}{9}(b_1 + \rho_2)^2\right]. \tag{9.36}$$

Given (9.36), the optimal monetary rule is to choose values for a_1 and b_1 such that

$$a_1 = -2\rho_1, \qquad b_1 = -\rho_2. \tag{9.37}$$

The above findings correspond to Fischer's (1977) equation (23).[21]

As Fischer (1977: 200) states:

> to interpret the monetary rule, examine [equation (9.33)]. It can be seen there that the level of output is affected by current disturbances ($\varepsilon_t + \eta_t$) that cannot be offset by monetary policy, by disturbances (ε_{t-1} and η_{t-1}) that have occurred since the signing of the older of the existing labor contracts, and by a lagged real disturbance, u_{t-2}. The disturbances, ε_{t-1} and η_{t-1}, can be wholly offset by monetary policy and that is precisely what equation [(9.37)] indicates. The u_{t-2} disturbance, on the other hand, was known when the older labor contract was drawn up and cannot be offset by monetary policy because it is taken into account in wage setting. Note, however, that the stabilization is achieved by affecting the real wage of those in the second year of labor contracts and thus should not be expected to be available to attain arbitrary levels of output – the use of too active a policy would lead to a change in the structure of contracts.
>
> [A] more general interpretation of the monetary rule, . . . is to accommodate real disturbances that tend to increase the price level and to counteract nominal disturbances that tend to increase the price level.

Fischer concludes by noting that:

> given a structure of contracts, there is some room for maneuver by the monetary authorities – which is to say that their policies can, though will not necessarily, be stabilizing.

Conclusion

This chapter presented the sticky money wage or Keynesian model of the macroeconomy. We find that in contrast to the neoclassical model, changes in the price level affect real variables and the amount of labor employed in the economy. Thus, money has real effects. The development of an upward-sloping aggregate supply curve has dramatic implications for the conduct of monetary policy. However, it is shown that the expectations of agents in the economy also play an important role in whether or not monetary policy is effective.

10 The Lucas model

Introduction

As we have seen, anticipated changes in prices have no impact on real variables in the neoclassical model. A key element of this model is the "essential presumption . . . that nominal output is determined on the aggregate demand side of the economy, with the division into real output and the price level largely dependent on the behavior of suppliers of labor and goods" (Lucas 1973). As such, this model implies no link between price changes and real output.

We have also seen how the natural rate model allows one to introduce a link between unanticipated price changes and real output. The seminal paper by Lucas (1973) formally develops a more complete model of the potential for "short-run supply behavior (resulting) from suppliers' lack of information on some of the prices relevant to their decisions." Lucas's explanation of a tradeoff between unemployment and inflation "is that the positive association of price changes and output arises because suppliers misinterpret general price movements for relative price changes."

As with the "illusion model," Lucas postulates "rational agents whose decisions depend on relative prices only, placed in an economic setting where they cannot distinguish relative from general price movements." That is, we retain the hypothesis that prices adjust to clear markets.

Lucas adds to the simple (static) natural rate model so far discussed by explicitly modeling the source of forecast errors. In doing so, he assumes that "inferences on these relevant, unobserved prices are made optimally (or 'rationally') in light of the stochastic nature of the economy." Below we outline Lucas's model.[1]

The "island" paradigm

Lucas's model begins by disaggregating the economy into a number of what have been called "sectors," "markets," or "islands." As Lucas says, "we imagine suppliers as located in a large number of scattered, competitive markets. Demand for goods in each period is distributed unevenly over markets, leading to relative as well as general price movements." In terms of our previous analysis, one could think of each of the n sectors in the economy as inhabited by firms producing the *i*th commodity ($i = 1, \ldots, n$). Associated with each sector or "island" is a set of workers and thus a labor market.

For firms producing commodity *i* in period *t*, the key relative price is the price of their output relative to the wage paid in sector *i*, or p_{it}/w_{it}, where p_{it} is the money price of commodity *i* (produced in sector *i*) and w_{it} is the money wage for labor in sector *i*. It is assumed that individuals (firms and workers) in sector *i*'s labor market know the money wage and price of commodity *i*. For labor suppliers in sector *i*, however, the key relative price is w_{it}/p_t, where p_t is the economy-wide price level, reflecting the fact that suppliers plan to use money wages to purchase a bundle of goods consisting of all *n* commodities.[2]

It is this setup of "dispersed markets" and "informational discrepancies" that Lucas uses to generate a correlation between price changes and output – the famous Lucas supply equation.

The supply function for a particular sector

The Lucas model assumes a competitive labor market for sector or "island" *i*, such that the equilibrium level of employment and money wage equate market demand and supply. With respect to the labor demand function, let us start by assuming the simple Cobb–Douglas production function, such that the marginal product of labor is given by:

$$a(N_{it})^{-\alpha} \qquad \text{where } a > 0.[3]$$

The profit-maximizing condition for the representative firm producing commodity *i* is to equate the money wage to the marginal product of labor multiplied by the money price of output. The resulting optimal labor demand can thus be defined by the equation:[4]

$$w_{it} = p_{it}a(N_{it}^d)^{-\alpha}.$$

Taking the natural log of this equation and rearranging, we have

$$\ln N_{it}^d = \frac{1}{\alpha}[\ln p_{it} - \ln w_{it} + \ln a]. \tag{10.1}$$

With respect to labor supply, let us assume for the moment that the real wage is known. Further, let us assume that the labor supply function takes the following logarithmic form:

$$\ln N_{it}^s = \frac{1}{\beta} \ln \frac{w_{it}}{p_{it}},$$

where β is a positive constant.

Employment contracts entered into at time *t* in sector *i* specify the money wage w_{it}, so that element of the real wage is known. However, if the price level is unknown, then the expected real wage based on information available at time t is equal to $w_{it}E_t(1/p_t)$. The associated expected logarithm of the real wage is then:[5]

$$E_t \ln(w_{it}/p_t) = \ln w_{it} - E_t(\ln p_t).$$

Given the assumed log-linear labor supply function and ignoring the implications of uncertainty for labor supply, we thus have

$$\ln N_{it}^s = \left(\frac{1}{\beta}\right)(\ln w_{it} - E_t(\ln p_t)). \tag{10.2}$$

Equilibrium in the labor market for sector i entails a level of employment N_{it} and money wage w_{it} such that the demand for labor equals the supply. In logarithmic form and using the specific labor demand and supply functions given by equations (10.1) and (10.2), equilibrium requires that the log of the money wage, $\ln w_{it}$, and the log of employment, $\ln N_{it}$, be such that

$$\ln N_{it} = \frac{1}{\alpha}(\ln p_{it} - \ln w_{it} + \ln a)$$

and

$$\ln N_{it} = \frac{1}{\beta}(\ln w_{it} - E_t(\ln p_t)).$$

Substituting the first expression into the second to eliminate the logarithm of the money wage, we have

$$\ln N_{it} = \frac{1}{\alpha}(\ln p_{it} + \ln a) - \frac{1}{\alpha}(\beta \ln N_{it} + E_t(\ln p_t)),$$

which, upon rearranging, becomes

$$\ln N_{it} = \ln N_{ni} + [1 + (\alpha + \beta)][\ln p_{it} - E_t(\ln p_t)], \tag{10.3}$$

where $\ln N_{ni} = (\ln a)/(\alpha + \beta)$.

Equation (10.3) indicates that the logarithm of equilibrium employment in the ith sector, and thus the production of commodity i, depends directly on the expectation of logarithm of the ratio of the price of commodity $i(p_{it})$ to the general level of prices, p_t. The term N_{ni} can be viewed as the "normal" level of employment. Note that we have abstracted from population growth and other factors that would result in this "normal" level of employment varying across time.

Given the assumption of a simple Cobb–Douglas production function of the form $y_{it} = (N_{it})^{1-\alpha}(\overline{K}_i)^\alpha$, we thus have

$$\ln y_{it} = \ln y_{ni} + \gamma[\ln p_{it} - E_t(\ln p_t)], \tag{10.4}$$

where $\gamma = (1 - \alpha)(\alpha + \beta)$ and $\ln y_{ni} = (1 - \alpha)\ln N_{ni} + \alpha \ln \overline{K}_i$. The term y_{ni} is denoted by Lucas as the "normal" level of output in the particular sector or market i

under consideration. As Lucas (1973: 327) states, the "quantity supplied in each market will be viewed as the product of a normal (or secular) component common to all markets and a cyclical component which varies from market to market. . . . The cyclical component varies with perceived, *relative* prices and with its own lagged value." Note that for the moment we do not include the lagged value of output in the above supply function. One can justify the inclusion of such by assuming adjustment costs.

The source of forecasting errors

According to (10.4), output of commodity i depends critically on suppliers' forecast of the log of the general level of prices, $E_t(\ln p_t)$. Now consider how such a forecast may be obtained in a stochastic environment. First, it is assumed that agents in sector i – in particular, suppliers of labor involved in the production of commodity i – know commodity i's price, p_{it}. However, the exact extent to which any change in the money price of commodity i reflects a change in the overall level of money prices as opposed to a change in commodity i's price relative to other prices is unknown. It is this uncertainty that leads suppliers in sector i to misinterpret a change in the general price level in terms of a change in a relative price.

To be concrete, suppose $E_{t-1}(\ln p_t)$ incorporates all information available at the end of period $t - 1$. The logarithm of the actual price level will vary from the logarithm of this expected price level to the extent that there are "surprises" with respect to the aggregate price level. Letting ξ_t denote this "surprise" for period t, we have

$$\ln p_t = E_{t-1}(\ln p_t) + \xi_t. \tag{10.5}$$

We assume that ξ_t, which is that part of the price level that cannot be predicted from past data, is a normally distributed random variable with zero expectation and variance σ^2.[6]

At the start of period t, suppliers in market i receive one additional piece of information, the logarithm of the price of commodity i, $\ln p_{it}$. This signal is assumed to contain some information about the logarithm of the overall price level in that

$$\ln p_{it} = \ln p_t + z_{it}, \tag{10.6}$$

where z_{it} is a normally distributed random variable with zero mean and variance σ_z^2. Thus, using equation (10.5) to substitute for $\ln p_t$,

$$\ln p_{it} = E_{t-1}(\ln p_t) + \xi_t + z_{it}. \tag{10.7}$$

In words, the logarithm of the nominal price for the sector, $\ln p_{it}$, is assumed to inform the supplier of the sum of the current "white noise" innovations to the relative price process in that sector (z_{it}) and the innovations to aggregate demand and thus the economy-wide level of prices (ξ_t).[7]

We can then express the expectation of the logarithm of the price level at time t for suppliers in sector i given the observed logarithm of the price of commodity i, $\ln p_{it}$, by

$$E_t(\ln p_t) \equiv E\{\ln p_t | E_{t-1}(\ln p_t), \ln p_{it}\}. \tag{10.8}$$

Formally, we have the joint distribution of two random variables, $f(\ln p_{it}, \ln p_t)$, where one of them, $\ln p_{it}$, is known to take a particular value. The problem is the basic one of "bivariate regression" in that we have to determine the conditional expectation, $E\{\ln p_t | \ln p_{it}\}$, namely the "average" value of $\ln p_t$ for the given value of $\ln p_{it}$.[8] As we shall see in the next section, the resulting expression for the expected general price level (in logs), given $\ln p_{it}$ is observed, can be expressed in linear form as

$$E_t(\ln p_t) = E_{t-1}(\ln p_t) + (1-\theta)(\ln p_{it} - E_{t-1}(\ln p_t)), \qquad \text{where } 0 \le \theta \le 1. \tag{10.9}$$

A digression on linear regression analysis

Let us assume a linear regression equation that links the observed logarithm of the price of commodity i to the logarithm of the general level of prices of the form[9]

$$E_t\{\ln p_t | \ln p_{it}\} = a_0 + a_1(\ln p_{it}). \tag{10.10}$$

We can express the regression coefficients a_0 and a_1 in terms of some of the lower moments of the joint distribution of $\ln p_t$ and $\ln p_{it}$, namely in terms of[10]

$$E\{\ln p_{it}\} = E_{t-1}(\ln p_t) \qquad \text{(from (10.7))},$$

$$E\{\ln p_t\} = E_{t-1}(\ln p_t) \qquad \text{(from (10.5)),}[11]$$

$$\text{Var}\{\ln p_{it}\} = \sigma^2 + \sigma_z^2 \qquad \text{(from (10.7))},$$

$$\text{Cov}(\ln p_{it}, \ln p_t) = E\{(-\xi_t - z_{it})(-\xi_t)\} = \sigma^2 + E\{z_{it} \cdot \xi_t\}.$$

In general, $E\{z_{it} \cdot \xi_t\} = \text{Cov}(z_{it}, \xi_t) + E\{z_{it}\}E\{\xi_t\}$. However, given that $E\{z_{it}\} = E\{\xi_t\} = 0$ and given the assumption that z_{it} and u_t are independent variables so that $\text{Cov}(z_{it}, \xi_t) = 0$, we have:[12]

$$\text{Cov}(\ln p_{it}, \ln p_t) = \sigma^2.$$

From (10.10), we have that[13]

$$E(\ln p_t | \ln p_{it}) \equiv \int (\ln p_t)\phi(\ln p_t | \ln p_{it})d \ln p_t = a_0 + a_1(\ln p_{it}), \tag{10.11}$$

where $\phi(\cdot)$ is the conditional density function of $\ln p_t$ given $\ln p_{it}$. If we then multiply the expression on both sides of (10.11) by the marginal density function of $\ln p_{it}$, denoted by $g(\ln p_{it})$, and integrate on $\ln p_{it}$, we obtain:

$$\iint (\ln p_t)\phi(\ln p_t | \ln p_{it}) g \ln(p_{it}) d\ln p_t d\ln p_{it}$$

$$= \int a_0 g(\ln p_{it}) d\ln p_{it} + \int a_1 (\ln p_{it}) g(\ln p_{it}) d\ln p_{it}$$

or

$$E\{\ln p_t\} = a_0 + a_1 E\{\ln p_{it}\}, \tag{10.12}$$

since $\phi(\ln p_t | \ln p_{it}) g \ln(p_{it}) = f(\ln p_{it}, \ln p_t)$. Had we multiplied the expression on both sides of (10.11) also by $\ln p_{it}$ before integrating on $\ln p_{it}$, we would have obtained:

$$\iint (\ln p_t)(\ln p_{it})\phi(\ln p_t | \ln p_{it}) g \ln(p_{it}) d\ln p_t d\ln p_{it}$$

$$= \int a_0 (\ln p_{it}) g(\ln p_{it}) d\ln p_{it} + \int a_1 (\ln p_{it})^2 g(\ln p_{it}) d\ln p_{it}$$

or

$$E\{(\ln p_{it})(\ln p_t)\} = a_0 E\{\ln p_{it}\} + a_1 E\{(\ln p_{it})^2\}. \tag{10.13}$$

Solving (10.12) and (10.13) for a_0 and a_1 and making use of the fact that

$$E\{(\ln p_{it})(\ln p_t)\} = \text{Cov}(\ln p_{it}, \ln p_t) + E\{(\ln p_{it})\}E\{\ln p_t\}$$

and

$$E\{(\ln p_{it})^2\} = \text{Var}(\ln p_{it}) + [E\{\ln p_{it}\}]^2,$$

we find that

$$a_0 = E\{\ln p_t\} - [\text{Cov}(\ln p_{it}, \ln p_t)E\{\ln p_{it}\}]/(\text{Var}(\ln p_{it})),$$
$$a_1 = (\text{Cov}(\ln p_{it}, \ln p_t))/(\text{Var}(\ln p_{it})).$$

Hence, we can write equation (10.10) as

$$E_t(\ln p_t) \equiv E(\ln p_t | \ln p_{it})$$
$$= E(\ln p_t) + [\text{Cov}(\ln p_{it}, \ln p_t)/\text{Var}(\ln p_{it})](\ln p_t - E\{\ln p_{it}\}).$$

Substituting in the above expressions for means, variance, and covariance, we have thus derived (10.9), with

$$1 - \theta = \sigma^2/(\sigma^2 + \sigma_z^2).$$

Equation (10.9) indicates that agents' rational expectation of the current price level is a "linear least-squares projection." That is, one could rewrite (10.9) as

$$E_t(\ln p_t) = \theta E_{t-1}(\ln p_t) + (1 - \theta) \ln p_{it}, \qquad (10.14)$$

where $\theta = \sigma_z^2/(\sigma^2 + \sigma_z^2)$. To see why this is called "linear least-squares," note that we could start with (10.14) (the "linear" part of the projection), and then pick θ to minimize the variance in this forecast or projection of $\ln p_t$ (the "least-squares" part of the projection). In particular, substituting in (10.5) for $E_{t-1}(\ln p_t)$ (i.e., $E_{t-1}(\ln p_t) = \ln p_t - \xi_t$) and (10.6) for $\ln p_{it}$ (i.e., $\ln p_{it} = \ln p_t + z_{it}$), (10.14) becomes

$$E_t(\ln p_t) = \ln p_t - \theta \xi_t + (1 - \theta)z_{it} \qquad (10.14')$$

The problem of picking θ to minimize the variance of this projection can then be expressed as[14]

$$\min_{\theta} E\{\ln p_t - \theta \xi_t + (1 - \theta)z_{it} - \ln p_t\}^2 = \theta \sigma^2 + (1 - \theta)\sigma_z^2.$$

Taking the derivative of the above expression with respect to θ, setting it equal to zero ("least squares"), and solving for θ, we verify that $\theta = \sigma_z^2/(\sigma^2 + \sigma_z^2)$.

As Sargent (1987a: 442) points out,

> the parameter θ is the fraction of the conditional variance in $\ln p_{it}$ due to relative price variation. The larger is this fraction, the smaller is the weight placed on $\ln p_{it}$ in revising $E_{t-1}(\ln p_t)$ to form $E_t(\ln p_t)$. This makes sense since the larger is θ, the more likely it is that a change in $\ln p_{it}$ reflects a relative rather than a general price change.[15]

Equation (10.14) can be substituted into the supply function for commodity i (10.4) to obtain

$$\ln y_{it} = \ln y_{ni} + \gamma \theta (\ln p_{it} - E_{t-1}(\ln p_t)) \qquad (10.15)$$

where, as before, $\ln y_{ni} = (1 - \alpha)(\ln N_{ni}) + \alpha(\ln \overline{K}_i)$. As noted above, if we assumed adjustment costs, then a lagged output term could be added to (10.15). In this case, we would have[16]

$$\ln y_{ni} = \ln y_{ni} + \gamma \theta [\ln p_{it} - E_{t-1}(\ln p_t)] + \lambda(\ln y_{it-1} - \ln y_{ni}). \qquad (10.15')$$

If suppliers were able to observe the actual value of the price level, so that $E_t(\ln p_t) = \ln p_t$, then, going back to (10.4), one could express the resulting "full information" output produced in sector i by

$$\ln y_{it}^* = \ln y_{ni} + \gamma[\ln p_{it} - \ln p_t]$$

which, given $\ln p_{it} = \ln p_t + z_{it}$, simply becomes

$$\ln y_{it}^* = \ln y_{ni} + \gamma z_{it}.$$

As you can see, since the expectation of the random shock to relative prices z_{it} is zero, $\ln y_{ni}$ has the natural interpretation as the expected output of sector i given full information.

The Lucas aggregate supply function

Equation (10.15) is close to what is known as the "Lucas aggregate supply function." Without adjustment costs, the Lucas supply function takes the form

$$\ln y_t = \ln y_n + \gamma \theta (\ln p_{it} - E_{t-1}(\ln p_t)). \tag{10.16}$$

With adjustment costs, the Lucas supply function takes the general form

$$\ln y_t = \ln y_n + \gamma \theta (\ln p_{it} - E_{t-1}(\ln p_t)) + \lambda (\ln y_{t-1} - \ln y_n), \tag{10.16'}$$

where y_n denotes the natural rate of output.[17] For simplicity we have assumed that the natural rate of total output is constant across periods.

The term $\ln y_n$ can be interpreted either as the logarithm of output for the "representative" sector or as the logarithm of total output across the n sectors. Let us assume the former interpretation. The average level of real output can be defined by

$$y_t \equiv \frac{1}{p_t} \left[\prod_{i=1}^{n} p_{it} y_{it} \right]^{1/n},$$

where $[\prod_{i=1}^{n} p_{it} y_{it}]^{1/n}$ is the geometric mean of nominal output across the n markets or sectors. Taking logs, we have the following definition for the logarithm of average output:

$$\ln y_t \equiv -\ln p_t + \frac{1}{n} \sum_{i=1}^{n} (\ln p_{it} + \ln y_{it}). \tag{10.17}$$

We will assume that the overall price level is constructed as a geometric mean of individual prices, such that

$$p_t \equiv \left[\prod_{i=1}^{n} p_{it} \right]^{1/n}.$$

Taking logs,

$$\ln p_t \equiv \frac{1}{n} \sum_{i=1}^{n} \ln p_{it}.$$

Substituting the above into (10.17), we have the following definition for the logarithm of average output:

$$\ln y_t \equiv \frac{1}{n} \sum_{i=1}^{n} \ln y_{it}. \tag{10.18}$$

Substituting into (10.18) the supply functions for the individual sectors as given by (10.15), we thus have[18]

$$\ln y_t \equiv \frac{1}{n} \sum_{i=1}^{n} [\ln y_{ni} + \gamma \theta (\ln p_{it} - E_{t-1}(\ln p_t))]. \tag{10.19}$$

Recall that $\ln p_{it} = \ln p_t + z_{it}$, where z_{it} is a normal random variable independently distributed across markets with a mean of zero and variance σ_z^2. Substituting this into (10.15) and rearranging, we have

$$\ln y_t = \frac{1}{n} \sum_{i=1}^{n} [\ln y_{ni}] + \gamma \theta (\ln p_t - E_{t-1}(\ln p_t)) + \frac{1}{n} \sum_{i=1}^{n} \gamma \theta z_{it}. \tag{10.20}$$

As the number of markets, n, approaches infinity, from the law of large numbers we know that the sum of the z_{it} divided by n approaches zero.[19] Thus for a large number of markets we may approximate (10.20) by

$$\ln y_t = \frac{1}{n} \left[\sum_{i=1}^{n} \ln y_{ni} + \gamma \theta (\ln p_t - E_{t-1}(\ln p_t)) \right]. \tag{10.21}$$

By definition, the logarithm of the geometric average of "normal" output across markets, $\ln y_n$, is given by $n^{-1} \sum_{i=1}^{n} \ln y_{ni}$. Thus we can rewrite (10.21) as (10.16), in which $\ln y_n$ is the logarithm of "normal" output that would occur if there were no surprises with respect to the aggregate price level, that is, when $\ln p_t = E_{t-1}(\ln p_t)$. Note that for simplicity we assume the natural rate is constant over time.

Equation (10.16) is the Lucas aggregate supply equation with the last term missing. As noted above, if we include adjustment costs then we obtain (10.16'), indicating that the deviation of real output from its "natural" level or trend is associated with a deviation in the price level from that expected and past deviations of output from the natural rate. This last term makes output serially correlated over time.

The Lucas supply function and the Phillips curve

The Lucas supply function predicts a direct correlation between unanticipated price changes and output, and thus a potential tradeoff between price changes and unemployment if one assumes that unemployment and output are inversely related. This potential inverse relationship between unemployment and inflation is sometimes referred to as the "Phillips curve," after A.W. Phillips, who noted the empirical relationship between wage inflation and unemployment for the British economy for the 100 years up to 1957 (see Phillips 1958). Later depictions of the Phillips curve replaced the rate of change in wages with the inflation rate.

To see this Phillips relationship more clearly, rearrange the aggregate Lucas supply function without adjustment costs (10.16) to obtain

$$\ln p_t = (\ln y_t - \ln y_n)/\gamma\theta + E_{t-1}(\ln p_t).$$

Subtracting $\ln p_{t-1}$ from both sides of this aggregate supply equation, we have

$$\ln(p_t/p_{t-1}) = (\ln y_t - \ln y_n)/\gamma\theta + E_{t-1}(\ln(p_t/p_{t-1})). \tag{10.22}$$

Let the term π_t denote the rate of inflation between periods $t - 1$ and t:[20]

$$\pi_t \equiv (p_t - p_{t-1})/p_{t-1} = (p_t/p_{t-1}) - 1.$$

It is common in macroeconomics to approximate the above rate of change in prices by the log of the ratio of the two prices. If the ratio equals one, then the log equals zero, which is the rate of inflation. If the ratio is $1 + x$ and x is a small proportion, then the log of this ratio approximately equals the actual inflation rate. For instance, if $p_t/p_{t-1} = 1.05$ so that inflation is 0.05 or 5 percent, then the log of 1.05 is 0.0488 which approximates this 0.05 rate of inflation. Thus we have

$$\pi_t \approx \ln(p_t/p_{t-1}) = \ln p_t - \ln p_{t-1}.$$

Using the above approximation for the rate of inflation, we can rewrite (10.22) as

$$\pi_t = (\ln y_t - \ln y_n)/\gamma\theta + E_{t-1}\pi_t \tag{10.23}$$

which, as Sargent (1987a: 443) states,

> is in the form of a standard natural rate Phillips curve relating inflation (π_t) directly to output ($\ln y_t$) and to expected inflation ($E_{t-1}\pi_t$). According to [(10.23)], the Phillips curve shifts up in the (π_t, y_t) plane by the exact amount of any increase in expected inflation. This characteristic of equation [(10.23)] is often taken as the hallmark of the natural unemployment rate hypothesis. It seems to offer an explanation for why the Phillips curve tradeoff worsened as average inflation rates increased over the 1970s in many western countries.

If we assumed that due to adjustment cost the lagged deviation in output from the natural level affects the current deviation, as the Lucas aggregate supply equation (10.16′) suggests, then in terms of rates of change in prices we would have

$$\pi_t = (\ln y_t - \ln y_n)/\gamma\theta + E_{t-1}\pi_t - (\lambda/\gamma\theta)(\ln y_{t-1} - \ln y_n). \tag{10.23′}$$

We could instead express (10.23) in terms of unemployment by assuming there is a linear inverse relationship between deviations in output from the natural rate and deviations in the actual level of unemployment, U_t, from its natural rate, U_n, such that

$$\ln y_{t-1} - \ln y_n = -\ell(U_t - U_n),$$

where ℓ is a positive constant. Substituting the above into (10.23), we thus have:

$$\pi_t = -(\ell/\gamma\theta)(U_t - U_n) + E_{t-1}(\pi_t), \tag{10.23''}$$

indicating the inverse relationship between unanticipated price changes and the actual level of unemployment. Rearranging (10.23″), we have that

$$U_t = U_n - (\gamma\theta/\ell)[\pi_t - E_{t-1}(\pi_t)], \tag{10.23'''}$$

where $\gamma\theta/\ell > 0$. Equation (10.23‴) is the typical expression of the Phillips curve found in the literature. It indicates that deviations in the unemployment rate below its natural level must be accompanied by deviations in the actual rate of inflation above that expected. It reflects the "natural rate of unemployment hypothesis" as originally coined by Friedman (1968: 11):

> There is always a temporary trade-off between inflation and unemployment; there is no permanent trade-off. The temporary trade-off comes not from inflation per se, but from unanticipated inflation, which generally means from a rising rate of inflation.

Recall that, as Barro and Gordon (1983: 592) observed, the term $E_{t-1}(\pi_t)$ in (10.23‴) is the

> prior expectation of inflation for period t [which is] distinguished from the expectation that is conditional on partial information about current prices. This distinction arises in models (e.g., Lucas 1972, 1973; Barro 1976) in which people operate in localized markets with incomplete information about contemporaneous nominal aggregates. In this setting the Phillips curve slope coefficient, $(\gamma\theta/\ell)$, turns out to depend on the relative variances for general and market-specific shocks.

Variability in prices and the tradeoff

As Lucas (1973: 333) states:

> demand policies [can] tend to move inflation rates and output (relative to trend) in the same direction, or alternatively, unemployment and inflation in opposite directions. The conventional Phillips curve account of this observed co-movement says that the terms of the tradeoff arise from the relatively stable

structural features of the economy, and are thus independent of the nature of the aggregate demand policy pursued. The alternative explanation of the same observed tradeoff is that the positive association of price changes and output arises because suppliers misinterpret general price movements for relative price changes.

Taking Lucas's alternative viewpoint, two aspects concerning the tradeoff are suggested. First, as Lucas states, "changes in average inflation rates will not increase average output." As we have seen, if we compare the expected price level for period t with the price level for the prior period, the difference would incorporate individuals' expectation of this average rate of inflation (along with a number of other potentially relevant variables). Second, "the higher the variance in average prices, the less 'favorable' will be the observed tradeoff." We consider this second point below by referring back to the simple Lucas supply function without lagged output (10.16).

Recall that the term ξ_t given by (10.5) denotes that part of the price level that cannot be predicted from past data. We have assumed that this "surprise" term ξ_t is a normally distributed random variable with zero expectation and variance σ^2. Substituting this into (10.16), we have that

$$\ln y_t - \ln y_n = \gamma\theta\xi_t, \tag{10.24}$$

where $\theta = \sigma_z^2/(\sigma^2 + \sigma_z^2)$ and $\gamma = (1 - \alpha)/(\alpha + \beta)$. Recall that θ is the weight attached to the expected price level prior to observing p_{it}.

Equation (10.24) indicates that deviations in output from the natural level depend solely on surprises. In his statement concerning the variance of prices, Lucas is pointing out that the impact of "surprises" on output relative to its natural level depends on the "slope" term $\lambda\theta$, which is given by

$$\lambda\theta = \frac{1 - \alpha}{\alpha + \beta}\frac{\sigma_z^2}{\sigma^2 + \sigma_z^2}.$$

As Sargent (1987a: 444) notes:

> a "favorable" tradeoff between output and unexpected inflation (that is, a large value of $\gamma\theta$) will exist only when σ^2 is small relative to σ_z^2. An attempt by authorities to exploit the tradeoff between output and unexpected inflation more fully by changing aggregate demand regimes might increase the variance σ^2 relative to σ_z^2, and thus change the slope $\gamma\theta$. This is yet another example of how agents' optimal decision rules change in response to changes in the random processes governing the exogenous variables they base their decisions on.

Sargent's last point is another example of the "Lucas critique," in this context with respect to the validity of using past econometric estimates of a tradeoff in predicting future tradeoffs.

Note that although the tradeoff worsens with higher variability in prices, the effect of higher variability in prices on the variance of output about the natural rate is unclear. In particular, from (10.16) we know that the variance in the difference between output and the natural rate is simply $(\gamma\theta)^2\sigma^2$. Given our definition of $\gamma\theta$, the variance of the logarithm of output becomes

$$\text{Var}(\ln y_t) = \gamma^2 \left(\frac{\sigma_z^2}{\sigma^2 + \sigma_z^2}\right)^2 \sigma^2.$$

Differentiating with respect to σ^2, we have

$$\frac{\partial \text{Var}(\ln y_t)}{\partial \sigma^2} = \gamma^2 \left(\frac{\sigma_z^2}{\sigma^2 + \sigma_z^2}\right)^2 - 2\gamma^2\sigma^2 \frac{\sigma_z^2}{(\sigma^2 + \sigma_z^2)} \frac{\sigma_z^2}{(\sigma^2 + \sigma_z^2)^2}$$

$$= \left(\frac{\gamma^2\sigma_z^2}{\sigma^2 + \sigma_z^2}\right)^2 \left(\frac{1 - 2\sigma^2}{\sigma^2 + \sigma_z^2}\right).$$

As the above expression indicates, by itself an increase in the variation in the average price level (σ^2) will increase the variation in the logarithm of output for a given "slope" ($\gamma\theta$). On the other hand, as Lucas pointed out, such an increase in the variation in price level will result in a reduction in the effect of any given price change on output, which by itself would decrease the variation in the logarithm of output.

Substituting (10.5) into the expanded Lucas supply function with lagged output, we have the Lucas supply function of the form

$$\ln y_t - \ln y_n = \gamma\theta\xi_t + \lambda(\ln y_{t-1} - \ln y_n)$$

where, as before, $\theta = \sigma_z^2/(\sigma^2 + \sigma_z^2)$. Substituting for prior differences in output from its natural level, we thus have

$$\ln y_t - \ln y_n = \gamma\theta \sum_{i=0}^{\infty} \lambda^i \xi_{t-i}, \tag{10.25}$$

which shows that the deviation of output from its natural rate depends on the current and all previous values of the "aggregate demand shock" that affects the equilibrium price level.

A complete model except for specifying the source of expectations

Equation (10.16) provides us with one part of the standard macroeconomic model, the "aggregate supply equation." To simplify the analysis, we will normalize output so that the natural level of real output is equal to 1. We have already assumed that the natural level of real output is constant over time. These two assumptions allow us to write (10.16) in the more compact form

$$Y_t = \gamma\theta(P_t - E_{t-1}P_t) + \lambda Y_{t-1}, \tag{10.26}$$

where Y_t denotes log of real output supply for period t (or equivalently the deviation in output from its natural level for period t), P_t denotes the log of the price level, and $E_{t-1}P_t$ denotes the expectation of log of the price level. What we now require is a characterization of the aggregate demand side of the economy as typically summarized by the LM and IS equations.

To obtain an explicit form for the portfolio or LM equation, we start by assuming a real money demand function for the end of period t of the form

$$L_t^d = y_t^{\alpha_1} \exp[-(\alpha_2 r_t)] \tag{10.27}$$

where y_t is real output, $\alpha_1 > 0$, and $\alpha_2 > 0$, indicating that real money demand is directly related to real output but inversely related to the nominal interest rate.[21]

Let M_t denote the nominal money supply at the end of period t (previously, this has been denoted by $\overline{M}$) and let m_t denote the logarithm of this money supply for period t, such that $m_t = \ln M_t$. Further, let us assume a logarithmic supply of money function of the form

$$m_t = \bar{m}_t + \varepsilon_t. \tag{10.28}$$

Equation (10.28) separates the logarithm of the money supply into two components, a deterministic component, $\bar{m}_t$, set by government authorities according to a rule tying money supply changes to past variables, and a random component, ε_t, which is assumed to be normally distributed with zero mean. This random term is also assumed to be serially independent (i.e., $E(\varepsilon_t\varepsilon_s) = 0$ for $s \neq t$).

The LM equation is simply the money market equilibrium condition equating the real supply of money to real money demand, and thus is given by

$$M_t/p_t = L_t^d. \tag{10.29}$$

Taking logs of the equilibrium condition (10.29) and substituting the logarithm of the money demand function (10.27) and the money supply function (10.28), we have

$$\bar{m}_t - P_t = \alpha_1 Y_t - \alpha_2 r_t - \varepsilon_t, \tag{10.30}$$

where $P_t = \ln p_t$. Equation (10.30) is the standard log-linear form of the portfolio or LM equation.[22]

To obtain an explicit form for the IS equation, which is the equilibrium condition in terms of equating output production to the demand for output, we must postulate a specific form for output demand. One common assumption is to include the expected real rate of interest, $r_t - \pi^e_{t+1}$, as a determinant of output demand. To do so, let

$$\pi^e_{t+1} \equiv (p^e_{t+1} - p_t)/p_t = (p^e_{t+1}/p_t) - 1.$$

As before, we can approximate the expected rate of change in prices by the expectation of the log of the ratio of the future to current price level (i.e., $\pi^e_{t+1} \approx P^e_{t+1} - P_t$, where P^e_{t+1} is the expected log of the price level for period $t+1$). Thus the expected real rate of interest becomes $r_t - \pi^e_{t+1}$.

Letting the term X_t denote a vector of exogenous variables that also affects output demand, we have in log-linear form the following equilibrium condition for the output market:

$$Y_t = X_t - \beta_1(r_t - \pi^e_{t+1}) + u_t, \tag{10.31}$$

where u_t is a serially independent, stationary random process with mean zero and finite variance equal to σ^2_u. The random terms for output demand and money supply, ε_t and u_t respectively, are assumed independent (i.e., $E(\varepsilon_t u_t) = 0$).

Summarizing, we have a model consisting of the aggregate supply equation (10.26), the LM equation (10.30) and the IS equation (10.31), which can be solved for the equilibrium output, price, and interest rate.

In particular, combining the LM and IS equations to eliminate the interest rate r_t, we obtain

$$Y_t = X_t + u_t - (\beta_1/\alpha_2) \cdot (-\bar{m}_t - \varepsilon_t + P_t - \alpha_1 Y_t) + \beta_1 \cdot \pi^e_{t+1},$$

which on rearranging becomes an "aggregate demand equation" of the form

$$Y_t = \frac{\alpha_2}{\alpha_2 + \alpha_1\beta_1} \left[X_t + u_t + \beta_1 \pi^e_{t+1} + \frac{\beta_1}{\alpha_2}(\bar{m}_t + \varepsilon_t - P_t) \right]. \tag{10.32}$$

Or, in terms of the price level, we have an "aggregate demand equation" of the form

$$P_t = \bar{m}_t + \varepsilon_t - \frac{\alpha_2 + \alpha_1\beta_1}{\beta_1} Y_t + \frac{\alpha_2}{\beta_1}(X_t + u_t + \beta_1 \pi^e_{t+1}). \tag{10.33}$$

Equations (10.32) and (10.33) indicate the inverse relationship between the price level and output that is shown graphically by a downward-sloping aggregate demand curve.

With respect to (10.33), note that the expected rate of inflation for the next period, π^e_{t+1}, is viewed as a distinct entity. Our prior assumption of unit elastic expectations concerning the expected log of the future price level P^e_{t+1} would imply that this term is, in fact, independent of changes in the current price level. Note also that *if output were unchanged*, then an x percent change in the money supply would result in an x percent change in the price level. This is the standard result of the "neoclassical" model.[23]

Combining the above aggregate demand equation (10.32) with the aggregate supply equation to eliminate the output term Y_t, we have[24]

$$\frac{\alpha_2}{\alpha_2 + \alpha_1\beta_1}\left[X_t + u_t + \beta_1\pi^e_{t+1} + \frac{\beta_1}{\alpha_2}(\bar{m}_t + \varepsilon_t - P_t)\right]$$
$$= \gamma\theta(P_t - E_{t-1}P_t) + \lambda Y_{t-1}.$$

Solving the above for the equilibrium price level, one obtains

$$P_t = \frac{1}{J_0 + \beta_1}\left[\beta_1(\bar{m}_t + \varepsilon_t) + \alpha_2(X_t + u_t + \beta_1\pi^e_{t+1})\right.$$
$$\left. + J_0\left(E_{t-1}P_t - \frac{\lambda Y_{t-1}}{\gamma\theta}\right)\right], \tag{10.34}$$

where $J_0 = \gamma\theta(\alpha_2 + \beta_1\alpha_1)$. Expression (10.34) is sometimes called the reduced-form equation for the price level.

Rearranging (10.34), we have

$$P_t - \frac{J_0}{J_0 + \beta_1}E_{t-1}P_t$$
$$= \frac{1}{J_0 + \beta_1}\left[\beta_1(\bar{m}_t + \varepsilon_t) + \alpha_2(X_t + u_t + \beta_1\pi^e_{t+1}) - J_0\frac{\lambda Y_{t-1}}{\gamma\theta}\right]. \tag{10.34'}$$

Let us assume perfect foresight, meaning that $E_{t-1}P_t = P_t$. Noting that $1 - J_0/(J_0 + \beta_1) = \beta_1/(J_0 + \beta_1)$, we can solve (10.34') for the equilibrium price level under this hypothesis of perfect foresight, obtaining:

$$P_t = \bar{m}_t + \varepsilon_t \frac{\alpha_2}{\beta_1}(X_t + u_t + \beta_1\pi^e_{t+1}) - J_0\frac{\lambda}{\beta_1\gamma\theta}Y_{t-1}. \tag{10.34''}$$

As equation (10.34'') makes clear, under the presumption of limited perfect foresight the predictions are those of the neoclassical model:

(a) a change in the money supply (in log form given by $\bar{m}_t + \varepsilon_t$) results in an equiproportionate change in the price level (in log form given by P_t);
(b) an increase in expected inflation π^e_{t+1} raises the price level;
(c) a higher level of lagged output (Y_{t-1}) lowers the price level;
(d) an increase in output demand ($X_t + u_t$) raises prices.

Following a procedure similar to that used to derive (10.34), if we combine the aggregate demand equation (10.33) and aggregate supply equation to eliminate the price level, we have

$$Y_t = \lambda Y_{t-1} - \gamma\theta E_{t-1}P_t$$
$$+ \gamma\theta\left\{\bar{m}_t + \varepsilon_t - \frac{\alpha_2 + \alpha_1\beta_1}{\beta_1}Y_t + \frac{\alpha_2}{\beta_1}(X_t + u_t + \beta_1\pi^e_{t+1})\right\}.$$

Solving for the equilibrium real output, we have

$$Y_t = \frac{\beta_1}{J_0 + \beta_1} \left[\lambda Y_{t-1} + \gamma \theta \left[\bar{m}_t + \varepsilon_t - E_{t-1}P_t + \frac{\alpha_2}{\beta_1}(X_t + u_t + \beta_1 \pi_{t+1}^e) \right] \right].$$
(10.35)

The above expression is sometimes call the reduced-form equation for real output. According to (10.35), changes in the money supply (in logs given by $m_t = \bar{m}_t + \varepsilon_t$) will affect real output to the extent that the impact of such changes on prices is not fully anticipated.

Note that with perfect foresight, we have $E_{t-1}P_t = P_t$. In this case, substituting (10.34'') into (10.35) for $E_{t-1}P_t$, we obtain

$$Y_t = \frac{\beta_1}{J_0 + \beta_1} \left(\lambda Y_{t-1} + J_0 \frac{\lambda}{\beta_1} Y_{t-1} \right) = \lambda Y_{t-1}.$$
(10.35'')

Thus we have the standard neoclassical result that output in the current period is independent of demand-side changes such as changes in expected inflation or the money supply.

One source of expectations: autoregressive expectations

As Shiller (1978) has noted:

> one of the most difficult problems which confronts builders of macroeco-
> nomic models is the need to model the mechanism by which the public forms
> its expectations of future economic variables. Many of the most important
> theoretical macroeconomic behavioral relations (e.g, the supply equation,
> investment, saving) depend critically on public expectations of future eco-
> nomic variables, yet we often do not even have any data on what these
> expectations are.

This and the next section suggest two approaches that have been taken to model expectations, in particular the expected price level that enters into the aggregate supply equations. These two approaches to expectation formation are the distributed lag (or adaptive) scheme and the rational expectations scheme.

To understand the ideas behind distributed lag schemes as the source of expectations, we start by noting that the price level p_t can be broken down into a combination of the price level for the previous period, p_{t-1}, multiplied by the ratio of the price level this period to last period:

$$p_t \equiv p_{t-1}(p_t/p_{t-1}).$$

Taking logs and recalling that $\ln(p_t/p_{t-1})$ is approximately equal to the rate of inflation π_t, we thus have

$$P_t \equiv \ln p_t = \ln p_{t-1} + \pi_t.$$

Taking expectations at time t assuming that at a minimum the price level for the prior period is known, we have

$$E_{t-1}P_t \equiv \ln p_{t-1} + E_{t-1}\pi_t. \tag{10.36}$$

Until the 1970s, the approach to modeling the source of the expected rate of inflation embedded in (10.36) was to assume individuals forecast the rate of inflation by looking at past inflation rates. A common quantitative representation of this hypothesis, originated by Fisher (1930), was to have individuals' expectation of the inflation rate behave like a weighted average or "distributed lag" of recent past inflation rates. That is,

$$E_{t-1}\pi_t = \sum_{i=1}^{q} \eta_i \pi_{t-i}, \tag{10.37}$$

where the η_i are fixed numbers. A typical idea behind this distributed lag approach to anticipated inflation was that individuals have "adaptive expectations," which meant that individuals adjusted or "adapted" their expectations of the rate of inflation in light of the actual forecast error made concerning the prior period's inflation rate. Specifically, adaptive expectations can be expressed as:

$$
\begin{aligned}
E_{t-1}\pi_t &= E_{t-2}\pi_{t-1} + \delta(\pi_{t-1} - E_{t-2}\pi_{t-1}) \\
&= \delta\pi_{t-1} + (1-\delta)E_{t-1}\pi_{t-1},
\end{aligned}
\tag{10.38}
$$

where $1 > \delta > 0$. Successive substitution allows us to rewrite (10.38) as:

$$E_{t-1}\pi_t = \delta\pi_{t-1} + (1-\delta)\delta\pi_{t-2} + (1-\delta)^2\delta\pi_{t-3} + \cdots$$

or

$$E_{t-1}\pi_t = \sum_{i=1}^{\infty} \delta(1-\delta)^{i-1}\pi_{t-i}. \tag{10.39}$$

As you can see, (10.39) is simply a specific form of equation (10.37) in which the η_i place declining weight on past inflation rates the more distant they are and $q = \infty$. Given declining weights, we can obtain a reasonable approximation of (10.39) even if we truncate the distributed lag on past inflation after q periods as long as q is reasonably large and/or δ is reasonably large.

Now let us place the above discussion not in terms of past rates of inflation but instead in terms of past price levels. Recalling the approximation

$$\pi_{t-i} \approx \ln p_{t-i} - \ln p_{t-i-1},$$

we can rewrite (10.37) in the form

$$E_{t-1}\pi_t = \sum_{i=1}^{q} \eta_i(\ln p_{t-i} - \ln p_{t-i-1}). \tag{10.40}$$

Writing this out, we have

$$E_{t-1}\pi_t = \eta_1(\ln p_{t-1} - \ln p_{t-2}) + \eta_2(\ln p_{t-2} - \ln p_{t-3})$$
$$+ \eta_3(\ln p_{t-3} - \ln p_{t-4}) + \cdots + \eta_q(\ln p_{t-q} - \ln p_{t-q-1}).$$

Thus, we may rewrite (10.40) as

$$E_{t-1}\pi_t = \eta_1 \ln p_{t-1} + (\eta_2 - \eta_1)\ln p_{t-2} + (\eta_3 - \eta_2)\ln p_{t-3} + \cdots$$
$$+ (\eta_q - \eta_{q-1})\ln p_{t-4} - \eta_q \ln p_{t-q-1}. \tag{10.41}$$

Combining (10.41) with equation (10.36), we obtain the following expression for the expectation formed at time t concerning the log of the price level:

$$E_{t-1}P_t = (1 + \eta_1)\ln p_{t-1} + (\eta_2 - \eta_1)\ln p_{t-2} + (\eta_3 - \eta_2)\ln p_{t-3} + \cdots$$
$$+ (\eta_q - \eta_{q-1})\ln p_{t-4} - \eta_q \ln p_{t-q-1}$$

or

$$E_{t-1}P_t = \sum_{i=1}^{q+1} v_i \ln p_{t-i}. \tag{10.42}$$

Equation (10.42) is what Sargent and Wallace (1975) refer to as "autoregressive expectations."

A second source of expectations: rational expectations

The papers by Lucas (1972, 1973) and Sargent and Wallace (1975) suggested that in macroeconomic model building a different approach to specifying the source of expectation is preferred. As Cukierman (1986) summarizes, this "rational expectations" approach to the modeling of inflationary expectations is

> based on the maintained hypothesis that individuals know the structure of the economy and of government's decision rule and that they use this structure in conjunction with the available information in order to form an optimal predictor of future inflation. . . . [this approach] requires a precise specification of the model of the economy as well as of the information sets of individuals. Empirical tests of this hypothesis are therefore joint tests of the validity of the expectational hypothesis as well as of the postulated structure of the economy and of the particular assumptions made about the information possessed by individuals.

A "structure of the economy" was derived based on the Lucas aggregate supply equation that included the assumption of market-clearing wages and prices. Suppose that individuals know this model and accept it as reflecting the structure of the economy. As we saw above, this model was solved to obtain (10.34), the reduced form for the equilibrium price level in period t. We assume that at time t individuals form their expectations $E_{t-1}P_t$ "rationally" in that

$$E_{t-1}P_t = E(P_t|\Omega_{t-1}), \tag{10.43}$$

indicating that $E_{t-1}P_t$ is the mathematical expectation of P_t conditional on the information set Ω_{t-1}, which is all information available at period $t-1$. As Sargent notes (1987a: 440):

> Lucas assumed that Ω_{t-1} included information on all *lagged* values of $\ln p_{it}$ and lagged values of real output in all markets. One could equally well conceive of less comprehensive definitions of Ω_{t-1}. For now, along with Lucas we suppose that Ω_{t-1} includes a comprehensive list of variables including lagged outputs and prices in all markets.

At the end of period $t-1$, individuals of course know $E_{t-1}P_t$, as well as Y_{t-1} and π_{t+1}^e. Thus, taking the expectation of (10.34) and subtracting it from P_t, we have:

$$P_t - E_{t-1}P_t = \frac{\beta_1}{J_0 + \beta_1}(\bar{m}_t + \varepsilon_t - E_{t-1}m_t) + \frac{\alpha_2}{J_0 + \beta_1}(X_t - E_{t-1}X_t + u_t). \tag{10.44}$$

In Sargent and Wallace (1975: 244), the deterministic part of the money supply, $\bar{m}_t$, is assumed to reflect a "linear feedback rule" of the form

$$\bar{m}_t = G\theta_t^*, \tag{10.45}$$

where "θ_t^* represents the set of current and past values of all of the endogenous and exogenous variables in the system as of the end of period $t-1$, and G is a vector of parameters conformable to θ_t^*." A simple example of a monetary feedback rule would be

$$\bar{m}_t = a_0 + a_1 Y_{t-1}, \tag{10.46}$$

where a_0 and a_1 are positive constants.

Let us assume that individuals' information set Ω_{t-1} includes not only the structure of the economy (as summarized by the above linear macroeconomic model) but also the money supply rule. In the particular example of (10.46), they know a_0, a_1, and Y_{t-1}, and thus $\bar{m}_t$. Then the assumption of rational expectations implies that $E_{t-1}m_t = \bar{m}_t$. Furthermore, since X_t represents the deterministic part of the vector of exogenous variables affecting output demand, we have that $E_{t-1}X_t = X_t$. Thus, (10.44) becomes

$$P_t - E_{t-1}P_t = \frac{1}{J_0 + \beta_1}(\beta_1\varepsilon_t + \alpha_2 u_t). \tag{10.47}$$

Substituting (10.47) into the aggregate supply equation, one obtains

$$Y_t = \gamma\theta\frac{1}{J_0 + \beta_1}(\beta_1\varepsilon_t + \alpha_2 u_t) + \lambda Y_{t-1}. \tag{10.48}$$

An important feature of (10.48) is that a deviation in output from its natural level, which is represented by the term Y_t different from zero given our assumption that the natural output level is normalized to equal one, is determined only by past deviations and "surprises" with respect to the money supply (the term ε_t) and output demand (the term u_t). The "deterministic" or predictable component of any money supply change has no real effects. Equation (10.48) should look familiar. Given $\lambda < 1$, it suggests that the times series for deviations of the logarithm of output from its natural rate is a stationary autoregressive process of order 1 or AR(1).

The above analysis is an example of a "linear rational expectations model." The result that "predictable" monetary policy has no real effects reflects the twin assumptions of the natural rate hypothesis and rational expectations. It should not be surprising that deterministic monetary policy has no effect, for the model is homogeneous of degree 0 in m_t, P_t, and $E_{t-1}P_t$. This is a critical characteristic of a "natural rate model."

Conclusion

The main focus of this chapter has been on the development of the Lucas supply function. The model is often discussed in the context of the "island" paradigm in which we specify the supply function for a particular sector in the economy. The role of forecasting errors is introduced and from that the Lucas aggregate supply function is constructed and the relationship of this function to the Phillips curve is discussed. A number of other issues were discussed involving variability in prices and the corresponding economic tradeoff, and then a complete model was introduced except for specifying the source of expectations. Two sources of expectations were then described, autoregressive expectations and rational expectations. The implications of expectations were then discussed in their historical context.

11 Policy

Introduction

This chapter extends the earlier discussions about the actions of the monetary authority and how these actions affect the macroeconomy. Perhaps the most interesting issue of monetary economics is addressed here, that is, the optimal role of monetary policy. The chapter highlights the differences in model results that depend on what type of expectations are assumed. Particular attention is given to the Sargent and Wallace "ineffectiveness propositions" and the Phillips curve. Other issues are then introduced, including the "rule versus discretion" debate, time inconsistency, and the role of credibility and enforcement.

Optimal monetary policy

In the 1970s, the articles by Sargent and Wallace (1975, 1976) and Lucas (1972, 1973) altered the view of how one should assess the impact of monetary policy on the economy, and by implication what is optimal monetary policy. The discussion starts with the premise that monetary policy should be conducted according to a rule or set of rules. As Sargent and Wallace (1976: 169) state:

> It is widely agreed that monetary policy should obey a rule, that is a schedule expressing the setting of the monetary authority's instrument (e.g., the money supply) as a function of all the information it has received up through the current moment. Such a rule has the happy characteristic that in any given set of circumstances, the optimal setting for policy is unique. If by remote chance, the same circumstances should prevail at two different dates, the appropriate settings for monetary policy would be identical.[1]

The Sargent–Wallace premise that monetary rules are preferred leads them to explore the form of the optimal rule. But as we will discover in going over the paper by Barro and Gordon (1983), there is a question of whether monetary rules can be enforced over time. If not, then what is typically left in these models is a "second best" solution involving the determination of optimal "discretionary" policy. Note that we use the term "second best," because enforceable rules tend to dominate discretion in these models.[2]

Accepting the premise that monetary policy can adopt *enforceable* rules still leaves open the specification of the optimal set of rules. The simplest rule, suggested by Friedman (1959), would increase the money supply at a constant rate each year, perhaps 3 percent.[3] More complex rules, known as "reactive rules," would specify *in advance* how the growth of the money supply will change based on new information on the state of the economy. One such rule suggested is that the growth in the monetary base, and thus the money supply, automatically adjust whenever the growth of nominal GNP deviates from its trend (McCallum 1985). Another reactive rule suggests that the government commit itself to holding the CPI to a preannounced target and adjust the monetary base, and thus the money supply, accordingly (Hall 1982).[4]

Below we begin our discussion of optimal monetary policy by reviewing the analysis of optimal, enforceable rules as suggested by the Sargent and Wallace (1975, 1976) papers and reviewed in Sargent (1987a: Chapter 17). This discussion is in the context of a natural rate model without rational expectations and then in the context of a model which assumes rational expectations.

Optimal monetary policy: exogenous expectations

As we saw previously, the reduced form for the log of the output in period t can be expressed as:

$$Y_t = H_0 \left[\lambda Y_{t-1} + \gamma \theta \left[-E_{t-1} P_t + \bar{m}_t + \varepsilon_t + \frac{\alpha_2}{\beta_1} (X_t + u_t + \beta_1 \pi_{t+1}^e) \right] \right],$$

$$(11.1)$$

where $H_0 = \beta_1/(J_0 + \beta_1)$ and $J_0 = \gamma \theta (\alpha_2 + \beta_1 \alpha_1)$. Recall that Y_t is the difference in period t between the logarithm of output and the logarithm of the natural level of output. Normalizing so that the natural level of output equals one, we can equivalently interpret Y_t in equation (11.1) as total output. As Sargent and Wallace (1976) state, "Y_t can be thought of as the unemployment rate or the deviation of real GNP from 'potential' GNP. This equation should be thought of as the reduced form of a simple econometric model."

Recall that the log of the money supply in period t, m_t, is the sum of a deterministic component $\bar{m}_t$ and the random component, ε_t, with variance σ_e^2.[5]

To understand the impact of monetary changes on real GNP, we must first consider how the expected log of the price level, $E_{t-1} P_t$, varies with changes in monetary policy. One approach, in the spirit of "autoregressive expectations," is to assume that the expected price level is independent of the current monetary policy. This essentially means viewing the expectation of the log of the price level $(E_{t-1} P_t)$ as exogenous.[6] Given this assumption, we may rewrite the reduced-form equation for output (11.1) as

$$Y_t = a_0 + a_1 Y_{t-1} + a_2 m_t + v_t, \tag{11.2}$$

where $v_t = H_0 \gamma \theta (\alpha_2 / \beta_1) u_t$ is a serially independent, normally distributed random variable with variance σ_v^2 and mean zero, m_t is the log of the money supply for period t, where $m_t = \bar{m}_t + \varepsilon_t$, Y_{t-1} is lagged output, and a_0, a_1, and a_2 are parameters.

Suppose that the monetary authority desires to set the money supply in order to minimize the fluctuation in the log of output around some desired level. Let us assume that the log of this desired level, denoted Y^*, is above the log of the natural level of output, Y_n.[7] Then the objective can be expressed as

$$\min E_{t-1}(Y_t - Y^*)^2.$$

We can break this expression into two terms, in that the objective can be equivalently expressed as

$$\min E_{t-1}(Y_t - E_{t-1}Y_t)^2 + (E_{t-1}Y_t - Y^*)^2. \tag{11.3}$$

The second way of expressing the objective allows us to see the objective as minimizing the sum of two terms: the variance of Y_t conditional on information up to the end of period $t-1$ and the "bias squared" around Y^*. The second term, the bias squared around Y^*, is the reason for an "activist" monetary policy. Equation (11.3) indicates that the optimal monetary policy entails:

1. minimizing the variance in the random component of the money supply. This follows since the first term in equation (11.3), the variance of Y_t, is given by $a_2^2 \sigma_e^2 + \sigma_v^2$.[8] If feasible, complete elimination of the random component to the money supply (i.e., a purely "deterministic" money supply) is optimal, such that $\varepsilon_t = 0$ for all t and thus $\sigma_e^2 = 0$.
2. setting $E_{t-1}Y_t = Y^*$, so as to make the second term in equation (11.3) equal to zero. From equation (11.2), this means a monetary policy such that

$$E_{t-1}(a_0 + a_1 \cdot Y_{t-1} + a_2 \cdot m_t + v_t) = Y^*.$$

Noting that $E_{t-1}Y_t = 0$ and that $E_{t-1}m_t = \bar{m}_t$, we see that this deterministic part of the optimal monetary policy is defined by the equation

$$a_0 + a_1 Y_{t-1} + a_2 \bar{m}_t = Y^*,$$

which can be solved for the optimal deterministic monetary policy rule:

$$\bar{m}_t = g_0 - g_1 Y_{t-1} \tag{11.4}$$

where $g_0 = (Y^* - a_0)/a_2$ and $g_1 = a_1/a_2$.

An equivalent expression for the optimal monetary rule (11.4) is derived in Sargent (1987a: Chapter 17) under the presumption of exogenous expectations. In particular, Sargent uses equation (11.2) to substitute out for Y_{t-1} in (11.4), so that the optimal (deterministic) monetary rule (11.4) becomes

$$\bar{m}_t = g_0 - g_1[a_0 + a_1 Y_{t-2} + a_2 m_{t-1} + v_{t-1}]. \tag{11.5}$$

Now substituting into (11.5) the expression for Y_{t-2} suggested by equation (11.2), we have

$$\bar{m}_t = g_0 - g_1[a_0 + a_2 m_{t-1} + v_{t-1}] - g_1 a_1[a_0 + a_1 Y_{t-3} + a_2 m_{t-2} + v_{t-2}]. \tag{11.6}$$

Continuing to successively substitute for Y_{t-i}, $i = 3, 4, \ldots$, we have Sargent's equivalent expression for the optimal (deterministic) policy rule as given by[9]

$$\bar{m}_t = g_0 - g_1 a_0 - \left(g_1 a_2 \sum_{i-1}^{\infty} a_1^{i-1} m_{t-i} \right) - \left(g_1 \sum_{i=1}^{\infty} a_1^{i-1} + v_{t-i} \right). \tag{11.7}$$

Following the above optimal monetary policy (i.e., reducing any random component to the money supply to its minimum level and establishing the rule for the deterministic component of the money supply as specified by (11.4) or (11.7)), we have by construction that

$$E_{t-1} Y_t = Y^* \quad \text{and} \quad Y_t = Y^* + a_2 \varepsilon_t + v_t,$$

where $v_t = H_0 \gamma \theta (\alpha_2 / \beta_1) u_t$ and the variance of the random component of the money supply, ε_t, is set at its lowest feasible level. Thus optimal monetary policy in essence sets output each period equal to Y^* plus irreducible noise. As Sargent and Wallace (1976: 171) note:

> the application of the rule eliminates all serial correlation in output since this is the way to minimize the variance in output. .... The basic idea is that where the effects of shocks to a goal variable (like GNP) display a stable pattern of persistence (serial correlation), and hence are predictable, the authority can improve the behavior of the goal variable by inducing offsetting movements in its instruments.

Note that without the lag term for output, g_1 in (11.4) equals zero.

Adaptive expectations and the accelerationist result

The well-known "accelerationist outcome" concerning the path of inflation is implied by the above analysis if expectations are adaptive and if the aim of monetary policy is to keep output above its natural level. To see this, let us go back to the aggregate supply equation that underlies the reduced form for output. To simplify, let us abstract from the stochastic elements in demand ε_t and u_t (as well as any supply-side disturbances) and also from adjustment costs (i.e., omit the lagged output term). Then the aggregate supply equation,

$$Y_t = \gamma\theta[\pi_t - E_{t-1}\pi_t] \tag{11.8}$$

reflects the actual path that output will take.[10]

To derive the accelerationist result, assume that $Y^* > Y_n$. By normalization $Y_n = 0$, so that to have $E_{t-1}Y_t = Y^* > Y_n$, we must have $E_{t-1}Y_t > 0$. Equation (11.8) suggests that to achieve an expected level of output greater than its natural level, the government must pursue a monetary policy that results in the actual rate of inflation typically being above that expected. In particular, the desire to keep output above its natural level means that monetary policy in period t results in the actual inflation rate π_t such that

$$\pi_t - E_{t-1}\pi_t = Y^*/\gamma\theta > 0.$$

If expectations are adaptive, then we have that

$$E_{t-1}\pi_t - E_{t-2}\pi_{t-1} = \delta(\pi_{t-1} - E_{t-2}\pi_{t-1}).$$

The assumption of adaptive expectations, coupled with $Y^* > Y_n = 0$, thus implies that

$$E_t\pi_{t+1} = E_{t-1}\pi_t + \delta(\pi_t - E_{t-1}\pi_t) = E_{t-1}\pi_t + \delta Y^*/\gamma\theta.$$

In words, the fact that individuals underestimate inflation this period (by the amount $Y^*/\gamma\theta$) leads them to adjust ("adapt") their expectations of inflation upward (by the amount $\delta Y^*/\gamma\theta$). The result is that to keep expected output at the level $Y^* > Y_n$ next period means an increase in the inflation rate by the amount $\delta Y^*/\gamma\theta$ each period. As Blanchard and Fischer (1989: 572) note:

> this is the famous *accelerationist* result derived by Friedman (1968) and Phelps (1968), using their Phillips curve together with the adaptive expectations assumption. The explanation is simple: if the government is trying to keep output above the natural rate, it has to produce inflation at a higher rate than expected each period. Since the expected inflation is a weighted average of past inflation rates, the actual rate must be increasing.

Now let us assume instead that $Y^* = 0$. To provide a role for an activist monetary policy, let us reintroduce the lagged output term λY_{t-1} into the right-hand side of (11.8). Thus, monetary policy can eliminate the effect of past deviations in output from the natural rate on current output. In other words, a policy aimed at setting $E_{t-1}Y_t = Y^*$ would imply altering inflation relative to expected *only* when lagged output deviated from the natural level. Rather than the prior result of an ever-increasing inflation with $Y^* > Y_n$, with $Y^* = Y_n$ we have that inflation simply wanders.[11] For instance, if logged lagged output Y_{t-1} fell below the log of the natural level of output, $Y_n = 0$, then the difference, Y_{t-1}, would be negative. Other things being equal, this would imply a lower output in the current period. To counteract this, the government would pursue a monetary policy that results in the actual rate of inflation being above that expected.

The above discussion helps us understand the comment of Hall (1976) that

> the benefits of inflation derive from the use of expansionary power to trick economic agents into behaving in socially preferable ways even though their behavior is not in their own interests ... The gap between actual and expected inflation measures the extent of the trickery ... the optimal policy is not nearly as expansionary when expectations adjust rapidly, and most of the effect of an inflationary policy is dissipated in costly anticipated inflation.

The above extract raises the following question: Can the monetary authorities systematically trick the public in order to exploit the link between inflation and output? For Sargent and Wallace and others, the answer is no, due to the existence of rational expectations.

Rational expectations and the Sargent–Wallace ineffectiveness proposition

As Sargent (1987a) notes, a critical aspect of the simple example of an optimal monetary rule as given by (11.4) (or equivalently (11.7)) "is the implicit assumption that agent's decision rules ... remain unchanged in the face of alternative stochastic processes for the control variable that different feedback rules imply." What Sargent means in this context is that the optimal monetary rule has been derived under the presumption that private agents do not take this rule into account in forming their expectation of the price level. Under this assumption, one could estimate the parameters of the reduced-form equation output (a_0, a_1, and a_2 in (11.2)) independently of the feedback rule (11.4).

However, Sargent and Wallace (1976) criticize this view. In particular, they argue that "in the reduced forms are embedded the responses of expectations to the way policy is formed. Changes in the way policy is made then ought not to leave the parameters of estimated reduced forms unchanged."[12] In other words, rational individuals would clearly seek out and use information on how monetary authorities act as well as on the structure of the economy in forming expectations of prices.

Let us now consider the following version of the reduced-form equation for output (11.2) that explicitly includes the potential role of expected monetary policy when individuals form expectations on prices:[13]

$$Y_t = a_0 + a_1 Y_{t-1} + a_2(m_t - E_{t-1}) + v_t. \tag{11.9}$$

For a given anticipated log of the money supply, $E_{t-1} m_t$, we have as before the optimal (deterministic) monetary rule of the form

$$\bar{m}_t = g_0 - g_1 Y_{t-1}, \tag{11.10}$$

so that

$$m_t = g_0 - g_1 Y_{t-1} + \varepsilon_t, \tag{11.11}$$

where ε_t is the irreducible random element in the money supply determination process. Now assume that the public knows the monetary authorities' feedback rule. Then our assumption of rational expectation (i.e., individuals use all available information in forming expectations) implies that

$$E_{t-1}(m_t) = g_0 - g_1 Y_{t-1}. \tag{11.12}$$

Combining (11.9), (11.11), and (11.12), the reduced form for output is now given by

$$Y_t = a_0 + a_1 Y_{t-1} + a_2 \varepsilon_t + v_t, \tag{11.13}$$

so that the biased squared term in the objective of the monetary authorities, $(E_{t-1} Y_t - Y^*)^2$, equals $(a_0 + a_1 Y_{t-1} - Y^*)^2$.

As is clear from (11.13), there is no role for systematic monetary policy to affect real output. As Sargent (1987a: 459) notes, "the bias squared is *independent* of the parameters of the money supply rule." The optimal policy is then to make monetary policy deterministic if feasible, for then the variance of output (given by $a_2^2 \sigma_e^2 + \sigma_v^2$) is minimized by setting $\sigma_e^2 = 0$. Until we add an inflation objective, any deterministic rule will be equally as good, for none will have any impact on output. This is once again an example of the neutrality of money.

As Sargent (1987a: 458) notes, "policy rules should be deterministic and involve no surprises." He goes on to argue that we

have therefore established the following stochastic neutrality theorem that characterizes our model: one deterministic feedback rule on the basis of the information set Ω_{t-1}, which is common to the public and to the authority, is as good as any other deterministic feedback rule. .... Via deterministic feedback rules, the monetary authority is powerless to combat the business cycle (the serial correlation in Y_t).

Naturally, if one abandons rational expectations or the natural rate hypothesis, then this "stochastic neutrality" result need not hold.

The Sargent–Wallace ineffectiveness proposition in the context of the Phillips curve

The above finding of the "neutrality of money" in the context of a stochastic, linear, natural rate model with rational expectations is viewed by Sargent (1987a: 459) as

> the antithesis of our earlier result rationalizing the activist Keynesian policy rules. . . . The reader is invited to verify that the truth of the neutrality theorem is not dependent on the particular information set assumed. It will continue to hold for any specification of Ω_{t-1} so long as the public and the authority share the same information set.

He concludes:

> The preceding results provide a [weak] defense for following rules without feedback. Simple x-percent growth rules do as well as any deterministic feedback rule, and dominate rules with a stochastic component.

Below we recast the Sargent–Wallace ineffectiveness proposition in terms of the expectational Phillips curve. This makes the discussion more in line with the next section's review of some implications of non-enforceable monetary rules. In addition, we add to the government goal's an inflation objective. In particular, we modify our analysis in the following four ways:

1   we alter the objective to be in terms of unemployment rather than output;
2   we expand our objective function to include inflation;
3   we link inflation to unemployment via a modified Lucas supply equation;
4   we incorporate rational expectations.

Our first task is to convert the objective of the government into unemployment terms. Before we assumed that the government simply sought to minimize the fluctuations in output about a particular level. In particular, if we let Z_t denote the cost incurred in period t, we assumed the objective was to:

$$\min E_{t-1} Z_t, \qquad \text{where } Z_t \equiv (Y_t - Y^*)^2. \tag{11.14}$$

We have previously assumed that the deviation of unemployment from its natural rate is linearly related to the deviation of the log of output from the log of its natural level. In particular, we assumed

$$-\ell(U_t - U_n) = Y_t,$$

given the normalization of the natural level of output such that $Y_n \equiv \ln y_n = 0$. Substituting the above into (11.14), the problem facing the government policy-maker becomes

$$\min E_{t-1}Z_t, \quad \text{where } Z_t = a(U_t - kU_n)^2, \quad a = \ell^2 > 0,$$
$$k = 1 - Y^*\ell/U_n. \tag{11.15}$$

Note in (11.15) that we assume $k < 1$, which is equivalent to assuming that the log of optimal level of output, Y^*, is greater than the log of the natural level of output, which by normalization has been set equal to zero. As Blanchard and Fischer (1989: 596–597) suggest:

> The most plausible justification [for $k < 1$] is the presence of distortions or imperfections that causes the natural rate of unemployment to be too high. This justification allows the loss function to be consistent with the single-period utility function of private agents. Another is that the government's objective function as shaped by the electoral process leads the government to seek to raise output above the natural level.

Having converted the objective function into unemployment terms, the next step is to expand the objective function to include an inflation goal. In particular, let us assume that the cost in period t includes a term reflecting differences between the actual inflation rate, π_t, and an optimal rate of inflation, π^*. Assuming a simple quadratic form, we have[14]

$$Z_t = a(U_t - kU_n)^2 + b(\pi_t - \pi^*)^2. \tag{11.16}$$

The problem of the government policy-maker is then:

$$\min E_{t-1}Z_t, \quad \text{where } Z_t \equiv a(U_t - kU_n)^2 + b(\pi_t - \pi^*)^2.$$

As before, we can decompose this objective to obtain the following equivalent expression for the object of the government policy-maker:

$$\min a[E_{t-1}(U_t - kU_n)^2 + (E_{t-1}U_t - kU_n)^2]$$
$$+ b[E_{t-1}(\pi_t - \pi^*)^2 + (E_t\pi_t - \pi^*)^2]. \tag{11.17}$$

Our third task is to link inflation to unemployment. Recall that if we ignore the lagged term with respect to output in the Lucas supply equation, assume unemployment is linearly related to real output, and approximate inflation by the log of the ratio of the price level this period to the price level last period, then we can manipulate the Lucas supply equation to obtain the expression

$$U_t = U_n - \alpha(\pi_t - E_{t-1}\pi_t), \tag{11.18}$$

where $\alpha = (\gamma\theta/\ell) > 0.$[15] Substituting (11.18) into (11.16), the government's objective becomes:

$$\min E_{t-1}\{a(1-k)U_n - \alpha(\pi_t - E_{t-1}\pi_t)^2 + b \cdot (\pi_t - \pi^*)^2\}.$$

Our fourth and final task is to introduce rational expectations. As we saw earlier, we obtain the reduced form for the deviation of the price level from that expected in period t,

$$P_t - E_{t-1}P_t = \frac{1}{J_0 + \beta_0}(\beta_1\varepsilon_t + \alpha_2 u_t), \tag{11.19}$$

if (a) the government follows a particular rule in determining monetary policy, (b) that rule is known to the public, and (c) there exist rational expectations.

An algebraic manipulation – simultaneously subtracting and adding the log of the price level for period $t-1$ to the left-hand side of equation (11.19) – brings us closer to having an expression that may be interpreted in terms of inflation:

$$\ln(p_t/p_{t-1}) - E_{t-1}(\ln(p_t/p_{t-1}) = \frac{1}{J_0 + \beta_1}(\beta_1\varepsilon_t + \alpha_2 u_t). \tag{11.20}$$

Using the log of the price ratio as an approximation for inflation, we thus can approximate (11.20) as

$$\pi_t - E_{t-1}\pi_t = \frac{1}{J_0 + \beta_1}(\beta_1\varepsilon_t + \alpha_2 u_t). \tag{11.21}$$

Substituting the above, which reflects the rational expectations approach to modeling expectations, into the new government objective, we have:

$$\min E_{t-1}\left\{a\left[(1-k)U_n - \frac{\alpha}{J_0 + \beta_1}(\beta_1\varepsilon_t + \alpha_2 u_t)\right]^2 + b(\pi_t - \pi^*)^2\right\}$$

or

$$\min a[(1-k)U_n]^2 + \left(\frac{\alpha}{J_0 + \beta_1}\right)^2 (\beta_1^2\sigma_e^2 + \alpha_2^2\sigma_u^2)$$
$$+ E_{t-1}\{b(\pi_t - \pi^*)^2\}, \tag{11.22}$$

since $E_{t-1}\varepsilon_t = E_{t-1}u_t = E_{t-1}\varepsilon_t u_t = 0$.

It is clear from (11.22) that with rational expectations, monetary policy can play no role in helping the government meet its objective concerning unemployment. In other words, in the context of the Lucas model the assumption of rational expectations means that the expected loss from deviations in unemployment from its desired level, and thus production from its desired level, is independent of the deterministic monetary rule. As a consequence, the minimization problem as given by the first half of equation (11.17) becomes simply one of specifying any deterministic monetary policy rule and eliminating any random changes in the money supply (i.e., setting $\sigma_e^2 = 0$ if feasible.)

But the objective of the government now also includes an objective concerning the rate of inflation, so we need an expression for the equilibrium rate of change in prices, π_t, that incorporates rational expectations. To do so, we start with the reduced form for the log of the price level obtained previously, which is given by

$$P_t = \frac{1}{J_0 + \beta_1} \left[\beta_1 \bar{m}_t + \varepsilon_t + \alpha_2 (X_t + u_t + \beta_1 \pi_{t+1}^e) + J_0 \left(E_{t-1} P_t - \frac{\lambda Y_{t-1}}{\gamma \theta} \right) \right].$$
(11.23)

Taking the difference between the reduced form for the log of the price level for period t and for period $t-1$, we can obtain an expression for π_t, the rate of inflation between period t and $t-1$, of the form

$$\pi_t = \frac{1}{J_0 + \beta_1} [\beta_1 \bar{m}_t + \alpha_2 (X_t - X_{t-1} + u_t - u_{t-1}) + \alpha_2 \beta_1 (\pi_{t+1}^e - \pi_t^w)$$
$$+ J_0 (E_{t-1} P_t - E_{t-2} P_{t-1}) - \frac{J_0 \lambda}{\gamma \theta} (Y_{t-1} - Y_{t-2})],$$
(11.24)

where π_{mt} approximates the rate of change in the money supply (i.e., $\pi_{mt} = m_t - m_{t-1} = \ln(M_t/M_{t-1})$). Assuming rational expectations, we have from equation (11.19) that

$$E_{t-1} P_t = P_t - \frac{1}{J_0 + \beta_1} (\beta_1 \varepsilon_t + \alpha_2 u_t)$$

and, similarly,

$$E_{t-2} P_{t-1} = P_{t-1} - \frac{1}{J_0 + \beta_1} (\beta_1 \varepsilon_{t-1} + \alpha_2 u_{t-1}),$$

so that

$$E_{t-1} P_t - E_{t-2} P_{t-1} = \pi_t + \frac{1}{J_0 + \beta_1} [\beta_1 (\varepsilon_{t-1} - \varepsilon_t) + \alpha_2 (u_{t-1} - u_t)].$$
(11.25)

Substituting this expression into equation (11.24), one obtains

$$\pi_t \frac{\beta_1}{J_0 + \beta_1} = \frac{1}{J_0 + \beta_1} [\beta_1 \pi_{mt} + \alpha_2 (X_t - X_{t-1} + u_t - u_{t-1})$$
$$+ \alpha_2 \beta_1 \cdot (\pi_{t+1}^e - \pi_t^e) - \frac{J_0 \lambda}{\gamma \theta} (Y_{t-1} - Y_{t-2})],$$
(11.26)

where we use the fact that $1 - J_0/(J_0 + \beta_1) = \beta_1/(J_0 + \beta_1)$. Solving for π_t, we have

$$\pi_t = \pi_{mt} + \frac{\alpha_2}{\beta_1}(X_t - X_{t-1} + u_t - u_{t-1})$$

$$+ \alpha_2(\pi_{t+1}^e - \pi_t^e) - \frac{J_0\lambda}{\gamma\theta}(Y_{t-1} - Y_{t-2}) \tag{11.27}$$

which, given $\pi_{mt} = m_t - m_{t-1} = \bar{m}_t + \varepsilon_t - (\bar{m}_{t-1} + \varepsilon_{t-1})$, can be rearranged to obtain:

$$\pi_t = \bar{\pi}_{mt} + \varepsilon_t - \varepsilon_{t-1} + \frac{\alpha_2}{\beta_1}(X_t - X_{t-1} + u_t - u_{t-1}) + \alpha_2(\pi_{t+1}^e - \pi_t^e)$$

$$- \frac{J_0\lambda}{\beta_1\gamma\theta}(Y_{t-1} - Y_{t-2}), \tag{11.28}$$

where $\bar{\pi}_{mt} = \bar{m}_t - \bar{m}_{t-1}$.

If we assume no change in exogenous (nonrandom) demand factors this period compared to the last period (i.e., $X_t = X_{t-1}$), no change in the expected future inflation between last period and this period (i.e., $\pi_{t+1}^e = \pi_t^e$), and ignore adjustment costs (i.e., $\lambda = 0$), we can simplify equation (11.28) to obtain

$$\pi_t = \bar{\pi}_{mt} + \varepsilon_t - \varepsilon_{t-1} + \frac{\alpha_2}{\beta_1}(u_t - u_{t-1}). \tag{11.29}$$

The three assumptions we made to derive equation (11.29) from equation (11.28) largely limit any differences between period t and $t - 1$ to differences in the size of the money supply. In fact, the two periods differ only by the deterministic component of the money supply and by random factors, where these random factors – the term $u_t - u_{t-1}$ with respect to output demand and the term $\varepsilon_t - \varepsilon_{t-1}$ with respect to the irreducible random component of the money supply – have mean zero. In other words, all potential changes in aggregate demand or production except money supply changes that would lead to different *expected* price levels in the two periods have been removed.

Substituting equation (11.29) into (11.22), we thus obtain the following complete government objective function under rational expectations:

$$\min a \left[[(1-k)U_n]^2 + \left(\frac{\alpha}{J_0 + \beta_1}\right)^2 (\beta_1^2\sigma_e^2 + \alpha_2^2\sigma_u^2) \right.$$

$$\left. + E_{t-1}\{b[\bar{\pi}_{mt} + \varepsilon_t - \varepsilon_{t-1} + \frac{\alpha_2}{\beta_1}(u_t - u_{t-1}) - \pi^*]^2\} \right],$$

from which we see that constant monetary growth will not achieve a constant rate of inflation unless we neglect the lagged disturbance terms.[16] To obtain the result of an optimal monetary rule in the form of a constant rate of growth in the money supply, we must further simplify and neglect the lagged disturbance terms. If we for the moment ignore the lagged stochastic terms ε_{t-1} and u_{t-1}, we have the objective:

$$\min a\left[[(1-k)U_n]^2 + \left(\frac{\alpha}{J_0 + \beta_1}\right)^2 (\beta_1^2 \sigma_e^2 + \alpha_2^2 \sigma_u^2)\right.$$
$$\left. + b(\bar{\pi}_{mt} - \pi^*)^2 + \sigma_e^2 + \left(\frac{\alpha_2}{\beta_1}\right)^2 \sigma_u^2\right].$$

As before, to minimize the loss requires that one reduces the random variation in the money supply to zero (if feasible), so that $\sigma_e^2 = 0$. That is, the optimal monetary rule is "deterministic." Further, given an inflation objective and no reason other than monetary policy for prices to change, the obvious optimal rule is simply to set the determinant rate of change in the money supply equal to the desired rate of inflation. That is, the optimal policy is

$$\bar{\pi}_{mt} = \pi^*.$$

Note that this rule assumes no shocks to the economy. If there were a steady rate of increase in output (and thus the real demand for output), then that would raise the optimal constant rate of change in the money supply to achieve a given rate of change in prices. Thus Friedman's "3 percent" rule for monetary growth presumed a 3 percent growth in real output so as to be consistent with a zero rate of inflation.

Rules versus discretion, monetary policy, and time inconsistency

The Sargent–Wallace ineffectiveness proposition has been used by many to support arguments for the government not adopting activist policy rules to offset fluctuations – particularly downturns – in an economy's real output reflecting demand-side disturbances. The reason, as we have seen, is that such policies have no real effects once one assumes rational expectations, although the attempt can lead to higher inflation.

Yet as Barro and Gordon (1983) point out:

> empirical studies ... indicate the presence of countercyclical monetary policy at least for the post-World War II United States – rises in the unemployment rate appear to generate subsequent expansions in monetary growth. Within the natural rate framework, it is difficult to reconcile this countercyclical behavior with rationality of the policymaker.

As Barro and Gordon go on to say, "a principal object of our analysis is to achieve this reconciliation." That is, rather than saying what policy rules government should follow, Barro and Gordon want to explain why government acts the way it does – thus the term "positive theory" in the title of their paper.

The Barro–Gordon approach combines a number of topics that we have considered before. First, they utilize a natural rate model like the Lucas model. Second, they assume rational expectations. And third, and most interestingly, they provide us with a nice example of the phenomenon of "time inconsistency" in the context of optimal monetary policy when there exists the potential Phillips curve tradeoff.

Contrasting the Barro–Gordon and Sargent–Wallace policy environments

In the Sargent–Wallace view of the optimal monetary policy choice, it is assumed that the policy-maker makes a once-and-for-all decision with respect to the particular monetary policy rule (reactive or not). Under certain assumptions, as we have seen, this leads to the natural conclusion that optimal monetary policy entails the simple rule of a constant rate of growth in the money supply so that the resulting average rate of inflation equals the desired level. If the desired level were zero, then inflation would be set equal to zero through appropriate monetary policy.

Barro and Gordon (1983: 598) have questioned this result on the basis that "there may be no mechanism in place to constrain the policymaker to stick to the rule as time evolves." The result is that the policy-maker decides each period the optimal monetary policy to follow. In other words, "though the objective function and decision rules of private agents are identical," Barro and Gordon obtain different results from Sargent and Wallace because "the problems differ in the opportunity sets of the policymaker." Below we illustrate the exact nature of this difference by first showing how Barro and Gordon's setup provides an example of the "time inconsistency problem" not present in the Sargent and Wallace problem and then derive the equilibrium for an economy characterized by the policy-makers who are allowed each period to pick a potentially new optimal monetary policy.

Time inconsistency: an example in the context of optimal monetary policy

In an important paper on the "time inconsistency" problem of optimal policy, Kydland and Prescott (1977) point out situations in which the optimal policies decided at time t would be changed at time $t + 1$.[17] In the context of monetary policy, as Kydland and Prescott note

> the reason that such policies are suboptimal is not due to myopia. The effect of (monetary policy) upon the entire future is taken into consideration. Rather, the suboptimality arises because there is no mechanism to induce future policy-makers to take into consideration the effect of their policy, via the expectations mechanism, upon current decisions of agents.

Let us see what this means by way of a concrete example.

A simple example of "time inconsistency" following Kydland and Prescott is constructed below. To simplify the discussion somewhat, for the moment we ignore uncertainty and restrict our attention to two periods. In this setting, the government, through monetary policy, can determine each period the actual inflation rate, rather than the expected rate of inflation. For periods 0 and 1, the choice variables facing the monetary policy-maker are thus π_0, the actual inflation in period 0, and π_1, the actual inflation in period 1. The inflation choice impacts the unemployment rate in that U_0 and U_1, the unemployment rates in periods 0 and 1, are given by the Phillips curve formulation (11.18)

$$U_0 = U_n - \alpha(\pi_0 - E_{-1}\pi_0),$$
$$U_1 = U_n - \alpha(\pi_1 - E_0\pi_1),$$

where the state variables $E_{-1}\pi_0$ and $E_0\pi_1$ denote the expected rate of inflation in periods 0 and 1, respectively. In periods 0 and 1, the objective for periods 0 and 1 is to minimize the simple quadratic forms

$$Z_0 = a(U_0 - kU_n)^2 + b(\pi_0 - \pi^*)^2,$$
$$Z_1 = a(U_1 - kU_n)^2 + b(\pi_1 - \pi^*)^2,$$

where the constants a and b are positive. It is assumed that $k < 1$, to capture the idea that distortions exist in the economy that an activist policy can address.[18] Substituting in the "Phillips curve" relations, in period 0 the present value of the objective function is

$$Z = Z_0 + \beta \cdot Z_1 = a[(1-k)U_n - \alpha(\pi_0 - E_{-1}\pi_0)]^2 + b[\pi_0 - \pi^*]^2$$
$$+ \beta a[(1-k)U_n - \alpha(\pi_1 - E_0\pi_1)]^2 + \beta b[\pi_1 - \pi^*]^2,$$

where β is the constant discount factor.

Let us presume that the expectations of inflation, the "state" variables, are exogenous and equal to the desired level each period (i.e., $E_{-1}\pi_0 = E_0\pi_1 = \pi^*$). In period 0, the optimal inflation rates for periods 0 and 1 (as determined by monetary policy) are then

$$\partial Z/\partial \pi_0 = -2a\alpha q_0 + 2b(\pi_0 - \pi^*) = 0,$$
$$\partial Z/\partial \pi_1 = \beta[-2a\alpha q_1 + 2b(\pi_1 - \pi^*)] = 0,$$

where $q_i = (1-k)U_n - \alpha(\pi_i - \pi^*)$, $i = 0, 1, \ldots$. In period 1, the objective is

$$Z_1 = a[(1-k)U_n - \alpha(\pi_1 - E_0\pi_1)]^2 + b[\pi_0 - \pi^*]^2$$

and the optimal solution given π_0 and $E_0\pi_1 = \pi^*$ is thus

$$\partial Z_1/\partial \pi_1 = -2a\alpha q_1 + 2b(\pi_1 - \pi^*) = 0.$$

Comparing this first-order condition to $\partial Z_0/\partial \pi_1$, it is clear that in the case of exogenous expectations, the optimal solution is time-consistent. Further, it implies a rate of inflation greater than the expected (optimal) rate of π^* each period to achieve an unemployment rate below the natural. This follows given that one of the objectives is to approach a level of unemployment equal to kU_n with $k < 1$.

What happens, however, if individuals' expectations of inflation for period 1 is a forecast that correctly anticipates the optimal future policy decision? That is, we have "rational expectations" such that in a deterministic world

$$E_0\pi_1 = h(\Omega_0) = \pi_1,$$

where Ω_0 is the information set at the end of period zero.

What the optimal inflation policy is now depends on whether policy-makers can "commit" to future policy actions. Let us start by assuming they can place constraints on future policy. We know that in period 0, the optimal solution for π_1 is then given by

$$\frac{\beta\partial Z_1}{\partial \pi_1} + \frac{\partial Z}{\partial E_0\pi_1}\frac{dh(\cdot)}{d\pi_1} = \beta[2b(\pi_1 - \pi^*)] = 0.$$

Since $dh(\cdot)/\partial \pi_1 = 1$, the optimal planned (at time 0) rate of inflation for period 1 is equal to the desired level π^*. This is the Sargent–Wallace ineffectiveness proposition.

However, once period 1 occurs, $E_0\pi_1$ is set (let us assume it equals π^*). If the policy-maker was not then constrained by the prior specification of a monetary policy to achieve a rate of inflation equal to π^*, they would choose π_1 such that

$$\partial Z_1/\partial \pi_1 = -2a\alpha q_1 + 2b(\pi_1 - \pi^*) = 0,$$

which implies $\pi_1 > \pi^*$. The "time inconsistency" arises, as you can see, because $\partial h(\cdot)/\partial \pi_1 \neq 0$. As Barro and Gordon state, "the term 'time inconsistency' refers to the policymaker's incentives to deviate from the rule when private agents expect it to be followed."

Equilibrium when monetary rules are not enforceable

As Barro and Gordon note, in the time inconsistency problem, "constraints on future policy actions are infeasible, by assumption." In contrast, in the Sargent–Wallace view,

> rules are enforceable, so that the policymaker can commit the course of future policy (and thus of expectations). In the former case, the time-inconsistent solution is not an equilibrium, given the problem facing the policymaker. In the latter case, the incentives to deviate from the rule are irrelevant, since commitments are assumed to be binding.
>
> (Barro and Gordon 1983: 599)

As the above extract suggests, in the "time inconsistency case" we have not yet characterized a rational expectations' equilibrium since in our example individuals' expectations of inflation for period 1 were incorrect. According to Barro and Gordon, there are three features of an equilibrium. The first is "a decision rule for private agents, which determines their actions as a function of their current information." These actions of private agents based on current information are summarized by the Phillips curve:

$$U_t = U_n + \zeta_t - \alpha \cdot (\pi_t - E_{t-1}\pi_t), \tag{11.30}$$

where ζ_t, a random variable with zero mean and variance σ_z^2, has been added to denote a real shock that affects the natural unemployment rate for the current period only.[19]

The second feature of an equilibrium is "a policy rule, which specifies the behavior of policy instruments as a function of the policymaker's current information set." This policy rule is given by the choice of inflation rates $\pi_{t+i}, i = 0, 1, 2, \ldots$, by the monetary authorities with the following objective:

$$\min E_t \left[\sum_{i=0}^{\infty} \beta^i Z_{t+i} | I_t \right]$$

where $Z_{t+i} \equiv a(U_{t+i} - kU_n)^2 + b(\pi_{t+i} - \pi^*)^2$, $a > 0$, $b > 0$, and $0 \le k \le 1$. The term I_t denotes the initial state of information and $1 > \beta > 0$ is the constant discount factor ($\beta = 1/(1+r_{real})$, where r_{real} is the exogenous real rate of interest). For simplicity we will assume that the optimal level of inflation is zero, so that $\pi^* = 0$.

The third feature is an expectations function, which determines the expectations of private agents as a function of their current information. Assuming that "the public understands the nature of the policymaker's optimization problem in each period," then $E_{t-1}\pi_t = \hat{\pi}_t$ where $\hat{\pi}_t$ is the optimal choice of inflation by the policy-maker for period t.

Combining the information contained in our discussion of the first and second features of equilibrium, the policy-maker's optimal choice of π_t minimizes

$$E_t Z_t = E_t[a(U_t - kU_n)^2 + b(\pi_t)^2]$$
$$= E_t[a((1-k)U_n - \alpha(\pi_t - E_{t-1}\pi_t))^2 + b(\pi_t)^2].$$

Given that $E\xi_t = 0$, the expression to be minimized by the policy-maker can be written as:

$$E_t Z_t = [a((1-k)U_n - \alpha(\pi_t - E_{t-1}\pi_t))^2 + b(\pi_t)^2].$$

A critical point to note is that each period the policy-maker inherits $E_{t-1}\pi_t$, and takes that expected rate of inflation as given in the above optimal choice of π_t.

The first-order condition for period t is thus

$$\partial E_t Z_t / \partial \pi_t = 2a((1 - k)U_n - \alpha(\pi_t - E_{t-1}\pi_t))(-\alpha) + 2b(\pi_t) = 0,$$

which can be simplified and rearranged to obtain the following expression for the optimal inflation rate:

$$\hat{\pi}_t = \frac{a\alpha}{b}[(1 - k)U_n - \alpha(\hat{\pi}_t - E_{t-1}\pi_t)]. \tag{11.31}$$

From the third feature of equilibrium, we know that the public realizes the problem faced by the policy-maker in terms of choosing the optimal rate of inflation for period t as defined by (11.31), and thus $E_{t-1}\pi_t = \hat{\pi}_t$, so that the second term drops out and we have

$$\hat{\pi}_t = \frac{a\alpha}{b}(1 - k)U_n = E_{t-1}\pi_t > \pi^* = 0, \tag{11.32}$$

as long as $k < 1$. We thus have that expectations are rational and individuals optimize subject to these expectations. Since $E_{t-1}\pi_t = \hat{\pi}_t$, we have that $E_t U_t = U_n$. Thus, "the equilibrium solution delivers the same unemployment rate and a higher rate of inflation at each date" than is the case in the Sargent–Wallace problem where there is a "rules-type equilibrium." Given the optimal rate of inflation, $\pi^* = 0$, a rules-type equilibrium with rational expectations would have the actual rate of inflation equal to zero.

As Barro and Gordon (1983: 608) conclude:

> under a discretionary regime, the policymaker performs optimally subject to an assumed inability to commit future actions. The framework assumes rationality within the given institutional mode. ... Excessive inflation, apparently unrewarding countercyclical policy responses, and reactions of monetary growth and inflation to other exogenous influences can be viewed as products of rational calculation under a regime where long-term commitments are precluded.
>
> The model stresses the importance of monetary institutions, which determine the underlying rules of the game. A purely discretionary environment contrasts with regimes, such as a gold standard or paper-money constitution, in which monetary growth and inflation are determined via choices among alternative rules (the Sargent/Wallace approach). The rule of law or equivalent commitments about future governmental behavior are important for inflation, just as they are for other areas that are influenced by possibly shifting public policies.

An alternative to the "rule of law" is reputation. As Blanchard and Fischer (1989: 599) state:

> reputation is the most interesting and persuasive explanation of how governments avoid dynamic inconsistency. Governments know that they can do

better than the shortsighted solution over the long run. They hope, by acting consistently over long periods, to build a reputation that will cause the private sector to believe their announcements. . . . The key to the answer [to the question of whether reputation can sustain the optimal policy] is the specification of private sector expectations of how the public reacts to broken promises.

Conclusion

This chapter has presented an overview of many of the major themes and issues faced in macroeconomics in terms of the conduct of monetary policy. The roles of expectations, the "ineffectiveness proposition," the modified Phillips curve, rules versus discretion, time inconsistency, credibility and enforcement are all dealt with in this chapter. Perhaps the major contribution of this chapter is that it highlights many of the issues and problems that real-world monetary authorities face when deciding what course of action to take.

12 Open economy

Introduction

The field of international economics can be roughly categorized as concerned with either the real side or the finance side of international issues. The "real" side focuses on such basic questions as why trade occurs between countries, what determines the terms of trade, and how government policies such as tariffs do or quotas affect trade. The "finance" side makes explicit the fact that countries differ in currencies in order to focus on such questions as what determines exchange rates and how macroeconomic shocks in one country (e.g., a change in the supply of money) affect its economy and the economies of the countries with which it trades.

In the discussion below, we examine questions more like those considered by the "finance" side. Namely, we extend simple macroeconomic analysis to an "open" economy, that is, an economy that incorporates a foreign sector. This analysis differs from traditional macroeconomic analysis of a "closed" economy in the following respects:

1   There is trade of composite commodities and financial assets between two countries. For the moment, we assume not only that the two countries produce differentiated output but also that the financial assets issued by the firms and government of one country are not perfect substitutes for the financial assets issued by firms and government of the second country.
2   The two economies are isolated in that individuals in each country can only purchase or sell labor services in their own labor markets.
3   The two economies are differentiated in that each has its own media of exchange. This means that an individual in the domestic economy who seeks to purchase foreign goods must exchange domestic money for foreign money.[1] Similarly, an individual in the foreign country must exchange his foreign money for the domestic money to purchase the domestic goods. Such exchanges take place in the foreign exchange market at the prevailing "foreign exchange rate," or the price of one currency in terms of the second currency. We will let e_t denote the exchange rate for domestic money. For instance, if the domestic country is the USA and the foreign country is Japan, then

e_t on December 1, 1989 was 143.4 yen, in that 143.4 yen = 1 dollar. This implies that $1/e_t$, the price of dollars in terms of yen, was 0.006973 dollars on December 1, 1989.

4   There is distinct government policy (fiscal and monetary) in each country, in that each country's government determines spending, taxation, and monetary policy for its economy.

To understand how macroeconomic analysis is altered in the above "open economy" setting, it is instructive to first consider the nature of the constraints faced by the various participants in an open economy. We then examine how the behavior of these participants is affected by changes in such variables as exchange rates. With that background, we are ready to consider some simple examples of open macroeconomic analysis, such as the effect of a change in the money supply in the context of an open economy neoclassical model.

Open economy participants, constraints, and Walras' law

To begin our task of modeling an open economy, recall that it is typical of macroeconomic models to simplify the economy by grouping markets into broad categories. In a closed economy, there were three important markets: the output, financial, and labor markets. One could add to this the money "market," since equilibrium required that the demand for money equaled supply. In an open economy, we add another market, the foreign exchange market, where the currency of one country is traded for that of the other country. In a closed economy, the participants in the various markets in the economy could be placed in one of five categories: households, firms, government (fiscal side), the central bank, and private depository institutions. In an open economy, we add one more participant, foreigners.

As we have seen, a common theme of macroeconomic models is their emphasis on the interdependencies among markets. Macroeconomics recognizes that events in one market imply changes in other markets as well. This "general equilibrium" approach contrasts with the "partial equilibrium" approach of microeconomics, which is less concerned with how changes in one market affect all other markets. To fully understand the links across markets, it is useful to specify the "financing constraints" faced by the participants in the various markets. Our discussion of open economy macroeconomics thus begins by introducing these financing constraints for firms, households, government (fiscal side), the central bank, private depository institutions, and foreigners. We then sum these constraints to obtain a modified Walras' law.

The financing constraints in an open economy

We start our discussion of the constraints faced by the participants in an open economy by considering the financing constraint faced by the new participant, foreigners. Foreigners purchase domestic output and financial assets. Let X_t^d denote foreigners' demand for domestic output (exports) and let net A_{ft}^d denote foreigners' desired real change in their holdings of domestic financial assets.

To purchase domestic output and financial assets, foreigners must first acquire domestic money. That is, foreigners must finance these purchases either from income generated from their previously acquired holdings of domestic financial assets or by supplying foreign currency in exchange for the domestic currency in the foreign exchange markets. In particular, we have the following foreigner financing constraint:

$$X_t^d + \text{net } A_{ft}^d - \alpha_f (z\overline{B}_f/p_t + d_t) - FC_t^s/e_t p_t = 0. \tag{12.1}$$

Note that for simplicity we limit foreigners' holdings of domestic financial assets to private financial assets (i.e., we not have them holding government bonds). Further, we assume foreigners' portfolio of holdings of domestic financial assets is identical to[2] that of domestic households, and that they own α_f, $1 > \alpha_f \geq 0$, of the total value of financial assets issued by domestic firms. Thus, $\alpha_f (z\overline{B}_f/p_t + d_t)$ is the real income foreigners gain from their holdings of domestic financial assets.[3]

In equation (12.1), the term $FC_t^s/e_t p_t$ denotes foreigners' real supply of foreign currency in the foreign exchange market. FC_t^s is foreigners' supply in units of the foreign currency in period t. Multiplying by $1/e_t$, the price of the foreign currency in terms of the domestic currency puts this in terms of the domestic currency. Dividing by the price level p_t then puts it in real terms (i.e., in terms of the domestic composite commodity). Embedded in the desired change in foreigners' holdings of domestic financial assets are changes in the desired holdings by foreign central banks (i.e., changes in foreign central banks "international reserves").

In addition to the above new constraint that accompanies the introduction of a new participant to the economy, foreigners, we have constraints faced by the domestic households, the central bank, private depository institutions, government (fiscal side), and firms. In the case of households and the central bank, we modify the constraints introduced in previous chapters to incorporate the exchanges of commodities and financial assets with foreigners. In particular, for households, the budget constraint in an open economy can be expressed by

$$b_t^d + c_t^d + z_t^d + (M_t^d - \overline{M})/p_t + \text{net } A_{ht}^d + \text{net } AF_{ht}^d - [y_t - \alpha_f (z\overline{B}_f/p_t + d_t)$$
$$+ \alpha(z\overline{B}_{ff}/p_{ft} + p_{ft}d_{ft})/e_t p_t - \delta\overline{K} - T_{nt}] = 0, \tag{12.2}$$

where the new term z_t^d denotes real imports, net A_{ht}^d denotes households' desired change in their real holdings of foreign assets, and $\alpha(z\overline{B}_{ff}/p_{ft} + p_{ft}d_{ft})$ denotes the income (in terms of the foreign currency) gained from holding the proportion a of the financial assets issued by foreign firms.[4] This income (in foreign currency) times the price of foreign currency in terms of domestic currency $(1/e_t)$ gives the domestic currency value of income from foreign asset holdings. Dividing by the price level p_t puts the income in terms of the composite commodity (i.e., in real terms).

Total consumption of commodities in period t is now the sum of c_t^d, purchase of output, and z_t^d, imports of commodities produced abroad.[5] Similarly, the total desired change in financial assets is the sum of net A_{ht}^d, the desired change in holdings of domestic financial assets, and net AF_{ht}^d, the desired change in holdings of foreign financial assets. Note that in incorporating the firm distribution constraint into the household budget constraint, we have taken into account the fact that not all domestic output y_t is income to domestic households since foreigners own the share α_f of domestic firms. On the other hand, households have an additional source of income from the ownership of foreign financial assets.

For the central bank, the (stock) financing constraint equates the sum of the change in real (domestic) financial asset holdings and international assets to the real change in the monetary base, or

$$\text{net } A_{ct}^d + \text{net } AF_{ct}^d - (MB_t^s - M\overline{B})/p_t = 0, \tag{12.3}$$

where net $A_{ct}^d = p_{bt}(B_{gct}^d - \overline{B}_{gc})/p_t, M\overline{B} = \overline{R} + \overline{C}$, and $MB_t^s = R_t^s + C_t^s$.[6] We have added the term net AF_{ct}^d to denote the real demand for additional international (foreign currency denominated) assets by the central bank. In particular

$$\text{net } AF_{ct}^d = p_{fbt}(B_{fct}^d - \overline{B}_{fc})/e_t p_t.$$

The quantity $p_{fbt}(B_{fct}^d - \overline{B}_{fc})$ is the change in the amount of foreign assets demanded by the central bank in terms of the foreign currency: p_{fbt} denotes the price of foreign bonds in terms of foreign currency, and the numbers of such bonds demanded and initially held by the domestic central bank are denoted, respectively, by B_{fct}^d and $\overline{B}_{fc}$. Multiplying this quantity by the price of foreign currency in domestic currency terms $(1/e_t)$ gives the domestic currency value of foreign assets demanded by the central bank. Then dividing by the price level p_t puts the net demand for international assets by the central bank, net AF_{ct}^d in terms of the composite commodity (i.e., in real terms).

For private depository institutions, the (stock) financing constraint indicates that private depository institutions can be viewed as financing additions to reserves and to financial assets holdings by creating deposits, or

$$\text{net } A_{pb}^t + (R_t^d - \overline{R})/p_t - (D_t^s - \overline{D})/p_t = 0, \tag{12.4}$$

where net reserves demanded or initially held are denoted by R_t^d and $\overline{R}$, respectively, and checkable deposits supplied or initially outstanding are denoted by D_t^s and $\overline{D}$, respectively. For simplicity, we assume that all private demands for foreign financial assets as well as for foreign commodities are captured in the household budget constraint. To the extent that private banks purchase foreign financial assets, they can be viewed as acting as financial intermediaries for households.

For the domestic government (fiscal side) the financing constraint is

$$g_{ct}^d - T_{nt}^* - \text{net } A_{gt}^s = 0, \tag{12.5}$$

where $T_{nt}^* = T_t - tr_t - z(\overline{B}_{gh} + \overline{B}_{gp})/p_t$, tr denotes transfer payments, and net $A_{gt}^s = P_{bt}(B_{gt}^s - \overline{B}_g)/p_t$. Equation (12.5) incorporates the "flow" financing constraint for the central bank. In doing so, it is assumed that the central bank claims on real resources just exhaust its interest payments on government debt holdings plus any income associated with central bank holdings of foreign assets. Finally, for firms the financing constraint on capital purchases is given by:

$$I_{nt}^d + \psi(I_{nt}^d) - \text{net } A_{ft}^s = 0. \tag{12.6}$$

Note that we assume for simplicity that neither firms nor the government purchase foreign commodities.

Walras' law and the balance of payments

We now sum the constraints faced by the six participants in an open economy (foreigners, households, the central bank, private banks, the government, and firms) as given by equations (12.1)–(12.6). In doing so, assume equilibrium with respect to the demand and supply of bank reserves (i.e., the R_t^s part of MB_t^s in the central bank constraint equals R_t^d in the private banks constraint) and note that the initial monetary base $\overline{MB}$ equals $\overline{R} + \overline{C}$, that the money supply is defined by $M_t^s = D_t^s + C_t^s$, and that the initial money supply is given by $\overline{M} = \overline{D} + \overline{C}$. We obtain

$$[B_t^d + C_t^d + X_t^d + g_{ct}^d + \delta\overline{K} + I_{nt}^d + \psi(I_{nt}^d) - y_t] + [M_t^d/p_t - \overline{M}/p_t]$$
$$+ [\text{net } A_{ht}^d + \text{net } A_{ft}^d + \text{net } A_{ct}^d + \text{net } A_{pt}^d - \text{net } A_{gt}^s - \text{net } A_{ft}^s]$$
$$+ [z_t^{d*} + \text{net } AF_{ht}^d + \text{net } AF_{ct}^d - FC_t^s/e_tp_t] = 0, \tag{12.7}$$

where $z_t^{d*} + \text{net } AF_{ht}^d + \text{net } AF_{ct}^d - FC_t^s/e_tp_t$ denotes households' imports not financed out of income generated from foreign asset holdings. Equation (12.7) is an example of the modified Walras' law for an open economy.[7] As we discuss below, (12.7) can be viewed as stating that the sum of excess demands in four markets must equal zero.

The first term in (12.7) reflects excess demand in the output market, where the demand now includes foreigners' demand for domestic output (exports). Note that, by adding and subtracting import demand, we could express the excess demand for output in the form:

$$b_t^d + c_t^{d*} + (x_t^d - z_t^d) + g_{ct}^d + \delta\overline{K} + I_{nt}^d + \psi(I_{nt}^d) - y_t \tag{12.8}$$

where the term c_t^{d*} denotes households' total consumption in terms of both domestic and foreign output (i.e., $c_t^{d*} = c_t^d + z_t^d$). Excess demand in the output market is often expressed this way, with the consumption term denoting total household consumption, such that the "net" export demand term $(x_t^d - z_t^d)$ appears.

Setting the excess demand for output term in (12.7) to zero gives us the IS equation in an open economy. The second term in (12.7) reflects the excess demand for money. Note that we assume that only domestic households desire to hold the domestic money (foreigners seek the domestic money in the foreign exchange market not to hold but as a means to purchase the domestic output or financial assets). Setting this second term in (12.7) to zero gives us the standard LM equation.

The third term in (12.7) reflects excess demand in the financial market. In going to an open economy, we add to the demand side of the financial market a demand for domestic financial assets by foreigners (which could include private foreign agents as well as foreign central banks). In addition, note that households' demand for domestic financial assets (net A_{ht}^d) no longer reflects households' total demand for financial assets, since they now have the option of purchasing foreign financial assets (net AF_t^d).

The fourth, and final, term in (12.7) reflects excess real demand for foreign currency in the foreign exchange market.[8] As before, we can view output (y_t) or the price of output (p_t) as determined in the output market, and the domestic interest rate (r_t) as determined in the financial market. Now we can view the foreign exchange rate (e_t) as determined in the foreign exchange market. The demand for foreign currency reflects z_t^{d*}, the demand associated with households' purchases of foreign commodities that could not be financed from the foreign currency earnings of their holdings of foreign financial assets, net AF_{ht}^d, the demand for foreign currency associated with households' purchases of additional foreign financial assets, and net AF_{ct}^d, the demand associated with the central bank's desired change in international reserves. Note that the real demand for the foreign currency could instead be stated as the real supply of the domestic currency in the foreign exchange market.

$FC_t^s / e_t p_t$ denotes the real supply of foreign currency or real demand for the domestic currency in the foreign exchange market, which from (12.1) reflects foreigners' purchases of financial assets and exports net of those financed through domestic currency earnings on financial assets held by foreigners. Foreigners' purchases of financial assets include both foreign private (i.e., foreign households') and foreign public (i.e., foreign central bank) purchases.

The balance of payments accounts

Let us assume for now that the domestic economy discussed above is the USA. The US Department of Commerce actually measures the various sources of the demand for and supply of dollars in the foreign exchange markets cited above. These data of international transactions are presented as the US balance of payments accounts. Table 12.1 summarizes its major components. Transactions are categorized as either sources of the real demand for or the real supply of dollars in the foreign exchange market for the US dollar.[9] Equivalently, they reflect the real supply of or real demand for foreign currency in the foreign exchange market.

Table 12.1 The US balance of payments accounts (in "real" terms)

	Real demand for dollars	Real supply of dollars
1	US exports of goods and services, x_t	US imports of goods and services, z_t
2	Transfers (interest and dividends to US holders of foreign financial assets, government grants, and gifts), $\alpha(z\bar{B}_{ff}/p_{ft} + p_{ft}d_{ft})/e_t p_t$	Transfers (interest and dividends to foreign holders of US financial assets, government grants, and gifts), $\alpha_f(z\bar{B}_f/p_t + d_t)$
3	Foreign purchases of US financial assets (capital inflow), net A_{ft}^d	US purchases of foreign financial assets (capital outflow), net AF_h^d + net AF_{ct}^d

The net demand for dollars associated with the first component of the balance of payments accounts (exports minus imports), is called the balance of trade. If the balance of trade is negative, as it has been recently for the USA, then the USA is said to experience a balance of trade deficit. If it is positive, as was the case for 106 consecutive years from the end of the Civil War to 1971 as well as through most of the 1970s, then a balance of trade surplus is said to exist.

The third component of the demand for and supply of dollars in the balance of payments accounts is the capital account. This capital account can be divided into a private part and a public part. On the demand side, the private part measures the real dollars demanded by foreigners other than foreign central banks to finance purchases of US financial assets. On the supply side, the private part measures the real dollars supplied by US households to buy foreign financial assets. These currency exchanges are called private international capital flows. Private international capital flows associated with the demand for dollars are referred to as US private international capital inflows, since they reflect the inflow of foreign currency due to private foreigners' purchases of US financial assets. Private international capital flows associated with the supply of dollars are referred to as US private international capital outflows, since they reflect the outflow of dollars due to US households' purchases of foreign financial assets.

Summing the net demand (demand minus supply) for dollars associated with the first two components plus the private international capital flows and adjusting for measurement errors (the discrepancy term) we obtain what is called the US balance of payments.[10] In years in which the balance of payments is negative it is referred to as a balance of payments deficit. On the other hand, a positive balance of payments is called a balance of payments surplus.

When there is a surplus or deficit in the balance of payments accounts, then equality between the real demand for and real supply of dollars is brought about by an offsetting deficit or surplus on what is known as "the official reserve transaction balance." The official reserve transaction balance reflects the intervention into the foreign exchange market by the US central bank (the Fed) and/or by foreign central banks. This is the "public" part of international capital flows. Whenever there exists a balance of payments deficit in the USA, then (on net) central banks demand US dollars in the foreign exchange markets. If this were solely the US central bank intervening, this means that net AF_{ct}^d was/is negative (the Fed was/is a net supplier of dollars in the foreign exchange market), and the US central bank would have lost/lose international reserves.

Behavior in an open economy

With an understanding of the constraints faced by the various participants in an open economy, we now consider the behavior of these participants, in particular the determinants of imports (z_t^d), exports (x_t^d), private international capital inflows (a part of net A_{ft}^d), and private international capital outflows (net AF_{ht}^d). In the first part of this section, we examine how a change in the foreign exchange rate for the domestic currency (to be concrete, the US dollar) can alter the relative price of foreign goods and thus lead to a change in the division of household consumption between purchases of domestic goods and purchases of foreign goods.[11] We also examine other factors that influence US imports of goods and services and thus the real demand for foreign currency (real supply of US dollars) in the foreign exchange markets.

In the second part of this section, we consider the factors that influence how households divide their real accumulation of financial assets between US stocks and bonds and the financial assets of foreign countries. As we saw above, household purchases of foreign financial assets constitute capital outflows, since in order to make these purchases households must demand foreign currency (supply dollars) in the foreign exchange market. We will see how differences in foreign and domestic interest rates and the expected appreciation or depreciation of the US dollar determine the relative returns on foreign and domestic financial assets. These relative returns in turn affect households' portfolio choices between foreign and domestic financial assets and the real demand for foreign currency (real supply of dollars) in the foreign exchange market.

In the third and fourth parts of this section, we turn to the other side of the foreign exchange market to examine determinants of foreigners' purchases of US goods and services and of US financial assets. In particular, we consider how such factors as exchange rates affect foreigners' demand for US goods (US exports) and how such factors as relative interest rates and the expected rate of change in the exchange rate affect foreigners' demand for US financial assets. We finish this section by illustrating graphically the behavior discussed in terms of the real demand for and supply of the domestic currency (the US dollar).

Households' demand for imports

When deciding whether to purchase foreign or domestic goods, households look at their relative prices. To be concrete, consider two countries. The domestic country is the USA and the foreign country is Japan. The relative price of Japanese goods is then the real quantity of US goods that must be sacrificed to purchase the foreign good. For example, if the price of a Japanese car is $6,000 and the price of a US computer is $1,500, then the relative price of a Japanese car in terms of US computers is 4 computers. If the relative price of Japanese cars rises, the USA will import fewer Japanese cars. The relative price of foreign goods, sometimes referred to as the terms of trade, is an important determinant of the quantity of imports. The relative prices of foreign goods depend on the dollar prices of US goods, the prices of foreign goods in their own currency, and foreign exchange rates (the price of one currency in terms of a second currency). The simple example that follows illustrates this point. Suppose that the price of a US computer is $1,500 and that in Japan the price of a Japanese car is 600,000 yen. The third "price" that we need to know in order to compute the relative price of a Japanese car in terms of US computers is the foreign exchange rate, in particular the price of a yen in terms of dollars. Suppose that it takes e_t yen to buy one dollar in the foreign exchange markets. Then it takes $1/e_t$ dollars to buy one yen. Returning to our example of Japanese cars and US computers, if $e_t = 100$ yen per dollar and the Japanese car had a yen price of 600,000, then its dollar price would be 6,000.

In general, the calculation of the relative price of Japanese goods is thus:

Relative price of Japanese goods (in terms of US goods)

$= \{$Yen price of Japanese goods (p_{ft})

$\times$ Price of yen in terms of dollars $(1/e_t)\}$

$/\{$Dollar price of US goods $(p_t)\}$

$$= \frac{p_{ft}}{e_t p_t}.$$

According to this expression, a rise in the yen price of Japanese goods (p_{ft}) raises their relative price. Similarly, a fall in the dollar price of US commodities (p_t) raises the relative price of Japanese goods. Finally, a rise in the price of yen in terms of dollars $(1/e_t)$ also increases the relative price of Japanese goods.[12] Since all three changes mean a higher relative price of Japanese goods, and thus an increase in the cost to US buyers of Japanese goods in terms of US goods forgone, all three changes reduce US imports of Japanese goods. The above relative price expression for a basket of foreign goods is sometimes termed the real exchange rate for foreign goods – that is,

Real exchange rates (foreign goods)

$$= \frac{\text{Dollar price of foreign goods}}{\text{Dollar price of US goods}} = \frac{p_{ft}(1/e_t)}{p_t} = \frac{p_{ft}}{p_t e_t}.$$

While a rise in the relative price of foreign goods will lead to a reduction in the quantity of foreign goods bought, we have to be careful not to infer from this that US import demand will necessarily be inversely related to the relative or real price of imports. The reason for this is that our measure of US real import demand is in terms of the US good and services, not in terms of the foreign good. An example will highlight this distinction.

Suppose that the dollar depreciates (e_t falls). With the implied appreciation of foreign currency ($1/e_t$ rises), the price of the foreign good in terms of US goods becomes greater, as our expression for the real exchange rate for foreign goods ($p_{ft}/p_t, e_t$) indicates. With a higher price, fewer foreign goods will be purchased – this is clear. This by itself would suggest a fall in the value of imports into the USA. But the higher price also means that each foreign good purchased will cost more in terms of US goods that must be sacrificed. This by itself would suggest a rise in the value of US imports (measured in terms of US goods that must be paid to obtain the imports). The net impact of a change in the relative price of foreign goods on US imports measured in terms of US goods depends on which of these two effects is stronger.

It is typically assumed that over time the effect of a change in the relative prices of imports on the quantity of imports purchased dominates, so that the value of imports in terms of US goods will fall with a rise in the relative price of imports. This is what we will assume.[13] Formally, this condition requires that the price elasticity of demand for foreign goods be greater than one. That is, a 1 percent increase in the price of foreign goods must cause a greater than 1 percent reduction in the amount of foreign goods that US households demand.[14]

Besides the relative prices of imports, real disposable income affects US import demand. An increase in disposable income can lead to a rise in household consumption demand. In an open economy with foreign trade, a rise in consumption demand means an increase in purchases not only of domestically produced goods but also of foreign goods. Thus households' import demand is directly related to their disposable income. To summarize, household real import demand z_t^d depends inversely on the relative price of foreign goods, $p_{ft}/e_t p_t$, and directly on disposable income, $y_t - \delta \overline{K} - T_{nt}$:

$$z_t^d = z_t^d(p_{ft}/e_t p_t, y_t - \delta \overline{K} - T_{nt}, \ldots). \tag{12.9}$$

Capital outflows: households' demand for foreign financial assets

When deciding whether to purchase US or foreign financial assets, households compare domestic and foreign rates of return. The nominal rate of return on US financial assets is simply the money interest rate r_t. The comparable nominal rate of return on foreign financial assets is not so simple to identify. To explain how to compute this return, which we will denote r_t^*, let us suppose that a household lends one dollar in the foreign financial market.

If the price of a dollar is e_t units of the foreign currency, say yen, then in terms of the foreign currency, the household lends e_t yen. If foreign financial assets offer the interest rate r_{ft} then one period from now the household will have $e_t(1 + r_{ft})$ yen. At that time, the household can convert these yen holdings back to dollars at the exchange rate then existing. At the time the money is lent, this future exchange rate may be uncertain.[15] Let households' expectation of this future exchange rate be denoted by e_{t+1}^e.[16] Then the household expects to convert its $e_t(1 + r_{ft})$ yen next year into $e_t(1 + r_{ft})/e_{t+1}^e$ dollars. Subtracting the one dollar with which the household started, the rate of return to lending in foreign financial markets, r^*, is given by

$$r_t^* = (e_t(1 + r_{ft})/e_{t+1}^e) - 1 = [e_t(1 + r_{ft}) - e_{t+1}^e]/e_{t+1}^e.$$

We can simplify the above equation by noting that the expected future dollar exchange rate, e_{t+1}^e yen per dollar, equals the current exchange rate of e_t yen times $(1 + \theta_{t+1}^e)$, where θ_{t+1}^e is the expected rate of change in the price of a dollar in terms of yen. Substituting the expression $e_t(1 + \theta_{t+1}^e)$ for the expected future dollar exchange rate, e_{t+1}^e, into the above expression for r_t^*, we have

$$r_t^* = [e_t(1 + r_{ft}) - e_t(1 + \theta_{t+1}^e)]/e_t(1 + \theta_{t+1}^e) = (r_{ft} - \theta_{t+1}^e)/(1 + \theta_{t+1}^e).$$

Since the expected rate of appreciation of a dollar is typically small, we can approximate the above expression by

$$r_t^* = r_{ft} - \theta_{t+1}^e. \tag{12.10}$$

Equation (12.10) has a straightforward interpretation. The return to lending in the foreign financial market equals the difference between the foreign interest rate and the expected rate of change in the price of the dollar. The return to lending in foreign financial markets increases with a higher foreign interest rate r_{ft} and decreases with a higher expected rate of increase in the price of the dollar (θ_{t+1}^e). The higher the expected rate of increase in the price of the dollar, the lower the expected return to lending in foreign financial markets since for a given number of dollars sold for foreign currency at the start of the period, fewer dollars can be bought back at the end of the period.

When households choose between purchasing domestic and foreign financial assets, they compare the domestic interest rate, r_t, with the rate of return to lending in the foreign financial markets, r_t^*. We can thus express household real demand for additional foreign financial assets as

$$\text{net } AF_{ht}^d = \text{net } AF_{ht}^d(r_t, r_{ft} - \theta_{t+1}^e, \ldots). \tag{12.11}$$

In (12.11), an increase in the US interest rate or a fall in the rate of return on foreign financial assets implies a reduction in households' real demand for foreign financial assets. The three dots in (12.11) reflect other factors that have been left unspecified. For instance, changes in the political stability of foreign governments are one unspecified factor that would likely impact on US households' demand for foreign financial assets. Equation (12.11) suggests that we should add another facet to our previous discussion on households' demand for US financial assets, net A_{ht}^d. In addition to such factors as real income, taxes, the US money interest rate, and the expected rate of inflation, household demand for US financial assets depends on the expected return to lending abroad, $r_{ft} - \theta_{t+1}^e$.

Foreigners' demand for exports

Just as US demand for foreign goods depends on relative prices, so too is foreigners' demand for US goods based on the relative prices of those goods. The relative prices of US goods to foreigners measure what foreigners have to give up of their own goods in order to purchase US goods. As we have seen, these relative prices depend on the money prices of US goods, the money prices of foreign goods, and the exchange rate. Considering "composite" goods for each country, the relative price of US goods to foreigners or the real exchange rate for foreign goods is given by

Real exchange rates (US goods)

$$= \frac{\text{Dollar price of US goods}}{\text{Dollar price of foreign goods}} = \frac{p_t}{p_{ft}(1/e_t)} = \frac{p_t e_t}{p_{ft}}.$$

Note that the real exchange rate for US goods is simply the inverse of the previously obtained real exchange rate for foreign goods. The price of a dollar in terms of an index of foreign currencies rose by 70 percent in 1984 and 1985. The resulting rise in the relative prices of US goods contributed significantly to a reduction in foreign demand for US goods and the large US trade deficit of the mid-1980s. Similarly, the dramatic fall in the price of a dollar in the subsequent period from late 1985 to 1988 led to an increase in US exports. Thus, we have

$$x_t^d = x_t^d(p_t e_t/p_{ft}, \ldots). \tag{12.12}$$

Equation (12.12) indicates that export demand falls with a rise in the relative price of US goods to foreigners.

We know from our previous discussion that an increase in US disposable income leads to a rise in household purchases of both domestically produced output and foreign goods and services. By the same token, an increase in foreigners' disposable income leads to a rise in their purchases of US goods. Thus, among the items missing in (12.12) that determine foreigners' real export demand, x_t^d, is foreign disposable income.

Capital inflows: foreigners' demand for financial assets

In 1960, purchases of US financial assets by foreigners were approximately one-half the amount of purchases of foreign financial assets by US citizens. In the US financial markets, foreign purchases of new US financial assets were less than 5 percent of household and depository institution purchases. Twenty-five years later, foreigners were purchasing four times as many US financial assets than the USA was purchasing abroad. In the US financial market, close to 30 percent of new US financial assets were being purchased by foreigners. This dramatic change in capital inflows to the USA is one indication of the growing importance to the US economy of international trade not only in goods but also in financial assets.

As with US households, we will assume that foreigners decide to purchase either US assets or financial assets of their own country by comparing the rates of return on the two types of financial assets. For foreigners, the nominal rate of return on domestic assets is the money interest rate in their own country (r_{ft}). The expected rate of return to foreigners on US financial assets equals the US interest rate plus the expected change in the price of the dollar in the foreign exchange market (i.e., $r_t + \theta^e_{t+1}$).

Not surprisingly, the expected return to foreigners lending in US financial markets increases when the US interest rate, r_t, increases. Not as obvious is that the return also increases with an increase in the expected rate of change in the price of the dollar, θ^e_{t+1}. This is because foreigners lending in US financial markets convert their currency to dollars to make the loans. When the loans are repaid, they then convert dollars back to their own currency. If the dollar is anticipated to appreciate during the course of the year, then part of their expected return to lending in the USA is the increase in the value of the dollars (in terms of their own currency).

Summarizing, we can express the foreign demand for US financial assets, net A^d_{ft}, as

$$\text{net } A^d_{ft} = \text{net } A^d_{ft}(r_{ft}, r_t, \theta^e_{t+1}, \ldots). \tag{12.13}$$

Equation (12.13) indicates that foreigners' demand for US financial assets increases if the US interest rate (r_t) rises, or the expected rate of change in the price of the dollar (θ^e_{t+1}) increases, or the foreign interest rate (r_{ft}) falls.

The foreign exchange market: the real demand and supply of dollars

The change in the price of a dollar (in terms of a second currency) affects the real quantity of dollars supplied and demanded in the foreign exchange market. Let us start with the price of a dollar set at the equilibrium level of $(e_t)_0$, let us say 100 yen. If the price of a dollar now falls to $(e_t)_1$, say 50 yen, then this depreciation of the dollar (appreciation of the yen) leads to a reduction in the real quantity of dollars supplied from Q_0 to Q_1.

A fall in the price of a dollar from 100 to 50 yen means a rise in the dollar price of a yen, from 0.01 to 0.02 dollars, or from 1 cent to 2 cents. Even though there is no increase in the yen price of Japanese goods, the dollar price of Japanese goods rises. For example, a 600,000 yen Japanese car that formerly cost 6,000 dollars ($600,000 \times 0.01$) now costs 12,000 dollars ($600,000 \times 0.02$). If the dollar prices of US goods have not changed, then the relative or real prices of Japanese cars have risen. In our example, this means that US households must give up an increased amount of US goods to obtain one more Japanese car.

The depreciation of the dollar, and resulting higher relative price for Japanese goods, leads US households to reduce the quantity of Japanese goods demanded. However, as we discussed above, the fact that the quantity of Japanese goods purchased falls does not necessarily mean that the quantity of dollars supplied in the foreign exchange market also falls. There are two countervailing forces at work here. While the purchase of fewer Japanese goods would reduce the quantity of dollars supplied, the fact that each Japanese good has a higher price would increase the quantity of dollars supplied. By assuming that the first effect outweighs the second effect, we conclude that a depreciation of the dollar causes the real quantity of dollars supplied in the foreign exchange market to fall. Thus, there is an upward-sloping supply of dollars curve.[17]

Naturally, behind the supply of dollars in the foreign exchange market is not only US real import demand but also the real demand by households and the US central bank for additional foreign financial assets (net AF^d_{ht} + net AF^d_{ct}). As we saw above, this sum of the US import demand and demand for foreign financial assets can be interpreted as representing not only a supply of dollars but also a demand for foreign currency.[18]

The above discussion also highlights the effect of a change in the price of a dollar (in terms of a second currency) on the quantity of dollars demanded in the foreign exchange market. The depreciation of the dollar (or appreciation of the yen) from $(e_t)_0$ to $(e_t)_1$ leads to an increase in the quantity of dollars demanded US in real terms. The fall in the price increases the quantity of dollars demanded because it lowers the relative price of US goods to foreigners. A fall in the price of a dollar from 100 yen to 50 yen causes a rise in the dollar price of the yen from 1 cent to 2 cents. Even though there has been no increase in the dollar price of US goods, the yen price of US goods falls, and the Japanese increase their demand for US goods. As a consequence, the real quantity of dollars demanded in the foreign exchange market increases.

Naturally, behind the demand for dollars in the foreign exchange market is not only foreigners' export demand but also their demand for US financial assets (net AF^d_{ht}). As we have seen, this sum of the export demand and foreigners' demand for US financial assets can be interpreted as representing not only a demand for dollars but also a supply of foreign currency.

Simple examples of open economy (static) macroeconomic analysis

The statement of Walras' law for an open economy indicates that for static macroeconomic analysis of an open economy, we need look at only three of the four excess demand conditions reflecting the output, financial, foreign exchange, and money markets. Standard practice is to look at the output, money, and foreign exchange markets. In the neoclassical model, these three equations would be solved to obtain the equilibrium price level, interest rate, and exchange rate (p_t, r_t, and e_t, respectively). In the Barro–Grossman disequilibrium analysis, these three equilibrium conditions could be solved to obtain the equilibrium output, interest rate, and exchange rate (y_t, r_t, and e_t, respectively). In the Lucas model or the Keynesian fixed money wage model, these three equilibrium conditions, along with the appropriate aggregate supply equation, could be solved for the equilibrium price level, output, interest rate, and exchange rate (p_t, y_t, r_t, and e_t, respectively).

With flexible exchange rates (i.e., exchange rates determined without the intervention of central banks), the basic change in the macroeconomic analysis is to recognize that the net export component of output demand (see equation (12.8)) is sensitive to interest rate changes, which implies the IS curve (in (interest rate, output) space) is flatter. The reason why a higher US interest rate reduces net export demand is that a higher interest rate increases capital inflows (net A_{ft}^d) and reduces capital outflows (net AF_{ht}^d). The first change increases the demand for dollars in the foreign exchange market, while the second reduces the supply of dollars in the foreign exchange market. The result is an appreciation of the dollar that reduces exports and increases imports. Note that, with flexible exchange rates, a change in either the price level or income does not affect net export demand.

Money supply changes in the neoclassical model: purchasing power parity

In general, when considering two countries, the country with the lower inflation rate will tend to have an exchange rate that is appreciating at a rate approximately equal to the difference in inflation rates between the two countries. This pattern of changes in foreign exchange rates is sometimes said to reflect the purchasing power parity condition. The condition of purchasing power parity means that the purchasing power of each country's currency is the same whether the currency is used to purchase domestic goods or foreign goods. Purchasing power parity exists for a monetary shock in the neoclassical model since a money supply change will lead to changes not only in domestic prices but also in foreign exchange rates such that relative prices remain constant.

Interest-rate parity

There are, of course, a number of variations to the above analysis. For instance we could assume that domestic and foreign financial assets are perfect substitutes and that the domestic country is sufficiently small in its interactions with foreign financial markets that it takes the foreign interest rate, r_{ft}, as a given. In this case of "interest rate parity," since the return to lending at home, r_t, must equal that of lending abroad, $r_t^* = r_{ft} - \theta_{t+1}^e$, we have that

$$r_{ft} = r_t + \theta_{t+1}^e \quad \text{(a constant).} \tag{12.14}$$

One use of (12.14) is in the well-known Dornbusch model (see Dornbusch 1976). Assume that output and the price of output are fixed initially. Assume $\theta_{t+1}^e = 0$ initially, such that $r_t = r_{ft}$. Now consider an increase in the money supply. To maintain equilibrium with respect to the demand and supply of money, the interest rate r_t must decrease. According to (12.14), the resulting increase in international capital outflows and reduction in international capital inflows must reduce the exchange rate such that it is expected to appreciate at a rate equal to the difference between x_t^d and the new lower r_t. This is Dornbusch's famous "exchange rate overshooting." That is, the analysis implies a fall in the exchange rate below what it will ultimately be after income or prices adjust.

A second use of (12.14) is to combine it with the assumption that exchange rates are fixed (through appropriate central bank intervention in the foreign exchange markets). An example taking this approach is the Mundell–Fleming model (Fleming 1962; Mundell 1968).

Conclusion

This chapter has brought together many of the issues associated with analyzing a macroeconomy that participates in the open or global economy. In keeping with the basic model framework of this book, the household is now viewed as having a demand for imported products as well as domestically produced goods and services. Additionally, firms are allowed to sell to agents in foreign countries. This flow of goods and services across borders logically leads to a flow of funds. Moreover, this interconnectedness among trading partners implies that the actions of one country, in particular those of the monetary authority, may influence conditions in the other country.

Notes

1 Introduction

1 Empirically an economy's total output is measured by real gross domestic product (or industrial production), employment is estimated from company records or household surveys, estimates of unemployment are compiled from household surveys or statistics on recipients of unemployment benefits, and price indexes are computed to measure changes in the overall level of prices.

2 Leon Walras first derived the result in his book, *Elements d'Economie Politique Pure*, first published in 1874–77 (see Walras 1954).

3 An endogenous variable is one that is determined by the model. An exogenous variable is one that is taken as given by the model.

4 An element that distinguishes both static and dynamic macroeconomic analysis from Arrow–Debreu analysis is the incorporation of money. The exceptions to this in macroeconomic analysis are real business cycle theories, which for the most part are purely "real" in the sense that money is not an intrinsic part of the analysis.

5 Note that an alternative to exogenous expectations is to specify an "expectation function." If this function relates expectations in certain specific ways to all current information, such that the expectation function reflects "rational expectations," then static analysis is converted to dynamic analysis.

6 In dynamic models, this would be termed "perfect foresight" in a deterministic setting, and "rational expectations" in a stochastic setting.

7 One could say that the effect of such a variable is implicit in the exogenous level of expected future prices of the static analysis.

8 A similar example of an incomplete listing of effects is a change in current government policies. A change in current government actions may require changes in government actions in subsequent periods that will impact future markets. Yet the construction of static analysis does not require such effects to be spelled out.

9 Forward markets are markets in which agreements are made that specify the prices at which goods will be exchanged in the future. Goods are thus in essence indexed by the date of trade.

10 This is the Arrow–Debreu contingent-claim interpretation of a competition equilibrium model (see Arrow 1964; Debreu 1959).

11 In some cases, one can attain the stationary state under the less restrictive requirement that certain exogenous variables simply grow at a steady rate over time.

12 While classical economists did not fully articulate their model, Patinkin (1965) is widely cited as providing a comprehensive review and formalization of many of the key ideas underlying the classical economists' views. The result may be denoted the prototype of the neoclassical (static) model. Dynamic neoclassical macroeconomic models are broadly based on neoclassical growth models with the addition of shocks of various kinds. Among the classic works developing neoclassical growth models are Solow (1956), Cass (1965), Koopmans (1965), and Sidrauski (1967a, 1967b).

13 Two of the most widely known proponents of new classical economics are Robert Lucas and Thomas Sargent. It has been suggested by some, however, that this line of analysis is less the extension of classical analysis than it is the antithesis of Keynesian analysis, as discussed below. See Niehans (1987) for this interpretation.

14 This is changing, as indicated by Howitt (1985), Shapiro and Stiglitz (1984), Weitzman (1985), and by the papers cited in the May 1988 *American Economic Review*.

15 Howitt goes on to say that there is the "reciprocal Keynesian question of how exactly the economic system manages to overcome all the obvious coordination problems that stand in the way of attaining the state of equilibrium common to new classical economics models."

2 Walrasian economy

1 A brief description of the theory is given in Patinkin (1965: note B).

2 In reality, of course, there is no auctioneer. In fact, some think that Walras would have been the first to question such a description of the economy as realistically capturing the true dynamic process by which the economy reaches the equilibrium described by supply and demand curves. See Walker (1987), who points out that Walras promoted a "disequilibrium-production model of tatonnement" as more representative of Walras' thought than the tatonnement model with an "auctioneer."

3 We use the letter T to denote the number of commodities because later we distinguish the T commodities according to time of availability (i.e., from period 1 to period T).

4 One could replace the assumption of known prices by the assumption that individuals form expectations at time t about prices at time t, and that such expectations are correct. This has been referred to as a situation in which expectations satisfy the assumption of "weak consistency."

5 With zero transactions costs, equality of purchase and sale prices could be viewed as forced by arbitrage conditions.

6 Walras was one of the first to note this point. Note that $\pi_{jj} = 1$.

7 See Debreu (1959, Chapter 2) for a discussion of such accounting prices.

8 A distinctive feature of macroeconomics is to alter traditional Arrow–Debreu general equilibrium analysis in such a way that we can reinterpret accounting prices as money prices and determine the level of money prices.

9 Others characterize transactions costs in similar fashion. For instance, Alchian and Demsetz (1972) cite the costs of "forming", "negotiating", and "enforcing contracts", while Dahlman (1979) writes of "search and information costs", "bargaining and decision costs", and "policing and enforcing" costs.

10 See Varian (1992) for a discussion on these points. By "well behaved," we mean that $\partial u^a / \partial c_{ai} > 0$ and u^a is strictly quasi-concave.

11 In this case, the Lagrangian is written ignoring the non-negativity constraints on consumption of commodity $i, i = 1, \ldots, T$. Below we provide an equivalent characterization of the constrained maximization problem that incorporates these constraints in the Lagrangian.

12 A function $y = f(x_1, \ldots, x_n, x_{n+1}, \ldots, x_m)$ is said to be homogeneous of degree k in the arguments x_1 through x_n if

$$f(\lambda x_1, \ldots, \lambda x_n, x_{n+1}, \ldots, x_m) = \lambda^k f(x_1, \ldots, x_n, x_{n+1}, \ldots, x_m).$$

3 Firms as market participants

1 With zero "adjustment costs," there could exist a market for capital at time t, such that the capital employed during the initial period, K_t, is conceptually distinct from capital inherited, $\overline{K}$. In this case, however, equilibrium in the capital market at time t would then imply that $K_t = \overline{K}$.

2 Note that output is a "flow variable." That is, for a period i of length h, the output produced is given by hy_i. The term y_i is thus the "rate of output" over period i. Since output is a flow variable, at a point in time the rate of production is not defined. (As you can see, for any rate of output, the limit of production as the length of the period goes to zero is zero.)

3 In general, for a period i of length h, labor services are denoted by hN_i such that total wage payments at the end of the period are $w_i hN_i$. Like the labor input, one should think of the capital input in flow terms, with the stock of capital determining the rate or flow of capital services.

4 For simplicity of notation, these expressions presume perfect foresight.

5 In general, for a period i of length h, the nominal interest rate from the end of that period to the end of the next period is given by $hr_i = hz/p_{bi} + (p_{b,i+h} - p_{bi})/p_{bi}$.

6 For simplicity of notation, these expressions assume perfect foresight with respect to future prices of equity shares. In addition, the expressions presume future dividends are known.

7 To minimize notational clutter, we have chosen to not denote such anticipations with the expectation operator. We do presume that agents (firms and households) have common expectations (assumed to be held with subjective certainty) concerning plans with respect to the issuing of equity shares.

8 For instance, if $r_i < r_{ei}$ for period i, there would be zero demand for bonds. The resulting excess supply of bonds would lead to a fall in the price of bonds, and thus a rise in the return on bonds, until equality across rates of return held.

9 We assume for the moment perfect foresight at time t with respect to prices at the end of the period (at time $t+1$).

10 As in the prior models, including money balances in the utility function reflects how money can save (leisure) time required to make exchanges within a period. For simplicity, we limit money holdings to agents labelled "households."

11 For the representative household, holdings of bonds issued by other households must be zero so that there is no real indebtedness effect with respect to the bonds exchanged among representative households.

12 In general, if we assume there are n_i firms producing commodity i and that there are m different commodities, then

$$y_t = \sum_{i=1}^{m} \left[\sum_{j=1}^{ni} (p_i/p) f_{ij}(N_{ijt}, \overline{K}_{ijt}) \right].$$

The above is a stylized view of how the empirical counterpart to total output, real gross domestic product, is actually computed by the Commerce Department.

13 Note that it is assumed that the capital stock $\overline{K}$ generates a fixed rate of capital services. That is, we do not consider variation in the "utilization of capital." If we did so, then variation in the services flowing from the capital stock could be considered an additional choice variable, with capital utilization presumably affecting the extent of depreciation in the capital stock over time.

14 Fama and Miller (1972) cite conditions under which the "owners of the firm," i.e., the holders of the $\overline{S}$ equity shares, will direct the managers of the firm at time t to maximize V_t.

15 In continuous time,

$$p_{e,t-1} = \int_t^{\infty} [p_s d_s / S_s] e^{-r(s-t)} ds,$$

where the interest rate r in the above expression is formally r_s.

16 Note that $S_{t-1} \equiv \overline{S}$. Assuming $r_i = r_t, i = t+1, \ldots$, we have

$$\overline{p}_e = [1/(1+\overline{r})] \left[p_t d_t / \overline{S} + \sum_{k=1}^{\infty} [p_{t+k} d_{t+k} / S_{t+k-1}] / (1+r_t)^k \right].$$

17 If the change is negative, net revenues available for distribution as dividends would be reduced.

18 We will explain more fully below the nature of these "adjustment costs."

19 As suggested earlier, if the utilization of capital were viewed as a choice variable, then it would be natural to have δ directly related to utilization of capital during the period.

20 Later we will say more about investment and the nature of adjustment costs.

21 Note that this discussion assumes for simplicity zero adjustment costs.

22 We follow Sargent and implicitly assume adjustment costs are related to net, not gross, investment. Net investment measures the change in the capital stock. As we will see later, the result is a slightly different expression for Tobin's Q than found elsewhere when adjustment costs depend on gross investment. We could also expand the nature of ψ so that adjustment costs depend on the size of the capital stock, as is done in such papers as Lucas (1967), Uzawa (1969) and Gould (1968).

23 In the National Income and Product Accounts of the USA that report various measures of the activity in the economy, depreciation is measured by what is called the "capital consumption allowance."

24 The presence of such markets reflects the existence of "perfect capital markets" in the macroeconomics literature. Remember that, with respect to the choice of investment for the individual firm, zero adjustment costs imply a potential discrete jump in the capital stock at a point in time, so that investment for the individual firm may not be defined.

25 L'Hospital's rule states that if a is a number, if $f(x)$ and $g(x)$ are differentiable and $g(x)$ does not equal zero for all x on some interval $0 < |x-a| < \varepsilon$, if the limit of $f(x)$ equals zero as x approaches a, and if the limit of $g(x)$ is zero as x approaches zero, then when the limit of the ratio $f(x)/g'(x)$ as x approaches a exists or is infinite, it equals the limit of $f(x)/g(x)$ as x approaches a.

26 In continuous-time or discrete-time models, such adjustment costs mean that the "capital market" at time t is eliminated.

27 Note that since bonds and equity shares are perfect substitutes, the optimization problem will not provide a breakdown into the optimal number of bonds versus equity shares.

28 Recall that we are holding the stock of equity shares outstanding constant.

29 Note that we ignore the potential choice of capital at time t, K_t, and associated choice of bonds, setting $K_t = \overline{K}$. This in fact would be the case with capital adjustment costs.

30 If we evaluated returns from the start of a period, each of the return functions would be multiplied by $1/\overline{R}$.

31 The equivalence of bond, equity share, and retained earnings financing of changes in the capital stock can be shown.

32 This expression reflects the envelope theorem. In particular, we have that

$$\frac{dW(K_{t+1})}{dI_{n,t+1}} \frac{dI_{n,t+1}}{dK_{t+1}} = \frac{dW(K_{t+1})}{dN_{t+1}} \frac{dN_{t+1}}{dK_{t+1}} = 0.$$

33 If the price of capital differed from the price of output, but both prices were expected to change at the same rate so that the relative price of capital was assumed to be constant over time, then the expected real user or rental cost of capital would be $(p_k/p)(m_t + \delta)$, where p_k/p denotes the relative price of capital.

34 Formally, at time t the inherited debt-to-equity ratio is given by $\bar{p}_b\bar{B}/\bar{p}_e\bar{S}$.
35 Naturally, there are other factors not discussed.
36 Note that during period t, when the length of the period between planned purchases of capital (at time t) and final installation (at time $t + 1$) is 1, then net investment I_{nt} is given by $I_{nt} = K_{t+1} - \overline{K}$ and adjustment costs are given by $\psi(I_{nt})$.
37 During period $t+1$, net investment is defined by $I_{n,t+1} = K_{t+2} - K_{t+1}$, and adjustment costs are given by $\psi(I_{n,t+1})$.
38 We can see from the general nature of the investment demand functions that if the production function were not separable, then the assumption of a constant real wage over time as well as a constant expected real rate of return over time would obtain this result.
39 See Sargent (1987a: 11) for a similar expression in continuous time. Note that the two expressions would be exact if we take the limit as the length of the period goes to zero. The equality between ψ'_{t+h} and ψ'_{t+2h} that typically would be an approximation in discrete time holds exactly in the limit. In addition, the definition of the real interest rate for a period of length $h, 1 + hm = (1 + hr)/(1 + h\pi)$ or $m = (r - \pi)/(1 + h\pi)$, indicates that in the limit (as h goes to zero) $m = r - \pi$. If we had assumed that adjustment costs were based on gross, not net, investment then the fraction on the left-hand side of (3.12) would include the term $-\delta\psi$ in the denominator.
40 The Q theory of investment demand was suggested by Tobin (1969). Sargent is one author who expresses investment demand in this way.
41 In fact, empirical measures of Tobin's average Q have been constructed, although such measures are more complex than those discussed here since they must incorporate influences of the tax system (such as investment tax credits, accelerated depreciation allowances and the like) on the optimal choice of the capital stock.
42 In a two-sector model, Tobin's average Q is given by pV/p_1K, where pV is the nominal value of the firm and p_1 denotes the price of capital, which differs from p, the price of output.
43 In our case, there is a single argument of the adjustment function – net investment. If one follows Hayashi (1982) and assumes, as he does, that adjustment costs depend on gross investment, then one must add the assumption that there is a linear homogeneous adjustment function, such that $\psi(\delta k) = \psi'\delta k$, over the appropriate range. Hayashi's adjustment cost function (like others) includes the stock of capital as well.
44 Euler's theorem (or law) is that if the function $f(\cdot)$ is a differentiable function homogeneous of degree 1 (linear homogeneous), with $f : R^n \to R$, then

$$f(x) \equiv \sum_{i=1}^{n}[\partial f(x)/\partial x_i]x_i.$$

Replacing the real wage with the marginal product of labor reflects the assumption that the firm is a price-taker in both the output and labor markets.
45 See, for example, Azariadis (1976). A second reason is that new workers and previously employed workers may not be considered perfect substitutes (e.g., see Oi 1962).
46 Taylor (1972) and Hall (1980) are among those who have examined this phenomenon.

4 Households as market participants

1 Time consistency means in this context that households will follow through on prior plans as the starting date advances. Strotz (1955–56) discussed this point in terms of a utility maximizing problem.

2 An example of nonseparable preferences is a "habit persistence model" in which utility is given by

$$\sum_{i=t}^{\infty} \beta^{i-t} u(c_i, c_{i-1}, \ldots),$$

so that consumption at time t depends on prior consumption. Alternatively, one could have utility given by

$$\sum_{i=t}^{\infty} \beta^{i-t} u(c_i, 1 - N_i, 1 - N_{i-1})$$

such that past work becomes a pertinent state variable for the current period. Kydland and Prescott (1982) is one important exception to the macroeconomic literature in assuming nonseparable preferences.

3 This is sometimes referred to as an "end-of-period" equilibrium specification in the market for assets. Alternative asset specifications for discrete-time analysis have been discussed by, among others, Foley (1975). As Edi Karni (1978) pointed out, Patinkin's model is an end-of-period model.

4 For simplicity, we ignore the financial asset markets at time t. If we assumed portfolio adjustment costs, then it would be the case that at time t desired bond and money holdings would be $\bar{B}$ and $\bar{S}$ respectively.

5 That is, $(\partial W(x_{t+1})/\partial c_{t+1}^d)(\partial c_{t+1}^d/\partial x_{t+1}) = 0$ since $\partial W(x_{t+1})/\partial c_{t+1}^d = 0$; similarly, the indirect effects of a change in x_{t+1} on $\partial W(x_{t+1})$ through its impact on optimal labor supply and real money balance holdings are zero.

6 For completeness, note that by substituting equation (4.3') into (4.5), we could have the equivalent expression

$$\partial W(x_{t+1})/\partial x_{t+1} = \beta[\partial u_{t+1}/\partial(M_{t+1}/p_{t+1})]R_{t+1}/[R_{t+1} - R_{m,t+1}].$$

7 These conditions appear in various forms throughout the macroeconomics literature; see, for instance, Mankiw *et al.* (1985) or Barro and King (1984).

8 The resulting demand for leisure function is termed a "Hicksian or compensated demand function" as it is constructed by varying the price of leisure (the real wage) and income so as to keep the individual at a fixed level of utility.

9 The resulting demand function for leisure that incorporates both the income and substitution effects of changes in the real wage is an example of a "Marshallian" demand function.

10 Borjas and Heckman (1978). See also Pencavel (1985) for a survey of estimates. For evidence on the effect of wage increases on the labor supply of working women, see Nakamura and Nakamura (1981) and Robinson and Tomes (1985).

11 Note that we continue to assume nonsatiation, such that $\partial u_t/\partial c_t > 0$.

12 The second statement presumes sufficient dispersion in preferences so that at each real wage there are some individuals who are just indifferent between a zero and positive labor supply. Thus any rise in the real wage will increase labor force participation.

13 This point was first formally developed in the classic paper by Lucas and Rapping (1970). The role of "market clearing" in macroeconomic analysis will be clearer later when we consider alternative characterizations of the labor market.

14 To be exact, this result assumes that utility is separable and concave in leisure. That is, it is assumed that $\partial^2 u/\partial c\partial N = \partial^2 u/\partial N\partial(M/p) = 0$ and $\partial^2 u/\partial N^2 < 0$.

15 Alogoskoufis (1987) provides a good review of the empirical analysis in this area.

16 Fisherian – or in Patinkin's (1965) terminology, "Fisherine" – analysis takes its name from the classic "time-preference" analysis of Fisher; see, in particular, Fisher (1930).

17 To assure this, one could let $du^a/dc_{ai} > 0$ with $\lim_{c_{ai}\to 0}(du^a/dc_{ai}) \to \infty$ and $\lim_{c_{ai}\to\infty}(du^a/dc_{ai}) \to 0$.

18 Equivalently, one could assume $\partial u^a/\partial(M_{ai}/p) \equiv 0$ for all i. Given the nonnegativity constraint on M_{ai}/p_i, $i = t,\ldots,t + T$, and the presumption of a positive nominal interest rate, $r_i, i = t,\ldots,t+T-1$, the optimal solution would be $M^d_{ai}/p_i = 0$ for all i. That is, bonds will dominate money as an asset, and only bonds will be held if asset holdings are positive. The reason is simple – the unique attribute of money holdings as a way to reduce "transaction costs" has not been introduced by providing a "utility yield" to holding money.

19 Note that the equality sign here rather than the $\geq$ sign reflects the fact that the first-order conditions imply that $\lambda_i > 0$, so that the condition $\lambda_i\partial L/\partial\lambda_i = 0$ must be met by $\partial L/\partial\lambda_i = 0$.

20 Note that we assume a time-invariant one-period utility function. The notation u^a_i reflects the fact that utility of agent a in period i depends on consumption in period i, c_{ai}.

21 In general, for a period of length h, we have that $1 + hm = (1 + hr_i)/(1 + h\pi_i)$. Solving for hm_i and then dividing through by h, we have that $m_i = (r_i - \pi_i)/(1+h\pi_i)$. Thus, in the limit as the length of each period goes to zero, $m_i = r_i - \pi_i$. Thus, in continuous-time analysis the real rate of interest is exactly defined by $r_i - \pi_i$.

22 In the discussion to follow, we maintain the assumption of a time-invariant utility function, such that $u^a_i(c_{ai}) = u^a(c_{ai})$ for $i = t,\ldots,t + T$.

23 At the point where $c_{at} = c_{a,t+1}$ the slope of the indifference curve is $-1/\beta$. Assuming $\bar{c}_{at} = \bar{c}_{a,t+1}$, and no initial assets or debt (i.e., $z\bar{B}_{at} = 0$), if $1/\beta = R_t$ then the result of the same consumption in each period would imply the individual would be neither a lender nor a borrower.

24 As Modigliani (1996) has stated, "the consumption and saving decisions of households at each point of time reflect a more or less conscious attempt at achieving the preferred distribution of consumption over the life cycle, subject to the constraint imposed by the resources accruing to the household over the lifetime." Modigliani summarizes his contribution to the analysis of consumption behavior in his Nobel lecture of December 1985 (see Modigliani 1986).

25 Examples of such discussions are Diamond and Hausman (1984) and Hurd (1987). However, what happens in the aggregate does mask different behavior among subgroups of the populations. For instance, Burbidge and Robb (1985) find for Canadian data that while an inverted U-shaped profile exists for the "average" Canadian household, "white collar" households do appear to continue to accumulate wealth years after both husband and wife have left the labor force.

26 If individual a were the representative agent, then consumption smoothing would imply that the aggregate endowment of the consumption good is identical across periods, i.e., $\bar{c}_i = \bar{c}_{i+1}, i = t,\ldots,t + T - 1$.

27 Note that in the case of multiperiod bonds, agent a's future income could include payments derived from the initial holdings of assets. Since the present value of such future "income" is incorporated in the current value of the assets, operationally future income $\bar{c}_{at}, i = t+1,\ldots,t+T$, is defined as income other than derived from initial asset holdings. In a production context, the source of such income would be compensation for labor services sold.

28 In an economy with production, this transitory component of current income can reflect such events as a temporary layoff, a short-run opportunity to work overtime, or a temporary tax rebate.

29 This discussion ignores the effects of uncertainty on optimal consumption plans.

30 Note that the equality sign here rather than the $\geq$ sign reflects the fact that the first-order conditions imply that $\lambda_i > 0$, so that the condition $\lambda_i \partial L/\partial \lambda_i = 0$ must be met by $\partial L/\partial \lambda_i = 0$.
31 Note that with one-period bonds, individual a has a zero initial endowment of bonds that continue into the future at time t.
32 Other papers on this topic include: Hansen and Singleton (1983) and Mankiw *et al.* (1985).
33 An example of a compositional change that could affect aggregate consumption but would not be accounted for in the analysis to follow is a change in the proportion of retired individuals in the economy. Thus, on this ground at least, Hall's empirical findings cannot be taken as the last word on consumption behavior at the level of the individual.

5 Summarizing the behavior and constraints of firms and households

1 Caballero and Engel (1999) provide an empirical study of investment dynamics in the context of manufacturing firms.
2 Weber (1998) provides empirical evidence on the link between the financial markets and consumption spending.
3 We refer to this perfect foresight as "limited perfect foresight" since it concerns only the current period. This focus on current markets alone, typical of static analysis, implies "expectations functions of the agents" with respect to prices in subsequent periods that do not reflect the underlying analysis of markets beyond the current period. Thus, beyond the current period expectations do not have the property of perfect foresight (or rational expectations in a nondeterministic setting).
4 In an open economy – that is, one which admits a foreign sector – we would add a fourth market, the market for foreign exchange.
5 Note that in a fully monetized economy, money enters on one side of every exchange – purchase or sale – in these three markets.
6 Note that money holdings and money demand arise only for "households." To the extent firms do hold money and make choices with respect to the size of such holdings, we presume their behavior would be similar to that of households, and so lump firms with households with respect to such activity. Thus, the behavior of the firm is restricted to labor demand, output supply, investment demand, and financial asset supply.
7 Recall that the expected real user cost of capital is $m_t + \delta$, where δ is the rate of depreciation of capital and m_t is the expected real rate of interest (i.e., $m_t \equiv (r_t - \pi_t^e)/(1+\pi_t^e)$, where r_t is the money interest rate and π_t^e is the expected rate of inflation between periods t and $t+1$).
8 As previously, for simplicity we continue to assume that expectations of future prices are held with subjective certainty.
9 If $\partial^2 f/\partial K \partial N = 0$, then the real wage would not enter as an argument in the capital demand function, nor would the existing capital stock affect labor demand.
10 That is, we can express a demand function in a form similar to one that would be obtained if the analysis were to consider only two periods.
11 Note that we do allow the expected wage inflation between period t and $t+1$, π_{wt}^e, to differ from subsequent wage inflation so that the expected real wage next period, $w_{t+1}^e/p_{t+1}^e \equiv w_t(1+\pi_{wt}^e)/p_t(1+\pi_t^e)$, can differ from the current real wage. This introduces the possibility of intertemporal substitution of labor supply in response to a change in the current real wage.
12 Assuming less than unit elastic expectations with respect to future income streams would assure from the standard Fisherian problem that the marginal propensity to consume would be less than one.
13 Recall that $\pi_t^e \equiv (p_{t+1}^e - p_t)/p_t$.

14 Recall that firms are presumed not to hold money balances, so there are no real balance effects to concern us with respect to firms' demands or supplies.
15 As Lucas and Rapping (1970) point out, introducing other expectation assumptions can retain the "intertemporal substitution hypothesis" in the context of changes in the current price level, but in doing so money illusion is introduced. In their own words, the

> labor-supply equation is not homogeneous in current wages and current prices (such that) there is "money illusion" in the supply of labor. . . . "money illusion" results not from a myopic concentration on money values but from our assumption that the suppliers of labor are adaptive on the level of prices, expecting a return to normal price levels regardless of current prices, and from the empirical fact that the nominal interest rate does not change in proportion to the actual rate of inflation. With these expectations, it is to a supplier's advantage to increase his current supply of labor and his current money savings when prices rise.
>
> (Lucas and Rapping 1970: 268–269)

Lucas and Rapping are particularly looking at the effect of a change in the current price level on the expected real rate of interest. Their assumption of "adaptive" expectations implies that an increase in p_t results in a fall in $\pi_t^e \equiv (p_{t+1}^e - p_t)/p_t$, a rise in the expected real rate of interest, and thus a rise in labor supply.
16 That is, future technology, capital demand, labor demand, the real wage, the rate of depreciation, and future real interest rates are all unchanged by such a change in prices and the money supply.

6 The simple neoclassical macroeconomic model (without government or depository institutions)

1 In particular, it is assumed that the money wage rate adjusts to continuously maintain equality between the demand for and supply of labor, the price of output adjusts to maintain equality between the demand for and supply of output, and the price of financial assets (and thus the interest rate) adjusts to maintain equality between the demand for and supply of financial assets. Patinkin (1965) provides one of the first complete accountings of this model.
2 That is, we would expect prices in the various markets to eventually adjust to eliminate any possible excess demands or supplies in the economy. We would also expect agents ultimately to correctly anticipate the price level. The neoclassical model can be modified to explain the workings of the economy in the face of incomplete information and price inflexibility.
3 As before, the "laws of motion" dictating how prices change to reach equilibrium are given by Walras' excess demand hypothesis, and we maintain the assumption that no exchange occurs until an equilibrium is reached (the recontracting assumption).
4 Alternatively, one could assume that expectations at time t concerning these future variables are constant.
5 Note that Patinkin has firms as well as households managing a portfolio of financial assets and money balances, which is why he includes the demand function for labor in the above statement. In our analysis, this statement applies to the labor supply function alone.
6 This last sentence anticipates the intertemporal substitution hypothesis.
7 We ignore the potential effect of changes in the interest rate on labor supply and thus employment.
8 This reflects the assumption that households and firms share common expectations concerning the price level (in fact, for both $p_t^e = p_t$).

9 Reasons such as these for changes in output form the basis of much of the current analysis in the literature with respect to "real business cycles."

10 This is, perhaps, too extreme a statement. To the extent that a higher price level is anticipated, the resulting lower real money balances could lead to an increase in labor supply at any given real wage and consequently increased employment and output. Also there is a potential effect of changes in the price level on aggregate labor supply through the impact of such changes on the expected real rate of interest if unit elastic expectations concerning future prices are not assumed. Recall that we follow macroeconomic tradition and abstract from these possibilities.

11 In a recent study, Ewing *et al.* (2002) develop a model of the equilibrium unemployment rate and examine how it responds to unanticipated changes in real output.

12 Fairlie and Kletzer (1998) discuss the issues revolving around job displacement.

13 Unemployment may also result if prices in the economy do not adjust quickly enough to ensure that all markets (particularly the labor market) are continuously in equilibrium. Unemployment associated with labor market disequilibrium is sometimes referred to as "involuntary" unemployment. We analyze such unemployment later.

14 See, for instance, the paper by Evans (1989) that examines the relationship between output and unemployment in the United States.

15 The "IS" equation is sometimes referred to as the aggregate demand equation, indicating that it reflects equality between total or aggregate demand for output and production. Note that equilibrium in the output market is being described in terms of demand equal to what is produced, y_t^*. The aggregate supply equation indicates what will be produced.

16 This is the case only for this simple aggregate model without government.

17 Such an assumption removes the anticipated real wage next period as an argument in these demand functions. Recall that earlier "static" assumptions concerning future interest rates and rates of inflation have already simplified the form of these functions.

18 However, "real" or "supply" shocks such as the above-mentioned changes in technology, capital stock, supply of other inputs such as oil, or in labor supply at prevailing real wages can affect real output.

19 This analysis should be familiar since we performed a similar analysis for the economy without production.

20 Note that unit elastic expectations imply that $\partial \pi_t^e / \partial p_t = 0$.

21 Note that without a real balance effect, the CC curve would be horizontal.

22 The lower interest rate abstracts from a real balance effect in the output market, so that the CC curve is horizontal.

7 Empirical macroeconomics: traditional approaches and time series models

1 To reduce notational clutter, we suppress time subscripts. All variables are period t variables.

2 Note that in Sargent (1987a: 20), equation (7.1) is replaced by the "representative" firm's first-order condition for the optimal use of the labor input given a competitive labor market, that is, the condition that the real wage equals the marginal product of labor: $w/p = F_n(n, K)$. Note that if the production function $F(n, k)$ is separable in the labor and capital inputs, such that $f(n, K) = v(n) + u(K)$ and $v(n) = (1/g)(fn - n^2/2)$, then equation (7.1) is identical to Sargent's equation since $f_n(n, K) = (1/g)(f - n)$.

3 Unless otherwise noted, all parameters in this model, such as $f, g, h,$ and j in equations (7.1) and (7.2), are assumed to be positive.

4 In this context, "lump-sum" taxes are taxes independent of income. Equation (7.3) is an example of the "consumption function."

5 Endogenous variables are variables whose values are determined by the analysis.

6 Sargent adds equations (7.3) and (7.4) to the system (7.12) in order to determine consumption and investment demand as well.

7 To derive w^*, start with the equilibrium condition $n^d = n^s$. Substituting the first two equations of 7.12, the equilibrium money wage satisfies

$$f - g \cdot (w^*/p) = h + j \cdot (w^*/p)$$

Then one can simply solve this equation for the equilibrium money wage w^*. We can then obtain the equilibrium employment level n^* by substituting the expression for w^* into either of the first two equations of 7.12.

8 This is a property of "classical" macroeconomic models, in that monetary changes that alter the price level do not affect real variables such as the real wage, output, and employment.

9 The IS equation indicates combinations of the interest rate r and output y at which, if the output were produced and that interest rate prevailed, output demand would equal output produced. The LM equation indicates combinations of r and y that will equate the demand for and supply of money.

10 For the model under consideration, the "aggregate demand curve" (a plot in (p, y) space of the aggregate demand equation) slopes downward and the "aggregate supply curve" (a plot in (p, y) space of the aggregate supply curve) is vertical. The intersection of the aggregate demand and supply curves graphically determines the equilibrium output and price level.

11 See Altonji and Siow (1987). Ewing and Payne (1998) examined the relationship between the personal savings rate and consumer sentiment in the context of a consumption model.

12 Note that Taylor assumes that certain demands, for instance consumption demand, may depend on past as well as current values of output and the money supply, so that the reduced-form expression estimated includes lagged values of income and the real money supply.

13 Time series analysis can be viewed as primarily the art of specifying the most likely stochastic process that could have generated an observed time series.

14 That is, forecasts generated by time series models have been used to proxy individuals' expectations of future events in tests of various theoretical macroeconomic models.

15 A histogram is a plot of the frequency distribution of a set of observations.

16 If the process is also "ergodic," these statistics give consistent estimates of the mean and variance. Ergodicity basically requires that observations sufficiently far apart should be almost uncorrelated. Then by averaging a series through time one is continually adding new and useful information to the average. For a rigorous explanation of this concept, see Hannan (1970: 201).

17 The variable $\gamma_k, k = 0, 1, 2, \ldots$, is termed the autocovariance function.

18 Or, more generally, $k \neq 0$. Note that $\rho_k = \rho_{-k}$.

19 Some have suggested that stock market prices follow a random walk. See Campbell *et al.* (1997).

20 Note that if y_t is taken to be the logarithm of real output, then the trend reflects a constant rate of growth of output equal to d in the absence of shocks.

21 This assumes y_0 is the initial value of the function y_t.

22 A random walk is an example of a class of nonstationary processes known as "integrated" processes that can be made stationary by the application of a time-invariant "filter." As defined by Granger and Newbold (1986) "if a series w_t is formed by a linear combination of terms of a series y_t, so that $w_t = \sum_{j=-s}^{m} c_j y_{t-j}$ then w_t is called a 'filtered' version of y_t. If only past terms of y_t are involved, so that $w_t = \sum_{j=0}^{m} c_j y_{t-j}$ then w_t might be called a one-sided or backward-looking filter."

23 This is a special case of a class of stochastic processes known as Markov processes.

24 Recall that for the random walk process, $\phi = 1$, in which case the process was not stationary as the variance of the process becomes larger and larger with time.

25 To obtain this result, note that

$$E\left[\sum_{j=0}^{\infty}(\phi^2)^j\varepsilon_{t-j}^2\right] = \sum_{j=0}^{\infty}(\phi^2)^j\sigma_e^2 = \sigma_e^2/(1-\phi^2).$$

26 Often the "lag operator" L, or equivalently the "backward shift operator" B, is used to express this equation: $L^\tau y_t$ (or $B^\tau y_t$) $= y_{t-\tau}, \tau = 1, 2, 3, \ldots$. There are associated polynomials in the lag operator, such that

$$d(L) = d_0 + d_1 L + d_2 L^2 + d_3 L^3 + \cdots + d_p L^p$$

Letting

$$\phi(L) = 1 - \phi_1 L - \phi_2 L^2 - \phi_3 L^3 - \cdots - \phi_p L^p,$$

we can thus express an AR(p) process for y_t as $\phi(L)y_t = \varepsilon_t$.

27 If y_t is an AR(p) process, it may be described in the following way: "an appropriate finite backward-looking filter applied to y_t will produce a white noise series" (Granger and Newbold 1986: 32).

28 If there were a single shock to y_t at time 0 (i.e., $\varepsilon_t = 0$ for all $t > 0$), then the deterministic component would signify the deviation of the time path from its equilibrium level. As we will see, in this case stationarity would imply "stability of equilibrium" in that y_t would converge to its equilibrium value over time.

29 A linear difference equation of order s is of the form

$$y_t = \sum_{j=1}^{s} a_j y_{t-j} + c.$$

30 Successive substitution (the "iterative method of solution") reveals this essential nature of the solution. In particular, substituting for past values of y_t in (7.25) results in $y_t = \phi^t y_0$.

31 The appendix to this chapter shows how one can reinterpret higher-order difference equations as a system of first-order difference equations.

32 Note that, in general, a quadratic equation of the form

$$ax^2 + bx + c = 0$$

can be solved using the quadratic formula:

$$x_1, x_2 = [-b \pm (b^2 - 4ac)^{1/2}]/2a$$

In our case, $a = 1$, $b = -(m_1 + m_2) = -\phi_1$ and $c = m_1 m_2 = -\phi_2$.

33 This assumes $m_1 \neq m_2$. The solution for repeated roots is discussed briefly below.

34 A variable x is said to be inside the unit circle if $x < |1|$. An alternative way of expressing this condition is in terms of the associated polynomial $1 - \phi_1 L - \phi_2 L^2 = 0$. This polynomial equation is similar to (7.30) except that b is replaced by $1/L$ and the whole equation is multiplied through by L^2. The stationarity condition is that the roots of this polynomial equation should lie outside the unit circle.

35 Recall that $\phi_1 = m_1 + m_2$ and $\phi_2 = -m_1 m_2$.

36 The following discussion follows Goldberg (1958: 171–172).

37 As discussed below, in this case the two roots are $m_1 = h + vi$ and $m_2 = h - vi$, where $h = \phi_1/2$, $v = (4\phi_2 + \phi_1^2)^{1/2}/2$, and i is the imaginary number $(-1)^{1/2}$. The product of these two roots is $(\phi_1^2 - 4\phi_2 - \phi_1^2)/4 = -\phi_2$, which is the square of the modulus of the roots. We are assuming $(-\phi_2)^{1/2} < 1$, so we have the condition that $\phi_2 < 1$ or $\phi_2 > -1$.

38 Note that if y_t is an MA process, then it is a "backward looking filter" applied to a white noise process. As before, we can use a lag operator L (or backward shift operator B) to express an MA(q) process for y_t as $y_t = \mu + \theta(L)\varepsilon_t$ where the polynomial in the lag operator $\theta(L)$ is given by

$$\theta(L) = 1 + \theta_1 L + \theta_2 L^2 + \cdots + \theta_q L^q.$$

39 Recall that, as discussed above, we assume for simplicity zero mean for y_t, that is, $\mu = 0$.

40 For a more detailed description of invertibility, see Granger and Newbold (1986) or Box and Jenkins (1970).

41 Note that ARMA($p, 0$) $\equiv$ AR(p) and ARMA($0, q$) $\equiv$ MA(q). Using the lag operator, the ARMA model (in the case of a zero mean) can be simply expressed as $\phi(L)Y_t = \theta(L)\varepsilon_t$.

42 In general, if y_t is ARMA(p_1, q_1) and x_t is ARMA(p_2, q_2), the sum $z_t = y_t + x_t$ is ARMA(p_3, q_3), where $p_3 \leq p_1 + p_2$ and $q_3 \leq \max(p_1 + q_2, p_2 + q_1)$. A proof of this is found in Granger and Morris (1976).

43 A time sequence $T(t)$ is called "deterministic" if there exists a function of past and present values $g_t = g(T(t - j)), j = 0, 1 \ldots$, such that $E[(T_{t+1} - g_t)^2] = 0$. If the function g_t is a linear function of $T_{t-j}, j \geq 0$, then T_t is called "linear deterministic."

44 For instance, for a stationary series of quarterly data, one could postulate a simple fourth-order seasonal AR process of the form:

$$y_t = \phi_4 y_{t-4} + \varepsilon_t.$$

This is a special case of AR(4) with $\phi_1 = \phi_2 = \phi_3 = 0$. The model could be extended to include both AR and MA terms at other seasonal lags, for instance the following ARMA(2,1):

$$y_t = \phi_4 y_{t-4} + \phi_8 y_{t-8} + \theta_4 \varepsilon_{t-4} + \varepsilon_t.$$

To add other than seasonal components, one could simply fill in the gaps (e.g., add terms such as $\phi_1 y_{t-1}$, $\theta_1 \varepsilon_{t-1}$, and the like to the above). Other options are discussed by Harvey (1993) and others.

45 Campbell and Mankiw argue that even if the log of output followed a random walk with drift, indicating that the effect of any shock persists indefinitely into the future, estimates using the detrended series would be biased and erroneously conclude otherwise.

46 Note that if the log of real output is an ARMA(p, q) process, then the differenced process will be an ARMA($p, q + 1$) process. This means that to allow for stationarity with respect to the level of real output requires at least one moving average process for the differenced series.

47 Equivalently, for the logarithm of real output they are considering ARIMA($p, 1, q$) processes for $p = 0, 1, 2, 3$ and for $q = 0, 1, 2, 3$.

48 Such a finding is often termed as supportive of real business cycle theories.

8 The neoclassical model

1 The presence of money reflects the introduction of "imperfect" or costly information. A medium of exchange can arise to minimize costs incurred by participants in the economy when there exists imperfect information on potential exchange partners.

2 In so doing, we assume that the new equilibrium, like the initial one, exists. Further, we disregard the process of adjustment of the variables to the new equilibrium. Alternatively, we could introduce "laws of motion" for the equilibrium values (e.g., the excess demand hypothesis for price changes) and examine whether the equilibriums are stable.

3 For notational simplicity, we let $L^d = L^d_t$, $c^d = c^d_t$, $I^d = I^d_{nt}$, $p = p_t$, $r = r_t$, $y^d = c^d_t + I^d_{nt} + \delta \overline{K} + \psi(I^d_t)$, and $M = \overline{M}$.

4 For simplicity, we let the expected real rate of interest component of the expected real user cost of capital $((r_t - \pi^e_t)/(1 + \pi^e_t))$ be approximated by $r_t - \pi^e_t$, as represented by $r - \pi$.

5 One alternative is for the interest rate to adjust to equate the demand for and supply of money.

6 That is, we assume that consumption demand is a function of the expected gross real rate of interest, R_t, not its components (r_t and π^e_t). This would be the case if one could view the consumption decision from the point of view of the pure "Fisherian problem," in essence separating the allocation of consumption across time decisions from the "portfolio problem." Note that for notational ease, we not only let r_t denote the money interest rate r_t but also let π denote the expected rate of inflation π^e_t.

7 This would be the case if our focus was solely on the portfolio choice problem.

8 Examples of growth models with money include Tobin (1965) and Sidrauski (1967b). As Begg (1980: 293) notes, "in a steady state, any expectations generating mechanism will yield correct predictions ... thus the steady state analysis of growth models with money may be viewed as a special case of the rational expectations model with systematic monetary policy."

9 This asymmetry in information can reflect an aggregation across labor markets in which each firm determines labor demand based on its correct anticipation of the price of the particular commodity it produces while suppliers of labor determine labor supply based on their potentially incorrect anticipation of the overall level of prices, reflecting the idea that suppliers are concerned with the purchasing power of wages in terms of commodities not restricted to the particular commodity that they produce.

10 As before, for notational simplicity, we let $L^d = L^d_t$, $c^d = c^d_t$, $p = p_t$, $r = r_t$, $y = y_t$, and $M = \overline{M}$.

11 Recall that for simplicity we let the expected real rate of interest component of the expected real user cost of capital $(r_t - \pi^e_t)/(1 + \pi^e_t)$ be approximated by $r_t - \pi^e_t$, as represented by $r - \pi$.

12 Note that $\partial y / \partial p = 0$ for the neoclassical model given limited perfect foresight.

13 This is obvious from the graph of aggregate demand and supply curves if one compares the vertical aggregate supply curve of the neoclassical model, $dp/p = dM/M$ with the upward-sloping aggregate supply curve of the model with real wage illusion. Note that the shift in the aggregate demand curve for a given change in the money supply is identical in either case.

9 The "Keynesian model" with fixed money wage: modifying the neoclassical model

1 Typically, a union contract runs for three years. Often, however, there are provisions that permit parts of the agreement to be renegotiated at specific times during the three-year contract period.

2 As a general rule, labor agreements are specified in money terms. An exception to this is the cost of living agreements (COLAs) as part of union wage contracts in the United

States which became popular during the 1960s and 1970s. COLAs adjust money wages automatically to changes in prices, typically using changes in the Consumer Price Index to measure price changes. However, the percentage of all workers who have contracts with COLAs is fairly small as less than 20 percent of the total labor force is covered by collective bargaining agreements. Further, not all COLA clauses offer full protection against general price increases, as wages may rise by only some fraction of the increase of the CPI. Considering these qualifications, for the time being we simplify by assuming that all labor agreements are specified in money terms.

3   These seven variables for the classical model are made up of three "prices", along with four variables implied from the behavioral equations. The three "prices" are money wage, price level, and interest rate determined by the equilibrium conditions for the labor market and two of the three other markets (output, financial and/or money markets). The variable implied from the behavioral equations are employment (labor demand function), output (production function), consumption (consumption demand function), and investment (investment demand function).

4   Note that this analysis is inconsistent with the idea that long-term employment contracts that fix the money wage for several periods arise due to adjustment costs with respect to the labor input.

5   As discussed before, one justification for this form is if real money balances are not part of household wealth, which can be the case when we introduce depository institutions into the analysis.

6   As before, for notational simplicity, we let $L^d = L^d_t, c^d = c^d_t, p = p_t, I^d_{nt} = I^d, r = r_t,$ $y = y_t,$ and $M = \overline{M}.$

7   Recall that for simplicity we let the expected real rate of interest component of the expected real user cost of capital $(r_t - \pi^e_t)/(1 + \pi^e_t)$ be approximated by $r_t - \pi^e_t$, as represented by $r - \pi$.

8   Note that $\partial y/\partial p = 0$ for the neoclassical model given limited perfect foresight.

9   The Lucas model was introduced in Chapter 8 and is covered in more depth in Chapter 10.

10   An exception to this statement occurs if monetary authorities can react to period t disturbances, that is, if monetary authorities' information set includes the values of the random shocks in period t which are not known to private agents.

11   Phelps and Taylor (1977) go on to state that they "do not pretend to have a rigorous understanding of [why prices and/or wages are set in advance]. In the ancient and honorable tradition of Keynesians past, we take it for granted that there are disadvantages from too-frequent or too-precipitate revisions of price lists and wage schedules."

12   Note that θ is affected by the variability of relative price shocks in relation to general price shocks.

13   We assume for simplicity that the coefficient on $P_t - W_t + \phi$ is one.

14   Note that, if $P_t - W_t + \phi = 0$, then equation (9.9′) is a first-order linear difference equation of the form $Y_t - \lambda Y_{t-1} = 0$ with solution $Y_t = c_0 \lambda^t$. In the limit as t approaches infinity, Y_t equals zero. Recall that the logarithm of the natural level of output is zero.

15   Recall our assumption that the scale factor in the determination of the real wage is equal to zero for convenience.

16   As Fischer shows, if wages were set only for the current period t, that is, $_{t-i}W_t = \phi + E_{t-i}P_t$, then his results would be like those obtained by the Sargent and Wallace model with rational expectations, for similar reasons. This can be seen clearly on substituting (9.10) into (9.9′), in which case one obtains the standard Lucas-like aggregate supply equation.

17   Later it will be assumed that u_t and u_{t-1} are correlated, so that information obtained during period $t - 1$ will help predict variations in output for period t. Like the lagged output term in the Lucas equation, this introduction of serial correlation in output is necessary (but not sufficient) if monetary policy rules that dictate the money supply

for period t based on information obtained up to the end of period $t - 1$ are to serve a stabilizing role.

18 Note that in Fischer's paper, $-v_t$ rather than v_t is used in (9.13). Our v_t is more in line with other models.

19 With the one exception, noted before, that Fischer has $-v_t$ replacing v_t.

20 Again, note that Fischer has $-\eta_t$ and $-\rho_2$ in the above equation since our v_t is his $-v_t$.

21 Fischer has $b_1 = -\rho_2$ since our v_t is his $-v_t$.

10 The Lucas model

1 The discussion follows that found in Lucas (1973) and Sargent (1987a: 438–446).

2 Or, as Sargent (1987a: 483) states, "an employee cares about his prospective wage measured not in terms of own-market goods but in terms of an economy-wide average bundle of goods ... the assumption is that the labor supplier works in one market but shops in many other markets."

3 The Cobb–Douglas production function would be given by $y_{it} = (N_{it})^{1-\alpha} (\overline{K}_i)^{\alpha}$, where $\overline{K}_i$ denotes the inherited capital stock for sector or "island" i, N_{it} is the employment of labor for sector i, and y_{it} is the production of commodity i by sector i during period t. In this case, the marginal product of labor is given by $\partial y_{it}/\partial N_{it} = (1 - \alpha)(N_{it})^{-\alpha}(\overline{K}_i)^{\alpha}$, which implies that $a = (1 - \alpha)(\overline{K}_i)^{\alpha}$.

4 Solving this expression for the demand for labor and differentiating with respect to the real wage relevant for a firm producing commodity i, we have

$$\partial N_{it}^d /\partial (w_{it}/p_{it}) = (1 - \alpha)^{-1/\alpha}(-1/\alpha)(w_{it}/p_{it})^{(-1-\alpha)/\alpha} < 0.$$

Note that our particular form for the labor demand function implies a constant elasticity. In particular, the elasticity of demand for labor is given by

$$\frac{\partial N_{it}^d}{\partial (w_{it}/p_{it})} \frac{w_{it}/p_{it}}{N_{it}^d} = -\frac{1}{\alpha}.$$

5 Up to this point, we have assumed that expectations are held with "subjective certainty," so that $E_t(1/p_t) = 1/E_t p_t$ and the expected real wage can be represented as $w_{it}/E_t p_t$. However, we now assume that individuals view the price level as a random variable. In this setting, the expression for the expected real wage is $E_t(w_{it}/p_t)$ or $w_{it}E_t(1/p_t)$, which is *not* the same as $w_{it}/E_t p_t$. In fact, the relationship between $w_{it}E_t(1/p_t)$ and $w_{it}/E_t p_t$ is shown by Jensen's inequality, $w_{it}E_t(1/p_t) \geq w_{it}(1/E_t p_t)$. This inequality reflects the fact that the function $f(p_t) = 1/p_t$ is convex rather than linear in p_t. For instance, if $p_t = p_0$ with probability t and p_1 with probability $1 - t$, then we have $E_t(1/p_t) = tf(p_0) + (1 - t)f(p_1) > f(tp_0 + (1 - t)p_1) = 1/E_t p_t$, where $1 > t > 0$. On the other hand, $\ln(1/p_t)$ is linear in $\ln p_t$, so the log of the real wage is linear in the log of the price level. Thus we express the labor supply function in logarithmic form and consider the expectation of the log of the price level.

6 The term ξ_t is assumed to be serially independent, which means that $E(\xi_t \xi_s) = 0$ for $t \neq s$.

7 We assume that z_{it} and ξ_t are statistically independent.

8 In problems involving more than two random variables – that is, a "multivariate regression" – we are correspondingly concerned with the term $E(z|x, y)$, the expected value of z for given values of x and y, and so on.

9 The discussion that follows is standard statistical theory. Note that if the joint distribution of the two variables is a bivariate normal density function, then the regression of $\ln p_t$ on $\ln p_{it}$ is linear.

10 In general, if $x_1, x_2, \ldots, x_n$ are random variables, $a_1, a_2, \ldots, a_n$ are constants, and $q = a_1 x_1 + a_2 x_2 + \cdots + a_n x_n$, then

$$E(q) = \sum_{i=1}^{n} a_i E(x_i),$$

$$\mathrm{Var}(q) = \sum_{i=1}^{n} a_i^2 \mathrm{Var}(x_i) + 2 \sum_{i<j} a_i a_j \mathrm{Cov}(x_i x_j),$$

where $\sum_{i<j}$ means that the summation extends over all values of i and j, from 1 to n, for which $i < j$. This expression is derived from the definition of the variance:

$$\mathrm{Var}(q) \equiv E([q - E(q)]^2) = E\left(\left[\sum_{i=1}^{n} a_i(x_i - \mu_i)\right]^2\right),$$

which can be expanded by means of the multinomial theorem according to which, for example, $(a+b+c+d)^2 = a^2 + b^2 + c^2 + d^2 + 2ab + 2ac + 2ad + 2bc + 2bd + 2cd$. Note that

$$\mathrm{Cov}(x_i x_j) = E[(x_i - \mu_i)(x_j - \mu_j)].$$

If the $x_i, i = 1, \ldots, n$, are independent, then

$$\mathrm{Var}(q) = \sum_{i=1}^{n} a_i^2 \cdot \mathrm{Var}(x_i).$$

11 Note that these first two expectations are taken without information on $\ln p_{it}$.
12 While it is true that if two random variables are independent they are also uncorrelated, the converse does not necessarily hold. That is, two random variables that are uncorrelated are not necessarily independent. However, two random variables having the bivariate normal distribution are independent if and only if they are uncorrelated.
13 In general, for any two random variables x_1 and x_2 with joint density function $f(x_1, x_2)$, the marginal density of x_2, $g(x_2)$, is obtained by integrating out, from $-\infty$ to $+\infty$, the other variable. Thus $g(x_2) = \int f(x_1, x_2) dx_1$. Similarly, we can obtain the marginal density of x_1 by integrating out x_2. The conditional probability density function of the random variable x_1 given that the random variable x_2 takes on the value x_2 is defined by $\phi(x_1 | x_2) = f(x_1, x_2)/g(x_2)$ assuming that $g(x_2)$ does not equal zero.
14 To obtain the following expression, we use the fact that the random variables ξ_t and z_{it} are independent with zero means and variances σ^2 and σ_z^2, respectively.
15 Note that this "signal extraction" problem appears in a number of different contexts such as in statistical theories of discrimination in labor economics (Aigner and Cain 1977; Lundberg and Startz 1983) and in the industrial organization literature.
16 If there were a trend in the natural level of output, then $\ln y_{nit}$ would replace the first $\ln y_{ni}$ and in the lagged term $\ln y_{nit-1}$ would replace the second $\ln y_{ni}$.
17 The last term in (10.16′) indicates the deviation of output in the prior period from its "normal" level. It is presumed that $\lambda < 1$.
18 Recall that this supply function assumes no adjustment costs and thus does not have a lagged output term in it.

19 In general, if $z_1, z_2, \ldots, z_n$ are independent random variables having the same distribution with mean μ and variance σ_z^2, and if $\bar{z} = (z_1 + z_2 + \ldots + z_n)/n$ then $E(\bar{z}) = \mu$ and $\text{Var}(\bar{z}) = \sigma_z^2/n$. Note that as n goes to infinity, the variance of $\bar{z}$ goes to zero.

20 Recall that we have let $\bar{\pi}(\pi_{t-1})$ denote $(p_t - p_{t-1})/p_{t-1}$. This was done so that the terms making up the expected real interest rate, $r_t - \pi_t^e$, would have the same time subscript, $\pi_t^e = (p_{t+1}^e - p_t)/p_t$. In the discussions to follow, however, we shift time subscripts, so that the previously denoted $\bar{\pi} = \pi$ and the previously denoted π_t^e becomes π_{t+1}^e.

21 Note that the natural log of real output is $\ln(y_t) = Y_t$.

22 Sometimes the money demand function is simplified by assuming $\alpha_2 = 0$, so that there are no effects of interest rate changes on real money demand.

23 This follows given $m_t = \bar{m}_t + \varepsilon_t$, so that $dP_t/dm_t = 1$. Recall that P_t and m_t are logs of the price level and the money supply, respectively, so that $dP_t = d(\ln p_t) = (1/p_t)dp_t$ and $dm_t = d(\ln M_t) = (1/M_t)dM_t$.

24 Note that we are somewhat imprecise in our statement that we are eliminating the term for output from the equation. Recall that the exact interpretation of Y_t would be as the difference between the logarithm of output and the logarithm of the natural level of output. Equivalently, we may call Y_t the log of the ratio of output to its natural level.

11 Policy

1 The alternative to a rule is called "purely discretionary monetary policy," in which money supply changes are made purely at the discretion of the government depending on its current reading of the economy and current set of objectives.

2 This view is not universally accepted. For instance, according to the Nobel prize winner James Tobin (1985), the government should be free to do as it sees fit, and he sees many reasons "for the Fed's reluctance to tie its own hands as much as 'rules' advocates ... wish." Sargent and Wallace (1976) identify as "Keynesians" individuals who believe government monetary policy should attempt to "lean against the wind" in an effort to attenuate the business cycle. In the view of Sargent and Wallace and others, the monetary authority has no scope to conduct countercyclical policy. Not surprisingly, those who disagree with this view suggest alternative models of the economy, such as those with "sticky" prices, more favorable to their alternative views.

3 Those who argue for a rule such as this are sometimes called "monetarists." Some advocates of a constant growth rate in the money supply would restrict the length of time during which a particular rate of growth was fixed. For instance, William Poole, former member of the President's Council of Economic Advisers (1982–1985), and now with the Fed, suggests that monetary rules should be adopted but that the rule should be "subject to change at any time upon presentation of a convincing case with supporting evidence" (Poole 1985).

4 Hall's suggestion echoes Simons' (1936) proposal for "a monetary rule of maintaining the constancy of some price index." Wayne Angell, a 1986 appointee to the Board of Governors of the Federal Reserve (the monetary authorities for the USA) has argued for a monetary policy that will stabilize a price index constructed from a basket of basic commodities (perhaps including gold).

5 Recall also that we assume the random variables ε_t and u_t (the random variable associated with output demand) are independent with zero mean and respective variances σ_e^2 and σ_u^2.

6 An example of such "exogenous" price expectations would be the autoregressive expectations.

7 Recall that the natural level of output was normalized to equal one so that $Y_n \equiv \ln y_n = 0$. Thus, if the optimal level of output is the natural level, then the objective would be to minimize $E_{t-1}(Y_t)^2$.

8 Recall that we are assuming that ε_t and v_t are independent random variables. From (11.2),

$$E_{t-1}Y_t = a_0 + a_1 Y_{t-1} + a_2 \bar{m}_t,$$

so that $Y_t - E_{t-1}Y_t = a_2\varepsilon_t + v_t$. Squaring this expression and noting that $E(\varepsilon_t) = 0$, $E(v_t) = 0$, and, given independence, $E(\varepsilon_t \cdot v_t) = 0$, we obtain

$$E_{t-1}(Y_t - E_{t-1}Y_t)^2 = a_2^2\sigma_e^2 + \sigma_v^2.$$

9 See Sargent's (1987a: 453) equation (13) for the corresponding expression. Recall that $g_0 = (Y^* - a_0)/a_2$.
10 Note that $\ln y_n = 0$ due to normalization.
11 To tie down the inflation rate, we would have to add an inflation objective to the goals of the government.
12 Note that this is another example of the Lucas critique, in which econometric estimates of a specific set of parameters based on past policies cannot be used to project the impact of new, different monetary rules to be followed in the future, for with these new policies the parameters will change.
13 This equation is derived from combining the price error expression with the aggregate supply equation given earlier.
14 The assumptions leading up to (11.16) have been chosen so that (11.16) matches the criterion found in Barro and Gordon (1983). We will contrast the results of that paper with our findings here shortly.
15 The form of this equation mirrors that in Barro and Gordon.
16 Consider what would happen if we did not neglect the lagged disturbance terms. For instance, let us say one of the disturbance terms (ε_{t-1} or u_{t-1}) is positive rather than zero while the other is held equal to zero. According to the reduced-form equation for the price level for period $t-1$, the result would be a higher price level in period $t-1$ with the positive lagged disturbance term. If the rate of growth in the money supply between period $t-1$ and t was the same in both cases, then the inflation rate would be higher in the case when both lagged disturbance terms are zero. Thus to maintain a constant inflation rate, a lower money supply growth is implied if lagged disturbance terms are zero instead of positive.
17 Kydland and Prescott were awarded the 2004 Nobel prize in economics for their work.
18 This form of the objective function, introduced above, is discussed in Barro and Gordon (1983). Without the assumption of $k < 1$, a zero average rate of inflation would be optimal regardless of the nature of expectation formation.
19 For simplicity, we assume there is no persistence in real shocks. Thus, we assume $\lambda = 0$ in the original Barro and Gordon model.

12 Open economy

1 For discussion purposes, the terms "domestic" and "foreign" are used with respect to the domestic perspective.
2 For simplicity, we assume foreigners do not desire to hold domestic money.
3 We assume for simplicity that foreigners are not taxed by the domestic government.
4 That is, the domestic households own the remaining share of bonds issued by foreign firms, $\bar{B}_{ff}$, and α of the equity share issues by foreign firms. The total dividends (in terms of the foreign currency) paid by foreign firms in period t are denoted by $p_{ft}d_{ft}$ where p_{ft} is the price level of the foreign country and d_{ft} are real dividends of foreign firms.

5 One might also include b_t^d, as purchase of output by private depository institutions is included in the household budget constraint. This reflects the replacement of dividends paid by private depository institutions to their shareholders (households) by the difference between banks' interest income and their purchases of the composite commodity. This definition of dividends for private banks has been termed the "flow" constraint for private depository institutions.

6 Recall that *MB* denotes the monetary base, *R* denotes reserves, and *C* denotes currency in the hands of the nonbank public.

7 Recall that we use the term "modified" as we have substituted the firm distribution constraint into the household budget constraint for labor income. We thus have effectively suppressed the labor market from the markets under consideration. This modified law is useful in understanding how the aggregate demand equation is derived.

8 By "real demand," we mean in units of the domestic commodity.

9 The term "real" means in terms of the domestic composite commodity.

10 In measuring the exports, imports, and international capital flows, a number of items are often missed. For instance, the clandestine transfer of funds from the Philippines to US bank accounts would generate a demand for dollars. On the other hand, secretive imports of heroin from Turkey result in a supply of dollars in international markets. The net of such unmeasured transactions are lumped under the heading of "statistical discrepancy" in the balance of payments accounts. We have omitted this item from Table 12.1.

11 For simplicity, we assume that the exchange rate affects only the division of total consumption between imports and purchases of the domestic output; total consumption is assumed to be unaffected by such exchange rate changes.

12 Note that an increase in the price of the yen, or an "appreciation" of the yen, means a fall in the price of a dollar in terms of yen, or a "depreciation" of the dollar.

13 If the price elasticity with respect to imports was less than one in short run, a rise in the relative price of imports due to a depreciation of the dollar could, in fact, lead to a rise in the value of imports as well. This short-run phenomenon when applied to the path of net exports over time is referred to as the "J-curve effect."

14 Actually, for much of the analysis to follow, we need only assume the weaker "Marshall–Lerner" condition that the sum of the price elasticity of demand for imports and the price elasticity of demand for exports exceeds one. This assures that a price of the dollar below its equilibrium level will be associated with an excess demand for dollars in the foreign exchange markets, while a price of the dollar above its equilibrium level will be associated with an excess supply of dollars.

15 Given future markets for foreign currency, this is not always the case.

16 We assume that such expectation is held with subjective certainty.

17 There are several reasons why, in the short run, the supply curve may not be upward-sloping. First, it often takes time for US purchasers to adjust purchases in light of a change in relative prices. Second, the prices of domestic goods that are close substitutes to the imported goods can rise significantly in the short run as domestic producers hit short-run production constraints. The third complication that has the effect of making the supply of dollars curve less likely to be upward-sloping is that foreign producers, at least in the short run, often adjust the foreign currency prices of goods they export to partially offset the impact of exchange rate changes on the prices of their goods in foreign markets. For instance, Knetter (1987) found that with a depreciation of the dollar (appreciation of the West German Mark), West German exporters often reduced the Mark price of their exports so as to minimize the rise in the dollar price of German goods that would result from the appreciation of the Mark. For the time being we abstract from such short-run considerations, although this is not to lessen the importance of this phenomenon, as the experience during the 1985–1987 period indicates. With a depreciation of the dollar, the dollar value of imports grew as the USA had to supply

more dollars for each unit of imported goods, and there was initially little reduction in the quantity of goods imported.

18 It is important to remember that while we talk of households as being the only private demanders of foreign goods and financial assets, this is purely a simplifying device. Firms also demand foreign goods and private depository institutions demand foreign financial assets. The analysis would be more complex if we explicitly recognized these demands, but our conclusions would be unchanged since we can subsume in household actions the actions of firms and depository institutions in foreign markets.

References

Aigner, D.J. and Cain, G.C. (1977) Statistical theories of discrimination in labor markets. *Industrial and Labor Relations Review*, 30(2), 175–187.

Alchian, A. and Demsetz, H. (1972) Production, information costs, and economic organization. *American Economic Review*, 62, 777–795.

Alogoskoufis, G.S. (1987) On intertemporal substitution and aggregate labor supply. *Journal of Political Economy*, 95, 938–960.

Altonji, J. and Siow, A. (1987) Testing the response of consumption to income changes with (noisy) panel data. *Quarterly Journal of Economics*, 102, 293–328.

Arrow, K. (1964) The role of securities in the optimal allocation of risk-bearing. *Review of Economic Studies*, 31 (April), 91–96.

Arrow, K. and Hahn, F.H. (1971) *General Competitive Analysis*. San Francisco, CA: Holden-Day.

Azariadis, C. (1976) On the incidence of unemployment. *Review of Economic Studies*, 43, 115–125.

Barro, R.J. (1976) Rational expectations and the role of monetary policy. *Journal of Monetary Economics*, 2, 1–32.

Barro, R.J. and Gordon, D. (1983) A positive theory of monetary policy in a natural rate model. *Journal of Political Economy*, 91, 589–610.

Barro, R.J. and Grossman, H.I. (1971) A general disequilibrium model of income and employment. *American Economic Review*, 61, 82–93.

Barro, R.J. and King, R.G. (1984) Time-separable preferences and intertemporal substitutions models of business cycles. *Quarterly Journal of Economics*, 99, 817–839.

Begg, D.K.H. (1980) Rational expectations and the non-neutrality of systematic monetary policy. *Review of Economic Studies*, 47, 293–303.

Blanchard, O.J. (1981) What is left of the multiplier accelerator? *American Economic Review*, 71, 150–154.

Blanchard, O.J. and Fischer, S. (1989) *Lectures on Macroeconomics*. Cambridge, MA: MIT Press.

Borjas, G.J. and Heckman, J.J. (1978) Labor supply estimates for public policy evaluation. NBER Working Paper No. W0299, November.

Box, G.E.P. and Jenkins, G.M. (1970) *Time Series Analysis*. San Francisco, CA: Holden-Day.

Burbidge, J.B. and Robb, A.L. (1985) Evidence on wealth–age profiles in Canadian cross-section data. *Canadian Journal of Economics*, 18, 854–875.

Caballero, R. and Engel, E. (1999) Explaining investment dynamics in US manufacturing: A generalized (S, s) approach. *Econometrica*, 67, 783–826.

Campbell, J.Y. and Mankiw, N.G. (1987a) Permanent and transitory components in macroeconomic fluctuations. *American Economic Review*, 77, 111–117.

Campbell, J.Y. and Mankiw, N.G. (1987b) Are output fluctuations transitory? *Quarterly Journal of Economics*, 102, 857–880.

Campbell, J.Y., Lo, A.W., and MacKinlay, A.C. (1997) *The Econometrics of Financial Markets*. Princeton, NJ: Princeton University Press.

Cass, D. (1965) Optimal growth in an aggregate model of capital accumulation. *Review of Economic Studies*, 32, 233–240.

Clower, R.W. (1965) The Keynesian Counter-revolution: A theoretical appraisal. In F.H. Hahn and F.P.R. Brechling (eds), *The Theory of Interest Rates*. London: Macmillan.

Coase, R.H. (1960) The problem of social cost. *Journal of Law and Economics*, 3, 1–44 .

Cukierman, A. (1986) Measuring inflationary expectations. *Journal of Monetary Economics*, 17, 315–324.

Dahlman, C. (1979) The problem of externality. *Journal of Law and Economics*, 22, 141–162.

Debreu, G. (1959) *The Theory of Value*. New York: Wiley.

Diamond, P.A. and Hausman, J.A. (1984) Individual retirement and savings behaviour. *Journal of Public Economics*, 23, 81–114.

Dornbusch, R. (1976) Expectations and exchange rate dynamics. *Journal of Political Economy*, 84, 1161–1176.

Enders, W. (2004) *Applied Econometric Time Series*, 2nd edn. Hoboken, NJ: Wiley.

Evans, G. (1989) Output and unemployment dynamics in the United States: 1950–1985. *Journal of Applied Econometrics*, 4, 213–237.

Ewing, B.T. (2001) Cross-effects of fundamental state variables. *Journal of Macroeconomics*, 23, 633–645.

Ewing, B.T. and Payne, J.E. (1998) The long-run relation between the personal savings rate and consumer sentiment. *Financial Counseling and Planning*, 9(1), 89–96.

Ewing, B.T., Levernier, W., and Malik, F. (2002) Differential effects of output shocks on unemployment rates by race and gender. *Southern Economic Journal*, 68, 584–599.

Fama, E.F. and Miller, M.H. (1972) *The Theory of Finance*. New York: Holt, Rinehart and Winston.

Fischer, S. (1977) Long-term contracts, rational expectations, and the optimal money supply rule. *Journal of Political Economy*, 85, 191–205.

Fisher, I. (1930) *The Theory of Interest*. New York: Macmillan.

Fleming, M.J. (1962) Domestic financial policies under fixed and under floating exchange rates. *IMF Staff Papers*, 9, 369–379.

Foley, K.D. (1975) On two specifications of asset equilibrium in macroeconomic models. *Journal of Political Economy*, 83, 303–324.

Friedman, M. (1959) *A Program for Monetary Stability*. New York: Fordham University Press.

Friedman, M. (1968) The role of monetary policy. *American Economic Review*, 58, 1–17.

Goldberg, S. (1958) *Difference Equations*. New York: Wiley.

Gould, J.P. (1968) Adjustment cost in the theory of investment of the firm. *Review of Economic Studies*, 35, 47–56.

Grandmont, J.M. (1977) Temporary general equilibrium theory. *Econometrica*, 45, 535–572.

Granger, C.W.J. and Morris, M. (1976) Time series modelling and interpretation. *Journal of the Royal Statistical Society, Series A*, 139, 246–257.

Granger, C.W.J. and Newbold, P. (1986) *Forecasting Economic Time Series*, 2nd edn. Orlando, FL: Academic Press.

Hall, R. (1976) The Phillips curve and macroeconomic policy. In K. Brunner and A.H. Meltzer (eds), *The Phillips Curve and Labor Markets*, Carnegie-Rochester Conference Series on Public Policy. Amsterdam: North-Holland.

Hall, R. (1980) Employment fluctuation and wage rigidity. In G.L. Perry (ed.), *Brookings Papers on Economic Activity*, pp. 91–123. Washington, DC: Brookings Institution.

Hall, R.E. (1982) Explorations in the Gold Standard and related policies for stabilizing the dollar. In R.E. Hall (ed.), *Inflation: Causes and Effects*. Chicago, IL: University of Chicago Press.

Hall, R.E. (1988) Intertemporal substitution in consumption. *Journal of Political Economy*, 96, 339–357.

Hannan, E.J. (1970) *Multiple Time Series*. New York: Wiley.

Hansen, B. (1970) *A Survey of General Equilibrium Systems*. New York: McGraw-Hill.

Hansen, L.P. and Singleton, K.J. (1983) Stochastic consumption, risk aversion, and the temporal behavior of asset returns. *Journal of Political Economy*, 91, 249–265.

Harvey, A.C. (1993) *Time Series Models*. Cambridge, MA: MIT Press.

Hayashi, F. (1982) Tobin's marginal q and average q: A neoclassical interpretation. *Econometrica*, 50(1), 213–224.

Hicks, J. (1939) *Value and Capital*. Oxford: Clarendon Press.

Howitt, P. (1985) Transaction costs in the theory of unemployment. *American Economic Review*, 75, 88–100.

Howitt, P. (1986) Conversations with economists: A review essay. *Journal of Monetary Economics*, 18, 103–118.

Hurd, M. (1987) Savings of the elderly and desired bequests. *American Economic Review*, 77, 298–312.

Karni, E. (1978) Period analysis and continuous analysis in Patinkin's macroeconomic model. *Journal of Economic Theory*, 17, 134–140.

Kester, W.C. (1986) Capital ownership structure: A comparison of the United States and Japanese manufacturing corporations. *Financial Management*, 15(1), 5–16.

Keynes, J.M. (1936) *General Theory of Employment, Interest, and Money*. London: Macmillan.

Kletzer, L.G. and Fairlie, R. (1998) Jobs lost, jobs regained: An analysis of black/white differences in job displacement in the 1980s. *Industrial Relations*, 37, 460–477.

Knetter, M. (1987) Export prices and exchange rates: Theory and evidence. Working paper, Stanford University, November.

Koopmans, T. (1965) On the concept of optimal economic growth. In *Proceedings Study Week on the Econometric Approach to Development Planning*. Chicago, IL: Rand-McNally.

Kydland, F.E. and Prescott, E.C. (1977) Rules rather than discretion: The inconsistency of optimal plans. *Journal of Political Economy*, 85, 473–491.

Kydland, F.E. and Prescott, E.C. (1982) Time to build and aggregate fluctuations. *Econometrica*, 50, 1345–1370.

Leonard, J.S. (1988) In the wrong place at the wrong time: The extent of frictional and structural unemployment. NBER Working Paper No. 1979.

Lucas, R.E. (1967) Adjustment costs and the theory of supply. *Journal of Political Economy*, 75, 321–334.

Lucas, R.E. (1972) Expectations and the neutrality of money. *Journal of Economic Theory*, 4, 103–124.

Lucas, R.E. (1973) Some international evidence on output–inflation tradeoffs. *American Economic Review*, 63, 326–334.

Lucas, R. Jr (1981) Methods and problems in business cycle theory. In *Studies in Business-Cycle Theory*. Cambridge, MA: MIT Press. First published in *Journal of Money, Credit, and Banking*, 12, November 1980.

Lucas, R.E. and Rapping, L.A. (1970) Real wages, employment, and inflation. In E.S. Phelps (ed.), *Microeconomic Foundations of Employment and Inflation Theory*. New York: W.W. Norton.

Lundberg, S. and Startz, R. (1983) Private discrimination and social intervention in competitive labor markets. *American Economic Review*, 73(3), 340–347.

McCallum, B. (1979) The current state of the policy-ineffectiveness debate. *American Economic Review*, 69, 240–245.

McCallum, B. (1985) On consequences and criticisms of monetary targeting. *Journal of Money, Credit, and Banking*, 17, 570–597.

Mankiw, N.G. (1987) The optimal collection of seigniorage: Theory and evidence. *Journal of Monetary Economics*, 20, 327–341.

Mankiw, N.G., Rotemberg, J.J., and Summers, L.H. (1985) Intertemporal substitution in macroeconomics. *Quarterly Journal of Economics*, 100, 225–251.

Marx, K. (1976) *Capital: Vol. 1. A Critique of Political Economy*. Harmondsworth: Penguin.

Mills, T.C. (1999) *The Econometric Modelling of Financial Time Series*, 2nd edn. Cambridge: Cambridge University Press.

Modigliani, F. (1966) Life cycle hypothesis of saving, the demand for wealth and the supply of capital. *Social Research*, 33, 160–217.

Modigliani, F. (1986) Life cycle, individual thrift, and the wealth of nations. *American Economic Review*, 76, 297–313.

Mundell, R.A. (1968) *International Economics*. New York: Macmillan.

Nakamura, A. and Nakamura, M. (1981) A comparison of the labor force behavior of married women in the U.S. and Canada, with special attention to the impact of income taxes. *Econometrica*, 49, 451–489.

Nelson, C.R. and Plosser, C.I. (1982) Trends and random walks in macroeconomic time series: Some evidence and implications. *Journal of Monetary Economics*, 10, 139–162.

Niehans, J. (1987) Classical monetary theory, new and old. *Journal of Money, Credit, and Banking*, 19, 409–424.

Oi, W.Y. (1962) Labor as a quasi-fixed factor. *Journal of Political Economy*, 70, 538–555.

Patinkin, D. (1965) *Money, Interest, and Prices*. New York: Harper & Row.

Pencavel, J. (1985) Labor supply of men: A survey. In Orley Ashenfelter (ed.), *Handbook of Labor Economics*. Amsterdam: North-Holland.

Phelps, E.S. (1968) Money-wage dynamics and labor market equilibrium. *Journal of Political Economy*, 76, 678–711.

Phelps, E.S. and Taylor, J.B. (1977) Stabilizing powers of monetary policy under rational expectations. *Journal of Political Economy*, 85, 163–190.

Phillips, A.W. (1958) The relationship between unemployment and the rate of change in money wage rates in the United Kingdom, 1861–1957. *Economica*, 25, 283–299.

Pindyck, R.S. and Rubinfeld, D.L. (1991) *Econometric Models and Economic Forecasts*, 3rd edn. New York: McGraw-Hill.

Poole, W. (1985) Comment on "On consequences and criticisms of monetary targeting." *Journal of Money, Credit, and Banking*, 17, 602–605.

Radford, R.A. (1945) The economic organization of a prisoner of war camp. *Economica*, 12, 189–201.

Robinson, C. and Tomes, N. (1985) More on the labour supply of Canadian women. *Canadian Journal of Economics*, 18, 156–163.

Sargent, T. (1987a) *Macroeconomic Theory*, 2nd edn. Boston, MA: Academic Press.

Sargent, T. (1987b) *Dynamic Macroeconomic Analysis*. Cambridge, MA: Harvard University Press.

Sargent, T.J. and Wallace, N. (1975) "Rational" expectations, the optimal monetary instrument, and the optimal money supply rule. *Journal of Political Economy*, 83, 241–254.

Sargent, T.J. and Wallace, N. (1976) Rational expectations and the theory of economic policy. *Journal of Monetary Economics*, 2, 169–183.

Shapiro, C. and Stiglitz, J.E. (1984) Equilibrium unemployment as a worker discipline device. *American Economic Review*, 74, 433–444.

Shiller, R.J. (1978) Rational expectations and the dynamic structure of macroeconomic models. *Journal of Monetary Economics*, 4, 1–44.

Sidrauski, M. (1967a) Rational choice and patterns of growth in a monetary economy. *American Economic Review*, 57, 534–544.

Sidrauski, M. (1967b) Inflation and economic growth. *Journal of Political Economy*, 75, 797–810.

Simons, H.C. (1936) Rules versus authorities in monetary policy. *Journal of Political Economy*, 44, 1–30.

Sims, C. (1972) Money, income, and causality. *American Economic Review*, 62, 540–552.

Solow, R. (1956) A contribution to the theory of economic growth. *Quarterly Journal of Economics*, 70, 65–94.

Strotz, R.H. (1955–1956) Myopia and inconsistency in dynamic utility maximization. *Review of Economic Studies*, 23, 165–180.

Stuart, C.E. (1981) Swedish tax rates, labor supply, and tax revenues. *Journal of Political Economy*, 89, 1020–1038.

Taylor, J. (1972) The behaviour of unemployment and unfilled vacancies: Great Britain, 1958–71. An alternative view. *Economic Journal*, 82, 1352–1365.

Taylor, J.B. (1979) Estimation and control of a macroeconomic model with rational expectations. *Econometrica*, 47, 1267–1286.

Tobin, J. (1965) Money and economic growth. *Econometrica*, 33, 671–684.

Tobin, J. (1969) A general equilibrium approach to monetary theory. *Journal of Money, Credit, and Banking*, 1(1), 15–29.

Tobin, J. (1985) Comment on "On consequences and criticisms of monetary targeting," or Monetary targeting: Dead at last? *Journal of Money, Credit, and Banking*, 17, 605–610.

Uzawa, H. (1969) Time preference and the Penrose effect in a two-class model of economic growth. *Journal of Political Economy*, 77, 628–652.

Varian, H. (1992) *Microeconomic Analysis*, 3rd edn. New York: W.W. Norton.

Walker, D.A. (1987) Walras' theories of tatonnement. *Journal of Political Economy*, 95, 758–774.

Walras, L. (1954) *Elements of Pure Economics*, trans. W. Jaffé. London: George Allen & Unwin.

Weber, C.E. (1998) Consumption spending and the paper-bill spread: Theory and evidence. *Economic Inquiry*, 36, 575–589.

Weitzman, M. (1985) The simple macroeconomics of profit sharing. *American Economic Review*, 75, 937–953.

Index

accelerationist outcome 170–2
aggregate demand 7, 86, 90–1, 94–5, 99;
  Keynesian model 133–4, 135, 139, 140;
  Lucas model 160–1; neoclassical model
  126, 127, 128, 146; shocks 158; *see
  also* demand
aggregate supply 82, 86–90, 91, 94–5, 98,
  113; Keynesian model 132, 133–4, 135,
  138, 140, 145; Lucas model 137,
  153–4, 155, 158, 160–1, 164, 166;
  monetary policy 170–1; neoclassical
  model 118, 123, 125–6, 127, 128, 133;
  see also supply
aggregation issues 5–6, 8, 14–15
Alchian, A. 203n9
Alogoskoufis, G.S. 51
Angell, Wayne 219n4
Arrow-Debreu theory 2, 202n4, n10,
  203n8
assets 51, 52, 53; portfolio decision
  39–40, 57–9; tangible 25–6; *see also*
  financial assets
autocorrelation function 102–3
autoregressive expectations 162–4, 168
autoregressive processes 103–5, 110, 111,
  113, 166

balance of payments 190–3
bankruptcy 32, 33
Barro, R.J. 156, 167, 179–80, 182–4
Begg, D.K.H. 122, 215n8
behavioral hypotheses 96, 98, 99, 100
Bellman equation: firms 29, 30, 31, 34,
  35; households 43, 44, 45, 48–9
Blanchard, O.J. 111, 112, 171, 175, 184–5
bonds 19–20, 23, 27–9, 32–3; financial
  market equilibrium 84–5; firm
  financing constraint 24–6, 64; Fisherian

problem 52; foreign 189; households
  39, 40, 43–4, 72, 204n11; money illusion
  59; portfolio choice 57, 58, 59, 93; real
  value 77; temporary equilibrium 80, 81
budget constraint 7, 16; household 43, 44,
  55, 65–6, 67, 70–1, 73–4; open economy
  188, 189
Burbidge, J.B. 208n25
business cycle 5, 6, 49, 50, 173; real
  business cycle theory 79, 136, 202n4;
  technological innovation 113

Caballero, R. 209n1
Campbell, J.Y. 111, 112, 113, 214n45
capital 23, 24, 31, 68, 69–70; cost of
  31–2, 36, 69, 70, 94, 120, 209n7; firm
  financing constraint 24, 25, 26, 64;
  international flows 192, 193, 195–6,
  197–8, 200; Tobin's Q 36; *see also*
  capital stock
capital account 192
capital adjustment costs 21, 26–7, 34–7,
  69–70
capital markets 27, 203n1, 205n24
capital stock 3, 18–19, 20–1, 23, 25, 27–9;
  optimal investment 30, 31, 69, 70;
  retained earnings financing 29–30, 32;
  superneutrality of money 120, 121, 122;
  Tobin's Q 35, 36
central banks 187, 188, 189, 190,
  191, 192–3
classical economics 4, 5, 79, 212n8
Clower, R.W. 117, 118
Coase, R.H. 11
Cobb–Douglas production function 147,
  148, 217n3
commodities 8, 9–10, 14, 16, 18–19, 20;
  individual experiments 11, 13–14;